Software Engineering

INTERNATIONAL COMPUTER SCIENCE SERIES

Consulting editors **A D McGettrick**
University of Strathclyde

J van Leeuwen
State University of Utrecht

Software Engineering

I SOMMERVILLE
University of Strathclyde

ADDISON-WESLEY PUBLISHING COMPANY
London · Amsterdam · Reading, Massachusetts
Menlo Park, California · Don Mills, Ontario · Sydney

©1982 by Addison-Wesley Publishers Limited
53 Bedford Square, London, WC1B 3DZ

Set by the author in elite-12 using NROFF, the UNIX text-processing system, at the University of Strathclyde, Glasgow.
Printed in Finland by Werner Söderström Osakeyhtiö, Member of Finnprint.

Library of Congress Cataloging in Publication Data
Sommerville, Ian.
  Software engineering.

  (International computer science series)
  Bibliography: p.
  Includes index.
  1. Electronic digital computers--Programming.
I. Title. II. Series.
QA76.6.S645   001.64'2   82–1652
ISBN 0–201–13795–X (pbk.)   AACR2

British Library Cataloguing in Publication Data
Sommerville, Ian
  Software engineering. – (International computer
  science series; 5)
  1. Computer programs
  I. Title   II. Series
  001.64'25   QA76.6

ISBN 0–201–13795–X

ABCDEF 898765432

Preface

The problems of implementing and testing large software systems are immense and not simply proportional to the size of the system. Some of these problems are akin to the problems which arise in large engineering projects – management and cost control, personnel management, tool selection, quality control and product design. This was first brought to prominence at a NATO conference in 1968 where the term 'software engineering' was coined.

Software engineering has now emerged as a discipline in its own right. Although its principal influence is computing science, it is also influenced by mathematics, psychology, ergonomics and management science. The software engineer must be able to assess and apply existing computing techniques in a cost effective and usable way. He or she must apply existing knowledge derived from more basic subjects in exactly the same way as the mechanical, electrical and civil engineer applies the basic sciences.

Since 1968, the problems of producing large software systems have been recognised and a good deal of work has been carried out in an attempt to solve these problems. There have been a number of important developments. High level languages have ousted machine languages for many applications, structured programming can increase programmer productivity and improve the readability and reliability of programs, some of the problems of software project management have been tackled, formal verification systems seem likely to become practicable in the next few years and preliminary steps for formal systems specification have been taken.

Low-cost microprocessor systems mean that more and more control tasks will be allocated to computer systems and the need for reliable, low-cost software systems is increasing. Many software systems are still being produced which are unreliable, over budget, poorly documented, and not well suited to the user. Existing, proven techniques are neither widely known nor applied. Software engineering education is of paramount importance if this situation is to be improved.

This book is designed as a software engineering textbook for use in advanced undergraduate or graduate classes in the subject. However, as well as being a student text, it is hoped that the book will be useful for practising software engineers in industry and commerce.

I consider the most important characteristics of a well-engineered software system to be reliability, understandability, and maintainability. The emphasis throughout the book is on topics relating to these software characteristics rather than on topics relating to the efficiency and performance of software.

The book has developed from courses in software engineering given to third and fourth year students of computer science at the University of Strathclyde and presupposes some knowledge of computing. It is assumed that the reader is familiar with at least one high level programming language such as ALGOL, Pascal or FORTRAN and also that he or she has attended at least one course in basic computer science covering algorithms, machine organisation and data structures.

Software engineering has developed remarkably quickly and it is impossible to cover all aspects of the subject in a single book. Indeed, any one chapter in this book could be expanded into a book in its own right. In selecting material for inclusion, techniques which have actually been found useful in the construction of practical systems have been described rather than research applications which may have future applicability. However, the most important of these research topics is probably the use of formal techniques in system validation and this is introduced but not covered in any detail. Examples of programs are mostly in Pascal but Ada is also used in some places where Pascal lacks constructs to illustrate the concept under discussion.

Broadly, the book is made up of two parts: Part 1 considers the technical aspects of the subject. It contains chapters covering software requirements, design, implementation and testing. Part 2 considers the human aspects of software engineering. Its chapters cover documentation, the design of user interfaces and psychological and practical considerations which are of relevance to software management.

Chapter 2 covers the specification of software requirements. It introduces the notion of a conceptual model which can be used to derive requirements, discusses the use of formal notations for requirements specification and shows how prototyping can be used for requirements validation.

Chapter 3 is concerned with the next stage in the software development process – design. This chapter concentrates on three notations – data flow diagrams, structure charts and design description languages for describing a software design. The methodology of top down design is described using examples derived from an office automation system and formal methods for design validation are illustrated by example.

Chapters 4 and 5 cover the implementation of a software design. Chapter 4 discusses programming languages and their importance to the software engineer. Language constructs and their impact on reliability and readability are discussed and guidelines provided on choosing a programming language for a major software project. Chapter 5 covers language independent aspects of programming. The chapter covers programming methodology, programming style, the use of software tools to assist program development and programming for portability.

Chapter 6 covers program testing and debugging. The complementary relationship between verification and testing, test case design and software tools to assist testing are described in the first part of this chapter and the second part covers debugging tools and techniques.

Chapter 7 is the link between the technically oriented chapters in the first part of the book and the final three chapters which cover non technical aspects of software engineering. User and system documentation are described, documentation tools discussed and hints on technical writing style are provided. The part of the chapter which covers system maintenance concentrates on the costs of maintenance and program understanding rather than programming for maintainability.

User interface design is the subject of Chapter 8. This topic is of increasing importance as computer applications broach on more and more areas of everyday life. User psychology, the design of mnemonics, the advantages and disadvantages of computer-initiated and user-initiated dialogues, error message design and the use of graphics in interface design are discussed here.

The final two chapters in the book are concerned with software management. Chapter 9 concentrates on psychological fundamentals which are of relevance to software management. A cognitive model of the programming process and its implications for management is described. This is followed by a discussion of individual programmer psychology and the psychology of programming groups. Chapter 10 is concerned with the practice of software management. Programmer team organisations, programmer productivity and software costing are covered here. The need for project planning is discussed and project scheduling and change control techniques are described.

I am grateful to a number of people who have carefully read the text and provided useful and constructive criticism. John Mariani of Strathclyde University and the series editors Andrew McGetterick and Jan van Leeuwen made a number of invaluable suggestions on how to improve initial versions of the text. Ron Morrison of the University of St Andrews clarified my thoughts on programming languages and also suggested a number of changes which have undoubtedly improved the book. To all of them, my thanks.

Ian Sommerville
February 1982

Contents

 # Introduction

The problems encountered in building large software systems are not simply scaled up versions of the problems of writing small computer programs. An analogy can be drawn with a road bridge over an estuary and a footbridge over a stream. Although both are members of the class 'bridges' and hence have some common properties, a civil engineer would never consider designing an estuarial bridge simply by enlarging a footbridge design. The complexity of small programs (or bridges) is such that it can be easily understood by one person and all details of the design and construction held in that person's head. Specifications may be informal and the effect of changes immediately obvious. On the other hand, the complexity of large systems is such that it is impossible for any single individual to mentally hold and maintain details of each aspect of the project. Formal techniques of specification and design are essential and each stage of the project must be carefully documented.

The term 'software engineering' was first introduced in the late 1960's at a conference held to discuss the so-called 'software crisis'. This software crisis resulted directly from the introduction of third generation computer hardware. These machines were orders of magnitude more powerful than second generation machines and their power made hitherto unrealisable applications a feasible proposition. The implementation of these applications required large software systems to be built.

There have been a number of definitions of software engineering proposed. Their common factors are that software engineering is concerned with building software systems which are larger than would normally be tackled by a single individual, uses engineering principles in the development of these systems and is made up of both technical and non-technical aspects. As well as a thorough knowledge of computing techniques, the software engineer, like any other engineer, must be able to

1

communicate, both orally and in writing. He or she should appreciate the problems which system users have in interacting with software whose workings they may not understand and should also understand the project management problems associated with software production.

Initial experience in building large software systems showed that that existing methodologies of software development were inadequate. Techniques applicable to small systems could not simply be scaled up. A number of major projects were late (sometimes years late), cost much more than originally predicted, were unreliable, difficult to maintain and performed poorly. Software development was in a crisis situation. Hardware costs were tumbling whilst software costs were rising rapidly. There was an urgent need for new techniques and methodologies which allowed the complexity inherent in large software systems to be controlled.

Since then, there has been much research into software development techniques. Hardware costs have continued to fall exponentially and software now accounts for about 85% of total computer systems expenditure. The new powerful hardware now available has made yet more complex applications feasible so the need for large software systems is even more acute. Some of the software development problems have been solved but many still remain.

The real costs of software development are immense. Although precise figures are very difficult to establish, it has been suggested (Lehman, 1980) that in 1977, software costs in the USA were in excess of $50 billion. This represented more than 3% of the American gross national product for that year. It can confidently be estimated that, at the time of writing (1982), these costs have at least doubled and are comparable in other developed countries. Even small improvements in software productivity can result in a significant reduction in absolute costs.

Software engineering is a practical subject. It is concerned with building usable systems economically and, to this end, utilises appropriate, rather than fashionable, techniques. The software engineer should be conservative - he cannot afford to experiment with each and every new technique put forward by research scientists. His principal responsibility is to produce a working system to specification, on time and within budget, and the use of untested methods might compromise this intention. On the other hand, he or she should not ignore new developments nor should they be rejected simply because they are new.

From its tentative beginnings, software engineering is now maturing into a fully fledged discipline. Many effective techniques have been developed and the problem now is to bring these techniques to a wider community of users.

In the remainder of this introduction, the notion of a software life cycle is introduced and the need to tailor software development to reduce total life cycle costs discussed. This is followed by a section which describes software evolution and the final section in the chapter discusses the importance of software reliability.

1.1 THE SOFTWARE LIFE CYCLE

Like all other large-scale systems, large software systems take a considerable time to develop and are in use for an even longer time. A number of distinct stages in this period of development and usage can be identified. Together, they make up what is termed the software life cycle.

The stages of the software life cycle are:

(1) Specification
The software requirements, that is, the system functions and operational constraints, must be established and specified.

(2) Design
A software design must be derived from an analysis of the software requirements.

(3) Implementation
The software design must be realised in a programming language which can be executed on the target computer.

(4) Testing
The implementation must be tested to ensure that the completed system meets the software requirements.

(5) Operation and Maintenance
The system must be installed and used. If system errors are discovered these must be corrected and

changes to the original requirements   may involve adding to the system.

The development of software is an iterative process with each stage in the life cycle feeding back information to earlier stages. As design proceeds, requirements may be clarified, implementation may reveal design flaws and testing may show up errors in any of the preceding stages.   When the system is in operation, errors, undetected at earlier stages, will be discovered and system requirements change.   To accommodate these changes involves repeating part of the earlier stages of the life cycle.

Each stage in the software life cycle accounts for an unequal proportion of the total software costs and it is the responsibility of the software engineer to build the system so that costs are minimised over the total life cycle.   Software development embraces the first four stages of the life cycle and Boehm (1975) provides figures which suggest that specification analysis and design account for about 40% of development costs, implementation 20% and testing also about 40%. However, the costs of stage 5 of the life cycle - operation and maintenance - far exceed total development costs, typically by a factor of 4 but in some cases, these costs may be up to 50 times the cost of system development.

To reduce total life cycle costs, efforts are best concentrated on reducing the costs of the maintenance stage of the life cycle.   As maintenance involves some person understanding and modifying parts of the system, maintenance costs are reduced by making the software system understandable and easy to change.   This implies that specifications be unambiguous, design and implementation tailored so that the system is made up of easy to modify, autonomous parts and the use of validation techniques so that the number of undetected errors is minimised.

Software validation is not synonomous with software testing. Testing is carried out when the implementation is fully or partially complete whereas any stage in the software life cycle may be validated. Validation of requirements and software design is essential as errors in these stages which are not detected until after implementation can be very expensive to correct.

Effective validation of these stages requires that an unambiguous specification of the requirements and design should be available. The use of informal notations, such as natural language, for requirements and design specifications makes validation extremely difficult because of the ambiguities inherent in the notation. If formal notations are used, however, unambiguous specifications can be produced and the specifications can be checked using software tools developed for this purpose.

In order to reduce overall costs, formal notations should be used wherever possible in all stages of software development. Each stage should be thoroughly and properly documented and, where feasible, automatically checked for consistency and completeness. This may actually increase the costs of software development although more emphasis on specification and design will reduce the testing costs of the finished system. However, any increased development costs are, generally, more than compensated for by a reduction in maintenance costs and hence an overall cost reduction.

1.1.1 Software evolution

Large software systems are not static objects. They exist in an environment which is subject to constant change and which may not be completely understood by the implementors of the software. As the environment changes or becomes more fully understood, the software system must either adapt to these changes or become progressively less useful until, ultimately, it must be discarded. This process of change has been termed software evolution and is discussed in an important paper by Lehman (1980).

Software maintenance is the process of correcting errors in the system and modifying the system to reflect environmental changes. For large systems, this maintenance is accomplished in a series of system 'releases'. Each release is a new version of the system with known errors corrected and which incorporates new or updated system facilities.

If the system is implemented in a number of installations it is unlikely that all installations will incorporate all changes in each system release. Furthermore, each installation may make local modifications tuning the system to the particular environment in which it operates. As a result of these factors, it is inevitable that the versions of the system at each installation drift further and further apart and that general maintenance, applicable to all installations, becomes more difficult. Special software tools are necessary for management of this situation.

Lehman suggests that the evolution of a software system is subject to a number of 'laws'. He has derived these laws from experimental observations of a number of systems such as large operating systems (Lehman and Belady, 1976). He suggests that there are five laws of program evolution:

(1)   A program that is used in a real-world environment necessarily must change or become less and less useful in that environment.

(2)   As an evolving program changes, its structure becomes more complex unless active efforts are made to avoid this phenomenon.

(3)   Program evolution is a self-regulating process and measurement of system attributes such as size, time between releases, number of reported errors, etc reveals statistically significant trends and invariances.

(4)   Over the lifetime of a program, the rate of development of that program is approximately constant and independent of the resources devoted to system development.

(5)   Over the lifetime of a system, the incremental system change in each release is approximately constant.

Lehman's laws are not universally accepted in the same way as physical laws but they do appear to have some validity in many cases. He has used them with some success in the management of new releases of a large operating system.

The fact that a program undergoes constant changes and that these changes inevitably degrade the structure of that program has probably been observed in every large software system that has ever been developed. The first two of Lehman's laws are almost certainly valid.

The universal validity of the latter three laws is more contentious. Whilst self-regulation of the development process can be explained by the inertia of the human organisations involved in that process, laws 4 and 5 seem to be contra-intuitive. Why is system development resource independent and why should the incremental change in each system release be constant?

Lehman suggests that these laws are direct consequence of organisational behaviour and the behaviour of individuals within an organisation but he does not attempt to explain them in more detail. His experimental work seems to have been done with the cooperation of a large organisation and it would be interesting to see if his observations were valid for systems developed by small or loosely structured groups. There is a need for more experimental studies to test the validity of the laws and to investigate why software evolution should be subject to such laws.

1.2   SOFTWARE RELIABILITY

As computer applications become more diverse and pervade almost every area of everyday life, it is becoming more and more apparent that the most important dynamic characteristic of computer software is that it should be reliable.

The reliability of any system (not merely software systems) is dependent on the correctness of the system design, the correctness of the mapping of the system design to implementation and the reliability of the components making up the system. For example, the reliability of a motor car depends on the car design, it depends on how well the car is put together, and on how long the components making up the car take to fail. In general, after initial teething troubles, the reliability of most systems is governed by how long it takes the system components to wear out. As the majority of systems have some moving parts, wear is inevitable and it is impossible for the systems to be 100% reliable.

Software systems are unique in this respect. They contain no moving parts and their reliability depends completely on design and implementation correctness. Hardware reliability can be achieved by duplication of components with a new component automatically switching in if component failure is detected. This approach cannot be taken by software systems. If a procedure gives the wrong answer there is no point in trying to execute another copy of the same procedure.

It is difficult to give a precise definition of what is meant by software reliability - some might say that software is reliable if it is correct. That is, if it meets its initial specifications and performs as specified. This is a possible definition but it does not take into account the possibility that the specifications themselves are incomplete or incorrect.

It is often the case that for large useful programming systems it is impossible to produce a specification which is complete and invariant. The reason for this is that these systems are not stand alone entities but operate in some environment which may not be wholly understood and which may be undergoing almost constant change.

The notion of absolute correctness of such systems is therefore of limited utility. Rather as Lehman (1980) points out, it is the usability of the program in the real world and the relevance of its output in a constantly changing environment that is the main concern.

A more realistic definition of program reliability is, therefore, that a program should meet its specifications, should never produce 'incorrect' output irrespective of the input, should never allow itself to be corrupted, should take meaningful and useful actions in unexpected situations and it should only completely fail when further progress is completely impossible.

To achieve this level of reliability inevitably involves a good deal of extra, often redundant, code to perform the necessary checking. This reduces the program execution speed and increases the amount of store required by the program. However, as computer users become more experienced, their principal criterion for system quality is reliability rather than efficiency. There are a number of reasons for this:

(1)   As equipment becomes cheaper and faster, there is no need to maximise equipment usage in preference to human convenience.

(2)   Unreliable software will be avoided by users and irrespective of how efficient it is it will soon become worthless.

(3)   For some applications (such as a reactor control system), the cost of system failure might be very much greater than the cost of the system itself.

(4)   An efficient system can be tuned with considerable success. An unreliable system is much more difficult to improve.

(5)   Inefficiency is predictable – programs take a long time to execute. Unreliability is much worse. Software which is unreliable can have hidden errors which can violate system and user data without warning and the results of an error might not be discovered till much later. For example, a fault in a design program used to design aircraft might not be discovered till a number of planes have crashed.

(6)   Unreliable systems can result in information being lost – hence much effort and money is expended in duplicating valuable data.

To achieve software reliability, the environment in which the software operates must be understood and a software specification prepared which, as far as possible, unambiguously defines the role of the software system in that environment.

The software design should implement all parts of the specification and each part of the design should be demonstrably correct. Although absolute correctness of the entire design is not necessarily meaningful because of constantly evolving specifications, each part of the design should be a well-defined function and hence susceptible to demonstrations of correctness.

A reliable implementation of the software design means that all parts of the design should actually be implemented and that the implementation should be a correct mapping of the design notation into a programming language.

Finally, irrespective of the measurable system reliability, unless the system documentation is accurate that reliability will not be visible to users of the system. The documentation must describe system facilities correctly and should point out areas where contra-intuitive results might be obtained from using the system.

As well as being reliable at any one point in time, programming systems ought to be reliable over their lifetimes. Because the environments in which these systems operate change, mechanisms must be built into the software so that it may readily evolve to reflect the changing environment. If the software cannot be readily maintained, its usability and relevance to users will decrease.

Throughout this book, reliability and maintainability are considered to be the most important attributes of a

well-engineered software system.   Whilst hard and fast
instructions on how to achieve this cannot be given, the
text provides guidelines which, if followed, should
simplify the production of well-engineered software.

# Requirements

The problems which software engineers are called upon to solve are usually immensely complex. Even understanding the nature of the problem can be very difficult particularly if the system is new and no comparable non-automated system exists to serve as a model for the software to be developed. This chapter addresses the initial stages of developing a solution to these problems – how the software requirements can be formulated and expressed. It covers the identification, understanding, and specification of problems for which a software solution is required.

It is important to make a distinction between needs and requirements. An organisation may decide that it needs a software system to support its accounting but it is unrealistic to present this simple need to a software engineer and expect an acceptable and usable software system to be developed. Rather, information about the problem to be solved must be collected and analysed and a comprehensive problem specification produced. From this specification, the software solution can be designed and implemented.

A software requirement is a property that the software system must satisfy. For example, in an accounting system, one requirement might be that the system should produce cash flow summaries according to a given specification. The precise description of the requirements for a software system is called the software requirements document (SRD). This is defined by Yeh and Zave (1980) as:

> a set of precisely stated properties or constraints which a software system must satisfy

The software requirements document is not a design document. It should specify exactly what the system should do without specifying how it should be done. As Yeh states:

> An SRD establishes boundaries on the solution space
> of the problem of developing a useful software system

An SRD allows a design to be validated - if the
constraints and properties specified in the SRD are
satisfied by the software design then that design is an
acceptable solution to the problem.

The task of developing an SRD should not be
underestimated. Bell et al. (1977) report that the
requirements document for a ballistic missile defence
system contains over 8000 distinct requirements and
support paragraphs and is made up of 2500 pages of text.

In principle, the requirements set out in such a
document ought to be complete and consistent.
Everything the system should do should be specified and
no one requirement should conflict with any other. In
practice, this is extremely difficult to achieve,
particularly if the requirements are stated as prose
text. Later in this chapter, formal notations which
allow some automatic consistency checking to be carried
out will be discussed.

The cost of errors in stating requirements can be
very high, particularly if these errors are not
discovered until the system is implemented.
Boehm (1974) reports that in some large systems up to
95% of the code had to be rewritten to satisfy user
requirements and also that 12% of the errors discovered
in a software system over a three year period were due
to errors in the original system requirements. The
majority of so-called program maintenance is not
actually correction of erroneous code but is code
modification to support changes to or errors in the
original system requirements.

The first section in this chapter describes how
requirements can be derived by establishing a conceptual
model of the system which is to be built. This is
followed by a discussion of notations which have been
developed for formally specifying requirements and a
requirements specification language is illustrated by
example. This description of specification languages is
followed by a discussion on how imprecise requirements
can be specified and also how system constraints - non-
functional requirements - may be expressed.

The final sections of the chapter cover the
specification of logical data structures, the structure
of a requirements document and the validation of
requirements.

2.1   DERIVING SOFTWARE REQUIREMENTS

The derivation of software requirements is not always considered the province of the software engineer. The systems analyst is sometimes considered responsible for this task, particularly where existing manual systems are to be automated. On the other hand, the specification of requirements for embedded systems and advanced systems is normally taken as a software engineering problem.

In fact, the roles of the systems analyst and the software engineer are complementary. The systems analyst should take responsibility for collecting data on the existing system and performing a critical analysis of that data to factor out relevant information. He should consult with the software engineer so that each understands the required system and to formulate a set of software requirements.

The derivation of software requirements requires that a conceptual model of the system be established. For trivial systems this model may exist only in the mind of the engineer responsible for establishing the requirements. He understands the systems and knows which functions must be provided and the constraints on the operation of these functions. For any non-trivial system, however, a mental model is likely to be inadequate. Because the system being modelled is inherently complex, mental models tend to be incomplete and contain ambiguities and conflicts. It is necessary to establish an explicit, formally specified system model at an early stage and to use this model to understand the system.

Salter (1976) has used finite state machines for system modelling and considers a general system model to be a function of three elements – control, function, and data. Intuitively, functions are the information transformers in the system, data are the inputs and outputs of functions and control is the mechanism that activates functions in the desired sequence. The notion of states and state transformations also underlies the conceptual modelling systems described by Yeh and Zave (1980) and Heninger (1980).

Heninger describes the derivation of requirements for an embedded software system used on board a military aircraft. This system receives 70 separate input items and transmits 95 distinct output data items. The system was modelled by considering each separate output item and associating a function with that item. It was found to be impossible to express each output as a function of one or more inputs so the requirements were expressed in terms of aircraft operating conditions. These conditions were then expressed in terms of input data items. As no direct functional relationship between input and output was specified, the system designer was not constrained by how particular operating conditions were detected.

In many systems, the system data is structured and it is necessary to establish a formal model of that data. This should describe system entities and the relationships between these entities. Examples of such data models are Codd's relational model (1970) and Chen's entity-relationship model (1976).

As an example of a conceptual model, consider an office document handling system which provides word processing, electronic mail and information retrieval facilities. Such a system might be modelled as Fig 2.1.

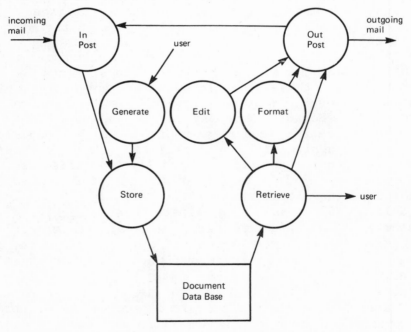

Fig. 2.1   Conceptual model of an office system

This model shows the major system functions in bubbles, and arrows represent the documents passing from one function to another. Using this model, the system requirements can be derived by considering the outputs of each of the major functions. Although similar to data flow diagrams described in the following chapter, this model does not imply an implementation. It simply identifies each major system function which must be provided without consideration of logical function grouping such as providing document generation and editing as a single subsystem.

If a system is completely new, the conceptual system model may be incomplete because the system specifier does not know exactly what is required of the system. Software requirements derived from such a model are inevitably imprecise. The Stoneman document (DoD, 1980), describing the requirements for an Ada programming environment, is an example of such an imprecise specification where the report states that more precise requirements can be formulated only after design experiments have been carried out. The results of these experiments are fed back to allow a more complete conceptual model to be established.

The Stoneman requirements specification document is typical of the state of the art of requirements specification. Examples from it are used throughout this chapter because it is publicly available. By contrast, most requirements specifications are proprietary documents and may not be freely quoted.

2.2   SPECIFYING SOFTWARE REQUIREMENTS

In specifying software requirements, it is useful to partition the requirements into two classes. These are:

(1)   Functional requirements – requirements which state the actual functions which the system must implement. For example, a functional requirement taken from the Stoneman requirements specification, setting out requirements for an Ada programming support environment (APSE), states:

> A virtual interface which is independent of any host machine shall be provided for APSE communication

> This specifies that a particular function, in this case a virtual interface, must be provided by an APSE.

(2)   Non-functional requirements – requirements which express practical constraints such as performance

specifications, memory requirements etc. An example of a non-functional requirement taken from the Stoneman document is:

It shall be possible for all necessary communication between the APSE and the user to be expressed in the standard Ada character set

Rather than describe a function to be provided, this is a practical limitation on the design of an Ada programming support environment.

The most common method of specifying software requirements is to use numbered paragraphs of prose text, with each paragraph specifying or qualifying some requirement. Typically, functional and non-functional requirements are not distinguished and the requirements statement may even include requirements which are so ill-defined as to be meaningless.

For example, requirement 4.C.1 of the Stoneman requirements states:

A virtual interface which is independent of any host machine shall be provided for APSE communication

This requirement is clearly a functional requirement and although it is imprecise, this is understandable considering the innovatory nature of the proposed system. On the same page, requirement 4.C.8 states:

It shall be possible for all necessary communication between the APSE and the user to be expressed in the standard Ada character set

This is a non-functional requirement which is precise and which places an understandable constraint on the system. However, also on the same page, requirement 4.C.2 states:

The virtual interface shall be based on simple overall concepts which are straightforward to understand and use and which are few in number

This 'requirement' cannot be classified as either functional or non-functional. In fact, it is a simply a platitude as there is no objective technique for judging the simplicity, straightforwardness, usability and overallness (whatever that is!) of the concepts on which the system is based. Although admirable in intent, such statements should not be included in a document which purports to specify software requirements.

The inherent ambiguity of natural language and the complexity of prose description means that it is difficult if not impossible to verify if requirements are complete and non-conflicting. Furthermore, the length and complexity of prose specifications makes such specifications difficult to understand. There is a high probability that they will be misinterpreted by the system designers and a design formulated which does not match the intentions of the system specifiers.

The inadequacies of unstructured paragraphs of natural language for requirements specifications are:

(1)   They rely on the shared linguistic experience of those responsible for reading and writing the requirements specification. The writer of a specification assumes that the terms which he uses in that specification mean the same to the reader as they do to him. This is a dangerous assumption partly because of the inherent ambiguity of natural language and partly because a standard computing terminology has not yet been established.

(2)   They are unable to express the functional architecture of the system in a clear and concise way. Schoman and Ross (1977) define the functional architecture of a system to be a description of the activities performed by the system and the interacting entities within the system. Essentially, it is a formalisation of the conceptual model built by the system specifier. As this model is based on abstractions, the notation provided for specifying the model should be capable of expressing these abstractions in an unambiguous manner.

(3)   They are over-flexible as they allow related requirements to be expressed in completely different ways. This means that the reader of the specification is left with the task of identifying and partitioning related requirements with the consequent likelihood of error and misunderstanding.

(4)   They do not partition requirements effectively. As a result, the effect of changes can only be

determined by examining every requirement rather than a group of related requirements.

Unstructured natural language is unsuitable for expressing requirements clearly and unambiguously. However, because of the high level concepts which are embodied in a requirements specification, no closed formal language such as a programming language can yet adequately express software requirements.

Notations which have been developed to specify requirements all rely on natural language. Instead of using it in an unstructured way, however, these notations impose some structure on the specification, limit the natural language expressions which may be used and, in some of these languages, enhance the natural language specification by use of graphics.

Languages which have been designed to express software requirements include PSL/PSA (Teichrow and Hershey, 1977), SADT (Schoman and Ross, 1977) and RSL (Bell et al., 1977). Although each language is intended as a general purpose notation for specifying requirements, these languages were originally designed with different types of application in mind. RSL is designed for specifying time-critical real-time systems, PSL/PSA for information processing systems and SADT for management information systems. RSL and PSL/PSA are designed to be used in conjunction with software tools which produce reports directly from formally stated requirements. By contrast, an SADT specification is intended to act as finished documentation so there is no need for an associated report generator.

SADT is the proprietary name of a notation developed by Ross (1977) based on a technique called Structured Analysis. Structured Analysis is not intended solely for specifying requirements but is designed as a technique for partitioning, structuring and expressing ideas, irrespective of the language in which these ideas are stated. Structured Analysis relies heavily on graphics to indicate structure and relationships, making use of about 40 distinct graphic symbols. Ross considers a description expressed in this way to bear the same relationship to the implemented system as a blueprint does to the engineering system which it describes.

Although Structured Analysis diagrams use special symbols, Ross maintains that they are easy to read and clear, even to the non-specialist. They are a tool for facilitating human communication but it is difficult to automatically collect the ideas expressed in these diagrams and check their consistency and completeness with software tools. This is not the case with PSL/PSA and RSL which have been specifically designed for machine processing.

RSL was designed as part of a requirements engineering methodology described by Bell et al. (1977) and Alford (1977). Statements in RSL are machine processable and information derived from these statements is collected into a database called the Abstract System Semantic Model (ASSM). A set of automated tools processes the information in the ASSM to generate simulators, produce reports and check the consistency and completeness of the requirements.

The language is simple in concept and based on only four distinct primitives. These are elements, relationships, attributes and structures. Elements correspond roughly to nouns in English, relationships to verbs, and attributes to adjectives. Structures model the flow of information through the functional steps which process that information. Fundamental elements, relationships and attributes are predefined in RSL and a facility exists for the user to add new elements, relationships, or attributes if this is necessary to express new concepts.

The basic structure of PSL/PSA is similar to that of RSL. It allows objects to be identified and named and allows relationships between objects to be specified. It also collects the specified information into a centralised database where it can be processed by software tools.

An alternative to the use of a requirements statement language to structure and restrict natural language is to use standard forms to achieve the same purpose. A project which used this approach is described by Heninger (1980). Special purpose forms were designed to describe the input, output and functions of an aircraft software system. The system requirements were specified by filling in these forms. Although the system described by Heninger is a manual one, standardisation of the forms would allow machine processing of the requirements to be carried out.

As some of the terminology used in these notations does not have an obvious meaning and space does not permit a full description of any language here, examples of these particular requirements specification languages are not provided. However, the example below is expressed in a formal, yet easily understandable notation which has been derived from PSL/PSA and RSL.

The example chosen is part of the office system whose conceptual model was discussed earlier in the chapter. The requirements for that part of the system dealing with incoming electronic mail are described.

The language uses keywords such as 'input', 'output', 'external' and 'define data object' to identify distinct sections of the specification. For each function, the requirements specification must provide a formal and informal specification of the actions of that function, a description of the data objects used by the function, a description of the actions to be taken in the event of an error and a specification of the constraints under which the function must operate. If the function makes use of objects which are defined globally, these objects must be explicitly named and identified using the keyword 'external'.

The notation used for the requirements specification uses the following conventions:

(1)   The names of external entities referenced in a specification must be explicitly declared.

(2)   Grouping of statements is indicated by indentation.

(3)   A description in free text may be included anywhere in the statement. This should be preceded by the keyword 'description'.

(4)   Elements in square brackets denote repetition. []* means zero or more repetitions, []+ means one or more repetitions and []n means n repetitions.

(5)   The operator ++ indicates catenation.

It is not appropriate to provide a full description of the language here; the example below, illustrating the notation, has been written so that it can be understood without detailed knowledge of the specification language.

```
in_post
   description
   in_post accepts and sorts incoming electronic
   mail. The recipient and sender are identified, the
```

mail placed in the recipients mail box and an
acknowledgement placed in the senders mail box.

input
    in_doc

output
    out_doc,mail_box_id
    acknowledgement,mail_box_id

description
out_doc is output with the mail box identifier of
the recipient.
acknowledgement is associated with the sender's
mail box id.

function
    out_doc := in_doc ++ time_of_receipt
    forward(outdoc)
    acknowledge
description
Forwards incoming mail and acknowledges receipt of
mail.

external functions
    date_and_time

error actions
    input error
    : Unidentified Recipient :
    recipient := DEAD.LETTER
    acknowledgement := Unidentified recipient
    : Unidentified Sender :
    sender := UNKNOWN
    acknowledgement := in_doc
    description
    if unknown sender, send copy of in_doc to
    system log of anonymous messages

    function error
    acknowledgement := system error -message not
    delivered
    description
    if functional error detected, output error
    message and in_doc to system error log.

 define data object mail_box_id

        description
        mail_box_id identifies a user's mail box in the
        system database. It has 2 components - the
        standard identifier MAIL_BOX and the user's
        name.

        syntax
            MAIL_BOX/[<char>]+

        structure
            MAIL_BOX/<user name>

    define data object in_doc
        description
        in_doc is an incoming document in the
        electronic mail system. As well as the text of
        the document, in_doc contains the following
        information
        -- the name and address of the recipient
        -- the name and address of the sender
        -- the time message was dispatched
        incoming documents are terminated by an END-
        OF-DOC control character on a line by itself.
        Each item of header information in in_doc
        occupies a line by itself.

        syntax
            [LINE]6[LINE]*

        structure
            <sender name> : NAME
            <sender address> : ADDRESS
            <recipient name> : NAME
            <recipient address> : ADDRESS
            <dispatch time> : TIME
            <message body> : TEXT
            END-OF-DOC

    external definitions
        NAME,ADDRESS,TEXT,LINE,TIME

    constraints
        SIZE(in_doc) <= 32766 lines

    define data object out_doc
        description
        out_doc is a transformed version of in_doc. All

information in in_doc is retained but the
header information is extended by an extra line
specifying the time of receipt.
Each item of header information occupies a line
by itself.

syntax
    [LINE]7[LINE]*

structure
    <sender name> : NAME
    <sender address> : ADDRESS
    <recipient name> : NAME
    <recipient address> : ADDRESS
    <dispatch time> : TIME
    <receipt time> : TIME
    <message body> : TEXT
    END-OF-DOC

external definitions
NAME,ADDRESS,TEXT,TIME,LINE

constraints
    SIZE(out_doc) <= 32767 lines

This specification describes the function and entities
associated with in_post but makes no attempt to describe
where the inputs come from or where the outputs are
sent.   The conceptual model illustrates this to some
extent - it shows outputs are passed to a store function
for entry in the document database.
   The conceptual model is a high level specification
and it is deliberately left uncluttered with detail.   On
occasion, it may be necessary to specify, in more
detail, where the inputs come from and how the function
is activated. This might be accomplished as follows:

input source

    file INCOMING_MAIL
    description
    This file containing all incoming electronic mail
    is created by the operating system communication
    functions.

output destination

```
function STORE(doc,store_id)
description
output from in_post is passed directly by
activating the store function.  The text to be
stored and a storage location are passed as
parameters.
```

activation
```
description
INCOMING_MAIL is examined periodically by the
system time daemon. If it is not empty, in_post is
activated and remains active  until all documents
in INCOMING_MAIL have been processed.
```

```
start
    function cron
```

```
stop
    INCOMING_MAIL = empty
```

```
period
    10 minutes
```

2.2.1 Specifying imprecise requirements

In principle, it ought to be possible to specify all system requirements formally using a notation such as that illustrated above. In practice, however, this is sometimes impossible because a sufficiently detailed conceptual model cannot be formulated by the requirements specifier. This is particularly likely when the system under development is completely new and not susceptible to detailed analysis. In such cases, an imprecise statement of the requirements must be formulated and subsequently refined as their ramifications become clear.

Formal notations are suitable for describing functional requirements once a clear, relatively detailed conceptual model of the system has been produced. Such notations, however, are not suitable for describing requirements such as the Stoneman requirements where only a nebulous conceptual model of the system has been formulated.

Natural language is the only realistic means of specifying these imprecise requirements. However, it must be used in such a way that the reader is led from the general to the particular. All technical terms which are used must be clearly defined. Requirements relating to the same entity should be grouped together under some subheading.

It should be possible to read the specification at different levels of detail so each entity should be described in a set of refinement steps. Forward references - references to some entity which is defined later in the specification document - should be clearly distinguished. In the example below, this is achieved by writing the first instance of terms which are introduced before definition in upper case letters.

To illustrate how an imprecise requirements specification might be described, part of the Stoneman requirements, the database requirements for a basic part of the Ada programming environment, have been rewritten below.

1.   KAPSE DATABASE REQUIREMENTS

1.1   The KAPSE database (hereafter termed the KDB) shall be made up of named entities termed OBJECTS.

1.2   The KDB shall not impose restrictions on the format of information stored in an object.

1.3   The KDB shall permit relationships between objects to be recorded.

1.4   The KDB shall allow APSE tools to access both the INFORMATION CONTENT and ATTRIBUTES of objects.

1.5   The KDB shall allow APSE tools to traverse the networks formed by relationships between objects.

1.6   The KDB interface shall permit provision of an archiving facility whereby information held in the KDB may be relegated to backing storage media. This relegation shall not compromise the integrity, consistency, or eventual availability of any information in the KDB.

1.7   KDB Objects

1.7.1   A KDB object is made up of two distinct components - INFORMATION CONTENT and ATTRIBUTES.

1.7.2   Each KDB object shall have a NAME which uniquely identifies that object.

1.7.3 It shall be possible for reading and writing of objects to be performed from within an Ada tool using the standard input-output facilities of the language as defined in the package INPUT_OUTPUT.

1.7.4 Object Names

1.7.4.1 An object name shall be constructed from a sequence of identifiers.

1.7.4.2 Each component of an object name shall conform to the Ada syntax for identifiers.

1.7.4.3 A version qualifier may be appended to an object name if appropriate.

1.7.5 Object Information Content

1.7.5.1 The information content of an object is defined as the raw information contained in the object.

1.7.6 Object Attributes

1.7.6.1 The attributes of an object are defined as meta-information which describes the object.

1.7.6.2 Each object must have at least 3 attributes - a HISTORY ATTRIBUTE, A CATEGORISATION ATTRIBUTE, and an ACCESS ATTRIBUTE.

1.7.6.3 An object may have an indefinite number of attributes in addition to the attributes specified above.

1.7.6.4 Access protection shall be applied to attributes so that attribute consistency is maintained.

This requirements specification can be continued by defining the history, categorisation and access attributes as well as any other undefined terms.

Because the specification of imprecise requirements such as those for the Ada programming environment is not amenable to formal description, responsibility for clear, concise and complete requirements specification is placed on the writer of that specification. This can be achieved by structuring the requirements hierarchically as illustrated above. Functional and non-functional requirements should be clearly delineated and unnecessary detail should be avoided

2.2.2 Specifying non-functional requirements

A non-functional requirement is a requirement which places some restriction on how a function or the system as a whole might be implemented. For example, the Stoneman requirement quoted above states that user communication with the system should make use of the standard Ada character set, is a non-functional requirement which precludes the use of special character sets in the interface design. A different kind of non functional requirement is the activation period of the in_post function described above. This is specified as 10 minutes - nothing to do with the function of in_post, simply a timing parameter.

Although both functional and non-functional requirements are liable to change, non-functional requirements are particularly affected by changes in hardware technology. As the development time for a large system may be several years, it is likely that the hardware available at the conclusion of the project will be more powerful than that available when the project is conceived. Furthermore, the hardware will evolve throughout the lifetime of the developed software and the non-functional requirements may be modified whilst the software is in use.

Such hardware changes as may occur whilst the software is being developed can be anticipated. Hardware dependent non-functional requirements can be specified so that they assume hardware capability will be available although that may not be the case when the project is started. No such anticipation can be made for changes during the project's lifetime and an important characteristic of hardware dependent requirements is that they should be specified in such a way that they may be easily changed.

The notion of a semi-formal language for requirements specification was introduced in a previous section. Although such a language can be used to specify non-functional requirements, it is often better suited to functional specifications. Non functional requirements are such that they tend to conflict - execution speed requirements and storage requirements is the obvious example. A non-functional requirements specification should set out these requirements in such a way that conflicts are made clear and which allows possible trade-offs to be discerned.

Boehm (1974) has described a notation called the requirements/properties matrix which is useful for determining the trade-offs to be made when considering requirements. He identifies program properties such as run speed, storage needs, reliability, maintainability, etc. and definite requirements such as size < 64K, user response time < 4 seconds, etc These are then put together in a matrix displaying requirements and system properties. An example of part of such a matrix is shown in Fig 2.2.

The use of such a matrix relates each requirement/property to an explicit specification. It reduces the probability that unrealistic requirements will be introduced by ensuring that a complete analysis of the implications of that requirement is made. Although the matrix does not show the results of analysis, it documents whether an analysis has been carried out or not. The implications of a particular requirement are unlikely to be overlooked.

Prop. Req.	Run speed	Maintainability	Reliability	Storage	. . .
< 64K	A	B	O	D42	
Standard character set	O	D32	O	O	
Response <4 secs	D17, D31	B	O	A	

Fig. 2.2   Requirements/Properties matrix

The matrix is filled in with one of the following:

    O -- irrelevant
    A -- analysed
    B -- in the process of analysis
    Di -- covered by specification Di
    Rj -- overlaps requirement Rj

2.2.3 Data specifications

For many applications, the logical structure of the data
that is to be processed by computer programs is complex.
For example, in the in_post function described above,
each incoming document has an associated sender, sender
address, time of posting, recipient and recipient
address.   In that example, the physical structure of
that data was simple, fixed and specified as part of the
functional specification.

In many other cases, however, the physical data
structure is not fixed and is determined by the
designers of the system.   It is important that the
notation used for logical data structure specification
does not imply a particular physical data structure.
This separation of logical and physical data
organisations is termed data independence.

One technique which has been used to define a data-
independent specification is to use a relational model
of data as described by Codd (1970).   Using the
relational model, the logical data structure is
specified as a set of tables, with some tables having
common keys.

As an example of a relational specification, consider
the document database in the previous model of an office
system.   Within that database, it may be desired to hold
information about each document such as the owner, the
time it was entered in the database, and the time of the
last access.   It may also be permitted to associate a
summary with each document.   Documents may be entered in
indexes (which are themselves documents) and the
structure of an index must also be specified.

If a unique identifier D# is associated with each
document when it is entered in the database, a document
may be specified as:

D# / text / owner / creation-time / last-access /
summary / access-permissions

An index entry may be specified as:

Index name/D#

Fields within these relations may also be defined as
relations. For example, creation-time may be specified
as:

hours/minutes/day/month/year

It is up to the designer to study the data specification and determine how that specification is best realised as a physical data structure. If a relational database management system is available it may even be possible to implement the logical specification directly.

Although a relational specification of the data does not compromise data independence, it does contain implications of how the data is to be physically structured. For example, it implies that document creation time and owner are stored in such a way that they are accessed via D# rather than in their own right. This may or may not be intended but it is difficult for the designer to ignore such implications as his design is obviously influenced by the specifications.

An alternative technique of data specification, described by Chen (1976) uses a modified relational model where each relation is simply a binary relation. Using binary relations, a document may be described as follows:

    D# 'is composed of' text
    D# ' is owned by' owner
    D# ' was created at ' creation-time
    D# ' was accessed at ' last-access
    D# ' has summary ' summary
    D# ' has permissions ' access-permissions

Using this type of specification, there is no implicit relationship between the document access permissions, say, and the document owner. Furthermore, each binary relation may have a converse:

    owner ' owns ' D#

so that access to documents need not all go through the document identifier D#.

Binary relations are used in the requirements specification language RSL, discussed above and a number of database systems have been implemented using this approach (Frost, 1981; McGregor and Malone, 1980; Sharman and Winterbottom, 1979).

2.3   THE SOFTWARE REQUIREMENTS DOCUMENT

It is very important that a requirements specification be set out in a formal document which may be referenced by system implementors, testers and maintainers. In this section, a possible structure for such a software requirements document is described. As set out by Heninger (1980), there are six requirements for such a document:

(1)   It should only specify external system behaviour.

(2)   It should specify constraints on the implementation.

(3)   It should be easy to change.

(4)   It should serve as a reference tool to those involved in system maintenance.

(5)   It should record forethought about the life cycle of the system.

(6)   It should characterise acceptable responses to undesired events.

The first two of these objectives have already been covered and most of the material in an SRD will be made up of functional and non-functional specifications. The last objective above, that acceptable responses to undesired events should be specified, can be accommodated by including this information in the detailed functional specifications.

Heninger considers that the SRD should serve as a reference tool and should record forethought about the system life cycle because it is used by maintenance programmers to find out what the system is supposed to do. In order to serve this purpose, information in the SRD must be precise and easily found. This implies that the SRD should have a detailed table of contents, one or more indexes, a glossary of terms used and a specification of the changes anticipated when the requirements are originally formulated. Bearing this in mind, a possible organisation for a requirements specification is:

(1)   Introduction
       This should describe the need for the system and should place the system in context, briefly describing its overall functions. It should also set out the structure of the remainder of the document and describe the notations used.

(2)   Hardware
If the system is to be implemented on special hardware, this hardware and its interfaces should be described.

(3)   The Conceptual Model
This section should describe the conceptual model on which the requirements are based. Data flow through the system should be described using a notation such as that of Constantine and Yourdon (1979).

(4)   Functional Requirements
The functional requirements of the system should be set out using some formal or semi-formal notation.

(5)   Non-functional Requirements
The non-functional requirements of the system should be described and related to the functional requirements.

(6)   Maintenance Information
This section of the SRD should describe the fundamental assumptions on which the system is based and describe anticipated changes due to hardware evolution, changing user needs, etc. Wherever possible, functions and constraints which are particularly subject to change should be explicitly specified.

(7)   Glossary
This should define the technical terms used in the document. In formulating the glossary, no assumptions should be made about the experience or background of the reader.

(8)   Index
It may be desirable to provide more than one kind of index to the document. As well as a normal alphabetic index, it may be useful to produce an index per chapter, an index of functions and so on. These indexes are best prepared with automatic aid so that changes to the SRD may readily be indexed.

Because requirements are liable to change, it is essential that the SRD be organised in such a way that changes can be accommodated without extensive rewriting. If this is not done, changes in the requirements may be incorporated in the system without recording these changed in the specification. This causes the program and its documentation to become out of step – a situation which can result in immense problems for the maintenance programmer. Techniques for producing maintainable documentation are described in chapter 7 of this book.

2.4   REQUIREMENTS VALIDATION

Once a set of system requirements has been established, these requirements should be validated. If no validation is carried out, errors in the requirements specification will be propagated to the system design and implementation and expensive system modifications may be required to correct these errors. There are four separate steps involved in validating requirements. These are:

(1)   The requirements must be shown to be consistent. Any one requirement should not conflict with any other.

(2)   The requirements must be shown to be complete. The specification should include all functions and constraints intended by the system user.

(3)   The requirements must be shown to be realistic. There is no point in specifying requirements which are unrealisable using existing hardware and software technology. It may be acceptable to anticipate some hardware developments but developments in software technology are much less predictable.

(4)   The needs of the user must be shown to be valid. A user may think that a system is needed to perform certain functions but further thought and analysis may identify additional or different functions which are required.

If the requirements are specified in some formal way, their consistency can be determined by reviewing the specification. This process is considerably simplified if the requirements specification is compilable and software tools for analysing the specification developed.

An example of such a tool, described by Boehm (1974) is a keyword analyser which, given particular keywords such as 'protection', 'store', 'access', etc., scans all requirements and extracts those requirements which include that keyword. These requirements can then be compared to ensure that they do not conflict. Other automated tools might ensure that duplicate terms for the same object are not introduced, or compare functional inputs and outputs. If a function A provides input for function B, A's output specification should match B's input specification.

The realism of requirements can be demonstrated, in some cases, by constructing a system simulator. The technique of system simulation is particularly useful to demonstrate that non-functional requirements can be met. One of the tools used in conjunction with the requirements statement language RSL, is a simulator generator. This tool analyses an RSL specification and automatically generates a system simulator in Pascal. Procedures which simulate each functional specification are provided by the specifier as part of the requirements definition.

Davis and Vick (1977) point out that, for complex systems, it can be as expensive and as time-consuming to develop the system simulator as it is to develop the system itself. Furthermore, it may be difficult to change the simulator so that changes in the requirements may be impossible to assess. As a result, simulation has not been extensively used in validating the requirements of large systems although Davis and Vick state that it can result in a significant reduction in requirements statement errors.

The other steps involved in requirements validation, checking the completeness of requirements and demonstrating that the system meets the actual needs of the user can only be carried out with the cooperation of the system user. The user must examine and understand the requirements and check that they specify the kind of system which is really needed. Unfortunately, many users do not clearly understand their own needs and cannot effectively compare a requirements statement with the application functions which are needed. Their needs can only be accurately identified if they have some kind of working software system to assess and criticise.

Ideally, a requirements specification should be

formulated according to the apparent needs of the user and the software built and delivered. After a period of use, the user then understands what is really needed and a 'correct' requirements specification can then be formulated. In practice, this procedure is usually impossible as it doubles the cost of the software and means that software takes twice as long to produce. In circumstances where software must be rewritten because of hardware developments, say, it is possible to use this technique. The existing system can be analysed and modifications specified. When the user understands a system, he is able to assess and validate the requirements for the new version of that system.

An alternative to implementing systems twice is to develop a system prototype and allow the user to experiment with this. On the basis of his experience with the prototype, accurate needs can then be formulated.

2.4.1 Prototyping

It is common practice for the developers of new engineering systems to assess their systems by building a prototype before committing themselves to final system specifications. The prototype is intended to act as a test vehicle and it need not satisfy every requirement of the final system. For example, if a prototype is intended to demonstrate functions, it may not be necessary for performance requirements to be met.

Prototyping has not been widely used in software evaluation. The principal argument against it is that the cost of prototype development represents an unacceptably large fraction of overall system costs. It is more economic to modify a finished system to meet unperceived needs than to provide an opportunity for the user to understand and refine his needs before the final system is built. By contrast, the cost of a prototype for a mechanical or electronic system which is to be mass produced represents a very small increment in the final unit cost of the system and the cost of modification after release is very large indeed.

Software prototyping is expensive if the prototype is implemented using the same tools and to the same standards as the final system. However, if a prototype is intended to demonstrate the functional rather than the non-functional aspects of a system it can be developed at a cost which is significantly lower than that of the final system. This can be accomplished by using very high level languages for prototype implementation, by ignoring considerations of error action, by compromising on the suitability of the user interface and by reducing reliability and program quality standards.

When a prototype is available it can be made available to the user for experiment. Not only does the prototype allow him to establish his requirements, it also demonstrates the feasibility of the system to management.

Because error detection and recovery and comprehensive user interface implementation comprise such a large part of most systems, their elimination drastically reduces the size of the system to be prototyped. Hence the prototype development time is much less than the final system development time. This time can be further reduced by lowering standards of reliability and program quality. As the prototype is thrown away after the final requirements have been established, there is no need for production software standards to be adopted.

By reducing the system size and standards, prototype software can be constructed in any programming language but prototype development time can be reduced by using a very high level programming language. Very high level dynamic languages are not normally used for large system development because they need a large run time support system. This run time support increases the storage needs and reduces the execution speeds of programs written in the language. As performance requirements can usually be ignored in prototype development, however, this is not normally a disadvantage.

The language APL (Iverson, 1962) is eminently suited to prototype development. It offers powerful operations such as matrix arithmetic, is concise so that little time need be spent typing and is implemented interactively. Using APL, the software engineer can often put together a prototype system in a fraction of the time required to implement the final software system. APL is unsuitable for large system programming because of its run time overheads, and because its syntax does not permit readable, well structured programs to be written.

Another useful prototyping tool is the shell programming language available under UNIX (Ritchie and Thompson, 1978; Bourne, 1978). The UNIX shell is a job control language which includes looping and decision

constructs.   It   provides   facilities   for   combining
commands which operate on files and strings.   In the
author's experience, a prototype for the information
retrieval   part   of   the   office   information   system
introduced earlier in the chapter was built, using the
shell, in a day.   By contrast, the final system took
several weeks to design and implement.

Design

Good software design is the key to effective software engineering. A well designed software system is straightforward to implement and maintain, is easily understood and is reliable. Badly designed systems, although they may work, are likely to be expensive to maintain, difficult to test properly and unreliable. The design stage is therefore the most critical part of the software development process.

Software design is a creative process. It requires a certain amount of flair on the part of the designer and the final design is normally an iteration from a number of preliminary designs. Design cannot be learned from a book – it must be practiced and learnt by experience and study of existing systems.

Until fairly recently, software design was very much an 'ad hoc' process. Given a set of requirements, usually in natural language, an informal design was prepared, often in the form of a flowchart. Coding then commenced and the design was modified as the system was implemented. When the implementation stage was complete, the design had usually changed so much from its initial specification that the original design document was a totally inadequate description of the system.

This approach to software design was responsible for many dramatic and very expensive project failures, as well as resulting in systems which were unreliable and expensive to run. Now it is realised that informal notations, and notations, such as flowcharts, which are close to the programming language are inadequate vehicles for formulating and expressing system design. A number of new, more formal notations such as data flow diagrams, HIPO charts, structure diagrams and design description languages have been developed and these are superior for expressing software designs.

A survey of these techniques has been compiled by Peters (1980).

This chapter introduces terminology used to discuss software designs and some of the many notations which

may be used to describe a software design. These
include data flow diagrams, structure charts and a
design description language. This is followed by a
description of a design methodology called top down
design. Top down design is illustrated using examples
selected from an office automation system. The final
part of the chapter discusses design validation and
introduces techniques which can be used to establish the
correctness of a design.

3.1   TERMINOLOGY

The communication of software design techniques is
hindered by the fact that no consistent terminology
exists to describe design elements. The term 'module'
is probably the most overloaded of any computing terms
and covers a range of entities from hardware units to
executable programs. Similarly, the terms task, job,
and process have different connotations for each
individual depending on that individual's background.

In such a young subject, this confusion of terms is
inevitable and at this stage, standardisation is
probably undesirable. However, this text requires a
consistent terminology and in this section a number of
terms are defined. These terms are used in a consistent
way throughout this chapter and the remainder of the
book.

Programming System
    A programming system is made up of a collection of
    autonomous programs possibly but not necessarily
    dedicated to a single application. Examples of
    programming systems are operating systems,
    command/control systems and office automation
    systems.

Subsystem
    A subsystem is a programming system which is itself
    part of a larger programming system but which is
    always dedicated to a single application. For
    example, an office automation system might be made up
    of a number of subsystems including a word processing
    subsystem, an electronic mail subsystem and a filing
    subsystem.

Program
    A program is a problem solution specification which
    may be executed by a computer.

Process

A _process_ is a program in execution. A number of processes may execute simultaneously on the same computer.

Program Object

A _program object_ or _object_ is any entity which may be named in a program. This term therefore covers named data objects, labels, _modules_, _procedures_, and _functions_.

Module

A _module_ is a named collection of program objects. These objects are referenced by specifying both the module name and the object name and their visibility to objects outside the module may be explicitly controlled. If an object declared within a module is a data object, it may retain its value from one module reference to another.

Procedure

A _procedure_ is an executable program object. If objects are declared within a procedure, they are deemed to come into existence when that procedure is activated and to go out of existence when execution of that procedure terminates.

Function

A _function_ is a procedure which always accepts at least one input value and returns a single output value.

Program Unit

A _program unit_ is either a module, a procedure or a function.

The definitions given here do not necessarily correspond with the intuitive notions of these terms held by the reader. This does not necessarily mean that the reader's understanding of the terms is incorrect - for the purposes of this text it is necessary to adopt a consistent terminology and the aim of this section has simply been to establish that terminology.

3.2   STAGES OF DESIGN

Given a requirements specification, the software

engineer must use this to derive the design of a programming system which satisfies these requirements. This derivation is accomplished in a number of stages:

(1)   The subsystems making up the programming system must be established.

(2)   Each subsystem must be decomposed into separate programs.

(3)   Each program must be designed in terms of interacting program units.

(4)   Each program unit must be refined. This normally entails specifying each program unit as a hierarchy of subordinate program units.

(5)   At some stage of this refinement process, the algorithms used in each program unit must be specified in detail.

As well as these various stages of programming system design, the software engineer may also be required to design communication mechanisms allowing processes in the system to communicate. He may have to design file structures, and almost certainly will have to design the data structures used in his programs. He will have to design test cases to validate his programs.

3.3   DESIGN NOTATIONS

Consistent and complete notations are immensely valuable in the creation of abstract objects such as computer programming systems. Without such notations, designs cannot be evaluated, compared, tested or communicated. Although the computer program itself is the absolute design specification, the level of detail presented in the program is such that it is unsuitable for conveying the design to human readers. This is particularly true of the higher levels of design where a large system is decomposed into functional units such as subsystems or programs.
    In this section, three design notations are introduced - data flow diagrams, structure charts/diagrams and an algorithmic description language called PDL. Data flow diagrams are particularly useful for describing stages 1, 2, and 3 of the design process,

structure charts, stages 3 and 4 and design description languages stages 4 and 5. Their roles are complementary and a complete design description may use all three techniques.

3.3.1 Data flow diagrams

The notation of data flow diagrams described here derives from the work of Constantine and Yourdon (1979), Yourdon (1975), and Myers (1975). These diagrams document how data input is transformed to output, with each stage in the diagram representing a distinct transformation.

Data flow diagrams are made up of 3 components:

(1)   Annotated arrows.

(2)   Annotated bubbles.

(3)   The operators * and ⊕.

The annotated bubbles represent transformation centres with the annotation specifying the transformation. The arrows represent data flow in and out of the transformation centres with the annotations specifying what the data is. The operators * and ⊕ are used to link arrows - * means AND and ⊕ means EXCLUSIVE OR. Data flow diagrams describe how an input is transformed to an output. They do not, and should not, include control information or sequencing information. Each bubble can be considered as a stand alone black box which, as soon as its inputs are available, transforms them to its outputs.

Fig 3.1 shows input data D1 and D2 being transformed to either D3.1 or D3.2. By convention, inputs enter

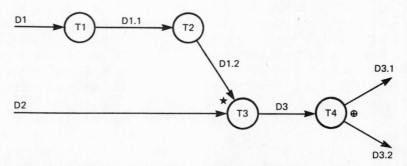

Fig. 3.1   A data flow diagram

from the left and outputs leave to the right. In this example, D1 is transformed by T1 to D1.1 which is transformed by T2 to D1.2. D1.2 is combined with D2 at transformation centre T3 to produce D3. D3 is transformed by T4 producing either D3.1 or D3.2.

Using a practical example, consider a spelling checker program which looks up each word used in a document in a dictionary. If a word appears in the dictionary it is deemed to be correctly spelled otherwise it is displayed on the user's terminal. The user may then decide if the word is misspelled or if it is correctly spelled. If misspelled, the word is held in a file of misspelled words, if correctly spelled, it is added to the dictionary.

There are a number of possible ways of implementing this system. The data flow diagram for one of these possibilities is shown in Fig 3.2.

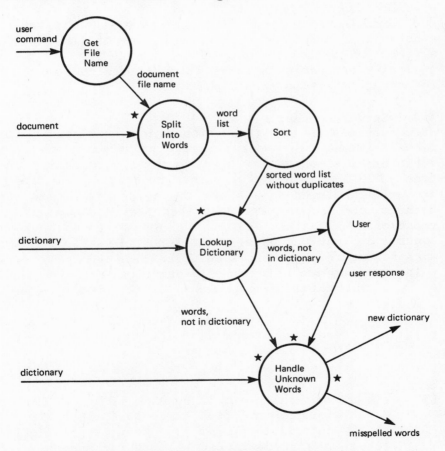

Fig. 3.2   Data flow diagram for spelling checker

One of the principal advantages of data flow diagrams is that they show transformations without making any assumptions about how these transformations are implemented.   In the above diagram, the user at a terminal is represented as a transformation and the other transformations might be implemented in a variety of ways.   For example, the system could be implemented as a single program using program units to implement each   transformation.   Alternatively,   it   might   be implemented   as   a   number   of   separate   interacting programs, using files to communicate with each other or, perhaps, the implementation might be an amalgam of these methods.

The   preparation   of   data   flow   diagrams   is   best approached   by   considering   system   inputs   and   working towards system outputs.   Each bubble must represent a distinct transformation - its output should, in some way, be different from its input.   There are no rules for determining the overall structure of the diagram and constructing a data flow diagram is one of the creative aspects of system design.   Like all design, it is an iterative process with early attempts refined in stages to produce the final diagram.

3.3.2 Structure charts
Structure charts are a notation which complements data flow diagrams.   They describe the programming system as a hierarchy of parts and display this graphically, as a tree. They document how elements of a data flow diagram can be implemented as a hierarchy of program units. The form of structure chart described here follows closely those of Constantine, Yourdon and Myers but without the control conventions used in their notation.

A structure chart shows relationships between program units without including any information about the order of activation of these units.   It is drawn using 3 symbols:

(1)   A rectangle annotated with the name of the unit.

(2)   An arrow connecting these rectangles.

(3)   A circled arrow o->, annotated with the name of data passed to and from elements in the structure chart. Normally, the circled arrow is drawn parallel to the arrow connecting the rectangles in the chart.

An example of a structure chart is shown in Fig 3.3.

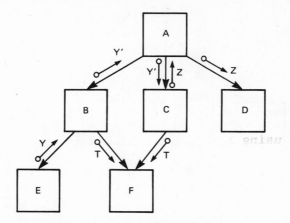

Fig. 3.3   A structure chart

Unit A calls on units B, C, and D. Unit B calls on units E and F and unit C calls on unit F. Notice that nodes at level n in the tree may be shared by two or more nodes at level n-1 but that nodes at level n may not utilise other nodes at the same level. The left to right ordering of B, C, and D does not imply that the units are called in that sequence.

In the above chart, data Y originates in unit E, is transformed by B to Y′ and passed to A. Unit B also passes data T to unit F. Unit A passes Y′ to C and C passes T to F. C returns Z to A which passes Z on to D. Data arrows which originate at a lower node are taken to be input and nodes which do not return data to a higher level node are assumed to output that data.

From any non-trivial data flow diagram, it is possible to derive a number of different structure charts. For example, Figs 3.4, 3.5, and 3.6 show three

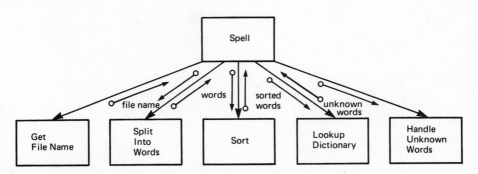

Fig. 3.4   Spell structure 1

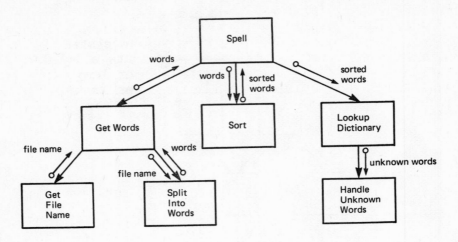

Fig. 3.5   Spell structure 2

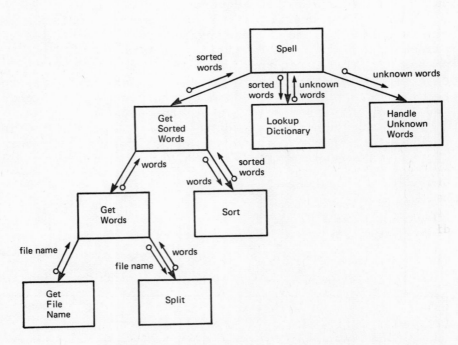

Fig. 3.6   Spell structure 3

structure   charts   representing   different   ways   of
organising a spelling checker program.

Structure   charts   derived   from   data   flow   diagrams
represent a first level structure of the system, where
each box on the structure chart represents a bubble in
the data flow diagram.   Naturally, deeper levels can be
described using the same technique.   For example, the
lookup rectangle might have a structure as Fig 3.7.

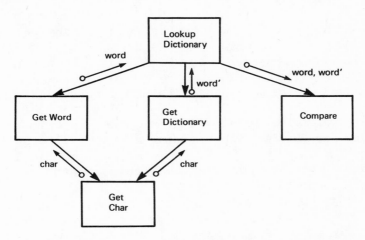

Fig. 3.7   Structure chart for lookup

A major problem facing the software engineer is how
to derive the most appropriate structure chart from a
data flow diagram.   This will be discussed later in the
chapter.

3.3.3 Software description languages
The lowest level of a software design is best described
using some formal notation.   It has been argued that the
most appropriate notation for this is a high level
programming language such as Ada or Pascal. Whilst this
has the obvious advantage that the design is executable
if a suitable language compiler is available, there are
disadvantages to this approach.   These are:

(1)   High level programming languages — because they
       must be compilable — are not easily extended to
       include new concepts.

(2)   The data types, structures and operations avail-
       able as primitives in programming languages are
       relatively   low   level.   This   means   that   the

representation of even intuitively simple high
level constructs such as an unbounded sequence of
data items sometimes tends to become detailed and
confused.

(3)   As thinking is constrained by language, the lower
the level of constructs available to the designer,
the more his thinking is liable to be influenced
by language constructs.

(4)   If an initial implementation of a design, specified in a programming language, must subsequently
be reimplemented, it is difficult to carry out
this reimplementation in a higher level language
than the design specification language.

Rather than using an existing programming language as a
vehicle for design expression, a better alternative is
to use a design description language specifically
intended for documenting and communicating software
designs. A number of such languages have been invented
such as those described by Chu (1978), Van Leer (1976)
and Linger et al., (1979). Space limitations do not
allow any of these languages to be described fully but
aspects of PDL, described by Linger et al. are covered
below and are illustrated by example. According to
Mills (1981), this design language has been used with
considerable success in a number of major projects.
    The language PDL (Process Design Language) is
specifically tailored for the specification of software
designs which are subsequently implemented in some
programming language. It embodies the notions of
structured programming, program correctness and
systematic programming suggested by Dahl et al., (1972),
Hoare (1969), and Wirth (1976).   PDL is not a fixed
formal language but is an extensible language which
provides constructs to express control and data
structures. Primitive data objects which are available
include scalars, stacks, lists, queues and sequences.
User types may be defined. The control constructs
include while-do, for-do, if-then, if-then-else, and
case but do not include either conditional or
unconditional gotos.
    PDL descriptions may include natural language to
describe some function. For example, a valid PDL
statement of a spelling checker program is:

```
proc spellcheck
    [ split document into words ]
    do
        get next word
        add word to word list in sort order
    while words remain in input document
    [ look up words in dictionary ]
    while all words not checked
    do
        if word not in dictionary then
            display word, prompt on user terminal
            if user response says word OK then
                add word to good word list
            else
                add word to bad word list
            fi
        fi
    od
    merge dictionary and good word list giving new
dictionary
corp
```

In this example, some PDL control constructs have been used to describe the decisions made in the program but all actual operations have been described in natural language. Statements enclosed in square brackets [], are logical commentary and in a typical PDL description represent a higher level (more abstract) design.

To illustrate further aspects of PDL, the operation of adding words to a list in sort order is described in more detail. Assuming the word is held in a string called 'word' and the list of words is held in a binary tree, the following PDL fragment describes the operation of adding a new word to the list.

```
record node
    left : node
    value : string
    right : node

[ run specifies that the named unit should be
activated ]
run enter_in_sort_order(word,node)

proc enter_in_sort_order(fix word, alt node)
    [ fix specifies word may not be changed
        alt specifies node may be modified   ]
```

```
            [ empty list case ]
            if node = nil then
               node := (nil,word,nil)
            else
            if word < node.value then
               if node.left = nil then
                  node.left := (nil,word,nil)
               else
                  run enter_in_sort_order(word,node.left)
               fi
            else
               if word > node.value then
                  if node.right = nil then
                  node.right = (nil,word,nil)
                  else
                     run enter_in_sort_order(word,node.right)
                  fi
               fi
            fi
            fi
            [ either new word entered or duplicate exists so
              no need to enter word   ]
         corp
```

Readers familiar with a high level programming language should have no difficulty understanding the above fragment as it uses only familiar programming language constructs. The final PDL example in this section uses a higher level PDL construct called a sequence.

A PDL sequence is an unbounded list which may be accessed sequentially. The keywords current, next and reset are used to access the sequence. Formally, a sequence can be defined as an ordered pair of lists, the first list (the past list) being those members already accessed and the second list (the future list) those members to be accessed. The keyword current refers to the last member of the past list, the keyword next to the first member of the future list. The keyword reset defines a new sequence whose past list is the empty list and whose future list is a catenation of the two lists of the old sequence. Informally, it sets an implicit list pointer to the beginning of the list.

If a sequence p is (a,b,c),(x,y,z), current refers to c, the last member of the first list and next refers to x, the first member of the second list. The operation reset(p) creates a new sequence p = (a,b,c,x,y,z). By convention, the first list is referred to as p-, the second list as p+. The sequence composition operator is '.' so p = p-.p+.

Sequences will be used in the example below which describes the final part of the spelling checker, namely the merging of the dictionary and the properly spelled words from the document which do not appear in the dictionary.

```
sequence dictionary,goodwords,newdict

run merge(dictionary,goodwords,newdict)

proc merge(fix a,b:sequence,alt c:sequence)
    scalar x,y
    if a = empty then
       c := b
    else
       if b = empty then
          c := a
       else
          x,y := next(a),next(b)
       fi
    fi
    while a ≠ empty and b ≠ empty
    do    [execute till one sequence exhausted]
       if x < y then   [select from 1st sequence]
          next(c),x := x,next(a)
       else
          next(c),y := y,next(b)
       fi
    od
    [ assign remainder of non exhausted sequence ]
    if a = empty then
       c := c.b+
    else
       c := c.a+
    fi
 corp
```

This example concludes this overview of PDL. However, PDL will be used throughout this chapter to describe software designs and these further examples illustrate some other aspects of the language.

3.4   TOP DOWN DESIGN

The design of software is a creative process which

cannot be formulated as a set of rules. Nevertheless, the use of a systematic design methodology simplifies the design process and results in software which is understandable, verifiable and reliable. One such methodology is called top down design or stepwise refinement. It makes use of the most fundamental human problem solving facility – abstraction.

According to the Concise Oxford Dictionary, abstraction is the 'process of stripping an idea of its concrete accompaniments'. The idea is considered as an abstract entity without details of how that entity is actually realised. The previous example of the spelling checker illustrated the process – checking spelling involved splitting the document into words, sorting these words then looking them up in a dictionary. These were identified as fundamental operations and, initially, how they actually worked was ignored. As the design progresses, each component is refined into its own fundamental operations with the process continuing until a low level design is formulated.

The formulation and description of a software design involves a number of different stages:

(1)   Study and understand the problem. Without this understanding, effective software design is impossible.

(2)   Identify gross features of at least one possible solution. At this stage it is often useful to identify a number of solutions and to mentally evaluate each of these. The simplest possible solution should be chosen. It is particularly important not to allow low level implementation details, of which the designer may be aware, to interfere with the choice of solution.

(3)   Construct a data flow diagram showing gross data transformations in the system. If this seems impossible, it is likely that the problem is not properly understood.

(4)   Using the data flow diagram, construct a structure chart showing the program units involved in the solution.

(5)   Describe each abstraction used in the solution in a description language such as PDL. It is likely

that at the first stages of the design this will
consist, almost exclusively, of natural language
description.

After the initial highest level, solution has been
formulated and described, the problem solving process
should be repeated for each abstraction used. This
process of refinement continues until a low level
specification of each abstraction has been prepared.
It is very important that the representation of each
stage of the design is clear and concise. A useful
convention which may be adopted is to express the design
in such a way that each part of the specification can be
described on a single, standard sheet of paper.

3.4.1 Deriving structure charts

An important stage in the design process is the
transformation of a data flow diagram to a structure
chart. This stage converts abstract transformations
into a hierarchy of program units thus representing an
important step in the transition from an abstract
problem solution to a concrete realisation of that
solution.
Recall that in the previous example of a spelling
checker program, 3 different structure diagrams were
derived from the system data flow diagram. No comment
was made at that stage as to which of these represented
the 'best' solution. Although this notion of a 'best'
solution is, to some extent, subjective, Constantine and
Yourdon (1979) suggest that the best solution is that
where program units exhibit a high degree of cohesion
and a low degree of coupling.
A program unit is said to exhibit a high degree of
cohesion if the elements in that unit exhibit a high
degree of functional relatedness. This means that each
element in the program unit should be essential for that
unit to achieve its purpose. For example – sort a file,
lookup a dictionary etc, etc. Elements which are
grouped together in a program unit for some other reason
such as to perform actions which take place at the same
time or which implement a number of distinct functions
have a low degree of cohesion.
Coupling is related to cohesion – it is an indication
of the strength of interconnections between program
units. Highly coupled systems have strong
interconnections with program units dependent on each
other whereas loosely coupled systems are made up of

units which are independent or almost independent.

The obvious advantages of highly cohesive, loosely coupled systems is that any program unit can be replaced by an equivalent unit with little or no change to other units in the system. This is important when designs are refined as loosely coupled units mean that a designer has the option of changing his mind about the design of a unit without adverse effects on the rest of the system. The identification of loosely coupled, highly cohesive units is simplified if units are considered to be principally responsible for dealing with one of four types of data flow.

(1)   Input – the program unit is responsible for accepting data from a unit at a lower level in the structure chart and passing that data on to a higher level unit. Yourdon and Constantine use the term 'afferent' to describe such units.

(2)   Output – the program unit is responsible for accepting data from a higher level unit and passing it to a lower level unit. This is termed 'efferent' by Yourdon and Constantine.

(3)   Transform flow – a program unit accepts data from a higher level unit, transforms that data and passes it back to that unit.

(4)   Coordinate flow – a unit is responsible for controlling and managing other units.

Typical representations for each type of unit in a structure chart are shown in Fig 3.8.

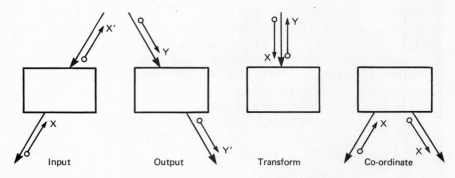

Fig. 3.8   Structure chart representation

The first step in converting a data flow diagram to a structure chart is to identify the highest level input and output units. These units are those which are still concerned with passing data up and down the hierarchy but are furthest removed from physical   input and output.   This step, generally, does not include all bubbles and the remaining transforms are termed central transforms.

The first level of the structure chart is produced by representing the input unit as a single box and each central transform as a single box. The box at the root of the structure chart is designated as a control unit. This factoring process may then be repeated for the first level units in the structure chart until all bubbles in the data flow diagram are represented. Consider again the data flow diagram for the spelling checker program shown in Fig 3.9.

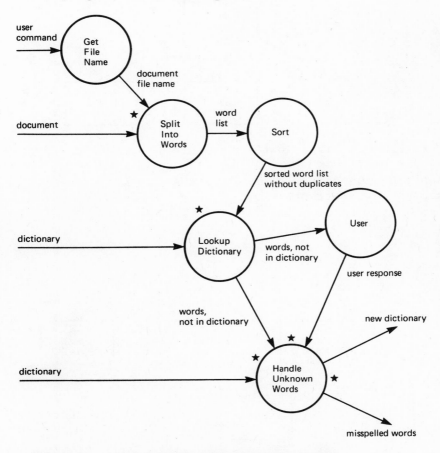

Fig. 3.9   Data flow diagram for spelling checker

Identifying the highest level input and output bubbles depends on the skill and experience of the system designer. One possible way to approach this task is to trace the inputs until a bubble is found whose output is such that its input cannot be deduced from output examination. The previous bubble then represents the highest level input unit. A similar criterion is used to establish the highest level output bubble.

Applying these criteria to the data flow diagram of the spelling checker suggests that the bubble 'lookup' represents a central transform whereas 'sort' represents the highest level input unit and 'handle unknown words', the highest level output unit. This results in the following first level structure being derived as in Fig 3.10.

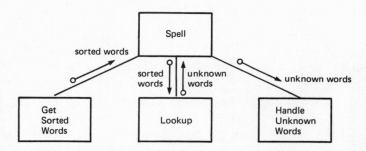

Fig. 3.10   First level structure for spelling checker

Applying the same process to the sort unit to derive the second level structure we get Fig 3.11.

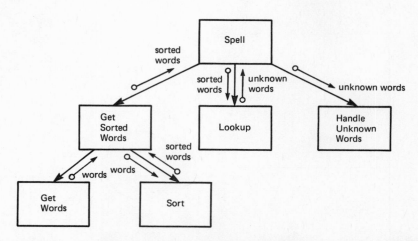

Fig. 3.11   Second level structure for spelling checker

Notice that sort has now taken on the role of a central transform. The derivation process is applied a third time to derive the final structure chart as Fig 3.12.

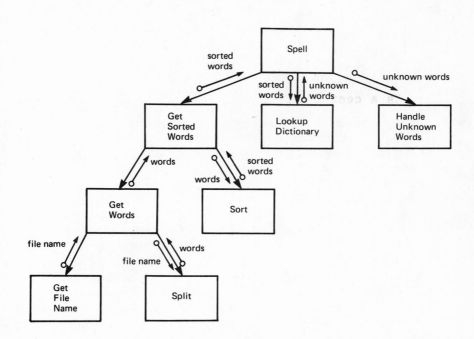

Fig. 3.12   Final structure chart for spelling checker

It is generally (although not necessarily) true that each node in the structure chart of a well structured design will have between two and seven subordinates. If a node has only a single subordinate, this implies that the unit represented by that node may have a low degree of cohesion – the unit encompasses more than a single function and the existence of a single subordinate means that one of the functions may have been factored out. If a node has many subordinates, this implies that the design has been developed to too low a level at that stage.

3.4.2 An example of top down design
The concepts of top down design are best illustrated by example and, in this section, an information retrieval system intended for use in an office is described. As a full system description is lengthy, only an overview of the system is presented. Aspects of the system will be expounded in more detail as required.

The Office Information Retrieval System (OIRS) is an automatic file clerk which can file documents under a number of headings, retrieve documents, display and maintain document indexes, archive documents and destroy documents. The system is activated by a request from the user's terminal and always returns a message to the user indicating the success or failure of his request.

When a document is filed, the location of the document, a document name and the indexes under which it should be filed must be specified. Retrieval requests involve the specification of one or more indexes along with the document name. Index examination involves specifying and index name and a qualifier. This qualifier is a condition determining which parts of the index are required for examination.

OIRS uses a file called currentdoc to communicate with the user. When a document is retrieved, it is copied to currentdoc, when an index is consulted, the relevant portion is copied to currentdoc and currentdoc is the default location for a document which is to be filed. Commands exist to create and display currentdoc and to transmit currentdoc to some other subsystem such as an electronic mail or word processing system.

OIRS maintains a history file of requests processed by the system. As well as being used to produce usage statistics, this file is a means of remembering specifiers provided by the user. Therefore, if the system is used to process a sequence of requests, command specifiers need not be provided in full by the user each time. They are assumed to be the same as that used in the previous command.

A full description of OIRS commands will not be given as it would be both lengthy and irrelevant - rather, some commands are illustrated by example below.

    file as smithletter under letters,smith

This command files currentdoc and names it smithletter. Entries are made in the indexes letters and smith.

    lookup letters s-v

This command retrieves part of the index called 'letters'. Only those names in the index whose initial lies between 's' and 'v' are retrieved. The output from lookup is placed in currentdoc.

```
get books on-loan
```

The document named 'on-loan' is assumed to be filed under the index books. This document is retrieved to currentdoc.

```
edit
```

Activates an editor to modify currentdoc.

```
file as on-loan
```

Files currentdoc as 'on-loan' under an index whose name is deduced from the history file. The index assumed is the last index or index list referenced by the user. If on-loan already exists in the index, the user specifies if the entry is to be duplicated or overwritten.

```
get tomsletter
```

This command specified that the document named tomsletter is to be retrieved. The index in which tomsletter is entered is deduced from examination of the history file.

3.4.3 Designing an office information system

The initial stage of the design of OIRS can be tackled by considering the system as a black box and examining the inputs and possible outputs of the system. This can be represented as a data flow diagram shown as Fig 3.13.

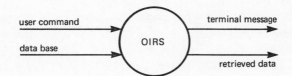

Fig. 3.13   Inputs and outputs of OIRS

A possible development of this is to consider that a data flow bubble should exist to handle each input and each output. Connecting these bubbles might be a transform converting input to output (see Fig 3.14). Examination of the problem description shows that there are a number of different user commands each of which may have parameters. There is, therefore, a need to

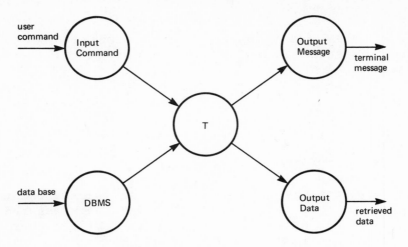

Fig. 3.14   Second refinement of OIRS

check command syntax and to 'understand' the command parameters before passing it on for transformation. This leads to a development of the input command bubble as shown in Fig 3.15.

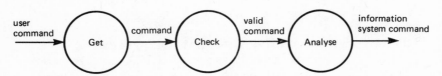

Fig. 3.15   Input command processing

After the user command has been analysed, it is transformed to a request for information retrieval.

Attention must now be paid to the other input bubble – that responsible for accessing the OIRS database. This database consists of many distinct files and, clearly, the function of this input bubble is fairly complex. A possible way of tackling this problem is to postulate the existence of a data base management system (DBMS) responsible for all information transfers to and from the OIRS database. This DBMS represents an abstraction and allows the database to be considered as a single entity rather than as a number of files. The data flow diagram for input therefore is as Fig 3.16.

The DBMS returns the information retrieved to bubble T and this must be transformed to appropriate user output. The output part of the system might be represented as shown in Fig 3.17.

In each of these diagrams, the bubble T has been shown as the sink for input and as the source of output.

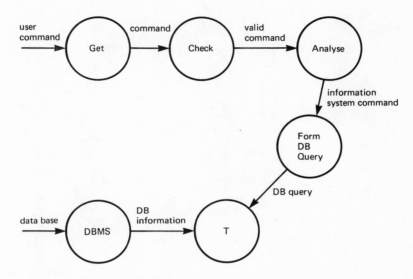

Fig. 3.16   Input transformations

However, examination shows that T is actually redundant and that the central transform is that carried out by

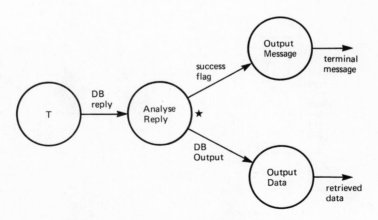

Fig. 3.17   Output data flow diagram

the DBMS. The highest level data flow diagram for OIRS therefore is illustrated as Fig 3.18.

The next stage in the design is to document it as a structure chart. The highest level 'input' bubble is

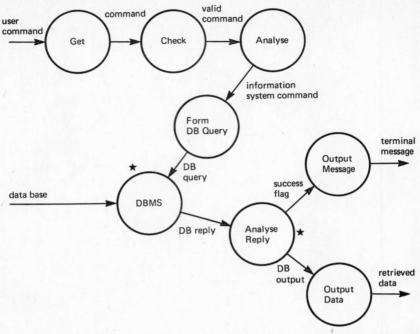

Fig. 3.18 First level data flow diagram for OIRS

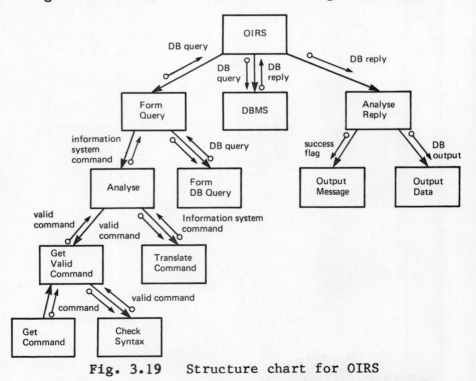

Fig. 3.19 Structure chart for OIRS

'form DB comm', the highest level output bubble is 'process DB reply' and the only central transform bubble is 'DBMS'. Therefore, the structure chart shown as Fig 3.19 can be derived.

The next stage in the design process is to consider the data flow diagram and specifications and work out which bubbles should be expanded in more detail.

Consider the bubble 'form DB command'. This accepts a 'compiled' user command and translates it to one or more database management system commands. Examination of the specifications shows that, on occasion, the compiled user command is incomplete – it may require additional information derived from previous commands. This is obtained from the a history file which stores all previous user commands. The expanded data flow diagram for this bubble is illustrated as Fig 3.20.

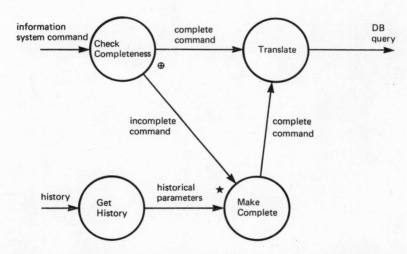

Fig. 3.20   Data flow diagram for form DB command

A similar expansion can be carried out for other bubbles in the data flow diagram and second order structure charts prepared for each of these.

Having prepared data flow diagrams and structure charts, the next stage in the design process is to derive and document the design using a description language. Before doing so, however, the data flow diagrams should be reexamined to see where error reports should be generated.

In the preparation of data flow diagrams, it is sensible to ignore data flows resulting from error conditions as these tend to clutter the diagram. In fact, they represent an unnecessary level of detail. However, as the design is documented in more detail, it is important to take errors into account. A modified data flow diagram for the system which includes error information is shown in Fig 3.21.

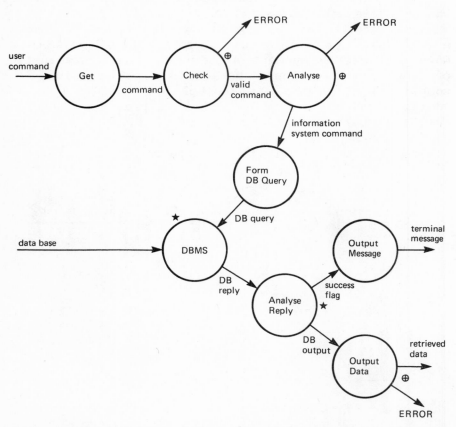

Fig. 3.21   OIRS data flow diagram showing error flows

For clarity, error data flow is not shown flowing to a bubble – it is clearly indicated by specifying ERROR in upper case letters.

The refinement of the design and specification in a description language is illustrated below by describing the design of 'analyse command' which generates a compiled OIRS request.   Such a request has the form:

```
record IRreq =
    [ set if request valid ]
    OK : logical
    [ command to be executed ]
```

```
command : integer(1..maximum_number_of_commands)
[ location of document ]
location : filename_type
[ name document is given by user ]
name : string
[ indexes under which document filed ]
indexes : index_list
```

The program unit 'analyse command' is called with a structure of this form as a parameter:

```
run analyse_command(request)
```

A high level description of 'analyse_command' is:

```
proc analyse_command(alt req : IRreq)
    scalar command_string : string, error_indicator :
    logical
    run
    get_valid_command(error_indicator,command_string)
    if error_indicator then
        req.OK := false
    else
        run compile_command(command_string,req)
corp
```

Now the design of each referenced unit in 'analyse_command' can be refined. This is illustrated by describing the design of 'compile_command'. The string returned by 'get_valid_command' has the form:

```
command_string ::= <command name> , <location> ,
<name> , <index list>:
```

The meaningful elements of the user command are presented as a string with elements separated by commas. The command string is terminated with a colon. This command is generated by another program unit so its syntax can be assumed to be correct. Therefore, 'compile_command' does not need syntax checking statements.

```
proc compile_command(fix command_string:string; alt
req)
    scalar sp:integer
    [ sp is pointer into command string ]
    sp := 0
```

```
run get_to_comma(sp,command_string,command)
run get_to_comma(sp,command_string,location)
run get_to_comma(sp,command_string,name)
run make_index_list(sp,command_string,indexes)
case
    command
part('file') [file command ]
    if name = '' then
        req.OK := false
        run error_message('file command needs a
name')
    else
        req := (true,FILE,location,name,indexes)
    fi
part('lookup')  [ lookup command ]
    if name ≠ '' or location ≠ '' then
        run error_message('only indexes needed in
lookup')
    fi
    req := (true,LOOKUP,'','',indexes)
part('get')
    .......
    [code for remaining commands]
    .......
corp
```

The final refinement step is to describe the program units get_to_comma and make_index_list but as the details of these are straightforward, they will not be shown here.

The design specification is continued for all other program units in a similar way. Notice that no account is taken of implementation details such as the efficiency of data representations or programming language control constructs. The intention of the designer is to develop a language-independent design which may be understood and validated. Taking implementation considerations such as efficiency and representation into account serves to confuse the design.

3.5   DESIGN VALIDATION

Validation of a software design is extremely important. Undetected errors and omissions which are carried forward to the implementation phase of the project and not detected until system testing can be extremely expensive to correct. They may require a complete redesign and reimplementation of parts of the system.

The validation of a software design is intended to achieve two objects:

(1)   To show that the software design is 'correct', that is, the design should correctly implement the intentions of the designer.

(2)   To show that the software meets the requirements in full, that is, for each requirement a design fragment should exist to meet that requirement.

The first of the objects above, the verification of design correctness is best achieved by providing a mathematical proof that each software fragment is correct. However, proving correctness is time consuming and intellectually demanding with the consequence that formally verifying a design is expensive. Because of this cost, formal verification is not yet generally used for demonstrating design correctness but it is the author's opinion that formal verification ought to be more widely used, particularly for critical parts of systems.

The second design validation objective, to check that all requirements have been met by the design is accomplished by the use of design reviews. At a design review, a set of requirements and the design to meet these requirements are studied and compared. This task is considerably simplified if the requirements are stated in a formal way. If requirements are stated informally, ambiguities in the requirements may result in uncertainties in the design which are difficult to resolve.

3.5.1 Design verification

The process of design verification is intended to show that each design unit fulfils its intended function. The only possible way of unambiguously doing so is to provide a mathematical specification of a unit's function and, by reference to the code of that unit, prove that that code implements the functional specification.

The verification of programs by providing a mathematical proof of their correctness was built on the work of McCarthy (1962), and a number of other authors such as Floyd (1967), Hoare (1969), Dijkstra (1976) and

Manna (1969). There are a variety of different techniques for proving program correctness but the general principle underlying these techniques is straightforward.

Assume that there are a number of points in a program where the designer can provide assertions concerning the program variables and their relationships. At each of these points, the assertions should be invariably true. Say the points in the program are P(1), P(2),...P(n). The associated assertions are a(1), a(2),...a(n). Assertion a(1) must be an assertion about the input of the program and a(n) an assertion about the program output.

To prove that the program statements between points P(i) and P(i+1) are correct, it must be demonstrated that the application of the program statements separating these points causes a(i) to be transformed to a(i+1). If this verification is carried out for all adjacent points in the program this will demonstrate that the input assertion plus the program leads directly to the output assertion. If the input and output assertions are correctly formulated and the program terminates(does not contain an endless loop), this process demonstrates the correctness of the program.

3.5.2 Examples of correctness proofs

A discussion of program proving techniques requires a book to itself so general techniques will not be covered here. Rather, two examples of program proofs are presented to demonstrate program verification. The first program is a trivial program which determines the maximum value in a sequence, and the second example is the well known binary search algorithm.

The notation used in these examples is not the familiar notation derived from predicate logic. The existential quantifier is replaced by a function MEMB so that MEMB(X) can be read as 'there exists a member of X'. If X is ordered, this ordering is denoted by ORD(X). The logical operators are written as 'and', 'or' and 'not' with 'not' having the highest precedence followed by 'and' then 'or'.

Rather than use the universal quantifier, the notation X, where X is a set, sequence or array, is taken to mean all members of X. Part of a sequence or array may be written as X(p..q) which means all members between X(p) and X(q). This notation may be extended to specify multiple parts. X(p..q,r..s) means all members

of X between X(p) and X(q) and all members between X(r)
and X(s).

[program accepts values from a sequence and sets max
to
 the same value as the largest member of that
sequence]
sequence I; scalar max,a

```
1.   max := next(I)
2.   while I+ ≠ empty do
2.1     a := next(I)
2.2     if max < a then
2.2.1         max := a
        fi
      od
```

Proof of Termination
The <u>next</u> operation is defined as reducing the length of
I+ by 1 each time it is applied and the test for an
empty sequence is defined to succeed when |I+| = 0. As
next is applied in every execution of the loop and no
reset statements are present, |I+| must eventually be
zero and the predicate (I+ ≠ empty) will be false. The
loop and hence the program will then terminate.

Initial Assertion
The program is valid iff the length of the sequence
I,|I| is greater than 0.

Final Assertion
The output assertion states that max is either greater
than or equal to all members of the sequence I.
    max >= I and max = MEMB(I)

Proof
To prove that this design is correct, it must be shown
that the output assertion follows from the input
assertion and the program. Consider each statement in
turn.

(1)   The assertion that can be made before statement 1
      is that max is undefined. This statement sets max
      to the first member of the sequence thus defining
      it equal to a member of I.

(2)   At statement 2, max is greater than or equal to

all members of the sequence considered so far.
    max >= I- and max = MEMB(I-)
This is true on first execution as I- consists of
the first member of I and statement 1 sets max to
this value.

(3)   The loop has no side effects so assertion 2 holds
before execution of statement 2.1. After execution either this assertion still holds or a > max.
    max >= I- and max = MEMB(I-) or max < a and a =
    MEMB(I-)

(4)   Statement 2.2 selects case where a > max.   After
this statement, a >max holds. Therefore:
    a >= I- and a = MEMB(I-)

(5)   Statement 2.2.1 assigns value of a to max. Therefore:
    max >= I- and max = MEMB(I-)
At this stage, statement 2 is executed. The invariant specified there subsumes this assertion(>=
includes >), so the invariant at 2 is true if this
statement is executed. On loop termination, therefore the assertion
    max >= I- and max = MEMB(I-)
always holds. But, the definition of the empty
condition specifies that I+ = empty is true when
|I+| = 0, that is, when I- = I.

(6)   Therefore, the final condition:
    max >= I and max = MEMB(I)
is true and the program is correct.

The assertions developed can be included in the program
as logical commentary.

```
sequence I;   scalar max,a

[ max = undefined and |I| > 0]
max := next(I)
[ max >= I- and max = MEMB(I-) ]
while I+ ≠ empty do
    a := next(I)
    [ max >= I- and max = MEMB(I-) or max < a and a =
    MEMB(I-) ]
    if max < a then
        [ a >= I- and a = MEMB(I-) ]
        max := a
```

```
        [ max >= I- and max = MEMB(I-) ]
      fi
  od

  [ max >= I and max = MEMB(I) ]
```

A proof of this trivial program has been covered in detail to demonstrate that even the verification of a simple program is lengthy.

As a further illustration of verification, consider a more complex program which describes a binary search routine. Assertions have been included as commentary in the program.

```
  proc binary_search(fix key:integer,T:array(m:n) of
  integer; alt l:integer)

    [ 1 -- m <= n and ORD(T) ]
    scalar mid,top,bott,l:integer; found : logical
    bott,top := m,n
    l := (m+n) div 2
    found := T(l) = key
    while
    [ 2 -- found and T(l) = key or
           not found and key ≠ T(m..bott-1,top+1..n) ]
        bott <= top and not found
    do
        mid := (top + bott) div 2
        if T(mid) = key then
        [ 3 -- key = T(mid) and found ]
            found := true
            l := mid
        else
            [ 4 -- key ≠ T(m..bott-1,top+1..n) ]
            if T(mid) < key then
            [5 -- key ≠ T(m..mid) ]
                bott := mid + 1
                [ 6 -- key ≠ T(m..bott-1) ]
            else
                [ 7 -- key ≠ T(mid..n) ]
                top := mid - 1
                [ 8 -- key ≠ T(top+1..n)]
            fi
        fi
    od
  [ 9 -- found and T(l) = key or
         not found and key ≠ T ]
  corp
```

Proof of Termination
The program terminates when found becomes true or when bott becomes greater than top.

   If search succeeds, that is if an element equal to the key exists, found is explicitly set true thus causing termination.

   Initially bott < top. If found is not set true, either the statement bott := mid +1 or the statement top := mid − 1 must be executed. The effect of these statements is to reduce (top − bott) until eventually it is negative in which case bott exceeds top and the program terminates.

Initial Assertion
The initial assertion specifies that T is in ascending order, that array bounds are positive and that the upper bound exceeds the lower bound.

   m <= n and ORD(T)

Final Assertion
The final assertion specifies either that an element in the table is equal to the key and that l is the index of that element or the table does not contain an element equal to the key.

   found and T(l) = key or not found and key ≠ T

Proof

(1)   Assertion 2 specifies either that the required value R does not lie in the portion of the table already examined or it is the value at the mid point of the table currently being examined.
      This is true on the first entry to the loop because none of the table has been examined so the required value does not lie in the portion of the table already examined.

(2)   Assertion 3 follows because of successful test, key = mid. If assertions 3, 5, and 7 are true then assertion 2 follows directly for subsequent entries to the loop.

(3)   Assertion 4 follows from the fact that T is ordered and T(mid) < key. All values between m and mid are less than V.

(4)   Assertion 5 follows by substituting bott-1 for mid.

(5)   Assertion 6 follows using similar argument to 4 for values greater than key.

(6)   Assertion 7 follows from 6 by substituting top-1 for mid.

(7)   On termination, it follows from the loop invariant that T(1) = key and found is true or, alternatively, found is false and there is no value in the part of the table searched so far that equals key. However, on termination bott is greater than top so the expression T(m..bott-1, top+1..n) includes the entire table so there is no value in T = key. Therefore, the binary search program is correct.

Notice that proofs above make the assumptions about the semantics of programming language operations such as the assignment and if-then-else statements. No justification of these assumptions will be made here but the interested reader is referred to Hoare (1969), and Strachey and Milne (1976) for a discussion of programming language semantics.

From the foregoing it is clear that a correctness proof is at least as long if not longer than the program whose correctness is being verified. The effort required to develop the proof normally exceeds the programming effort. Thus developing a proof is a difficult and costly exercise requiring specially trained and motivated staff. Although some progress has been made in implementing software tools to assist verification, the development of such tools is still a research problem.

For these reasons, authors such as Jensen and Tonies (1979) do not consider program proving to be a cost effective software engineering technique. On the other hand, reports of work at IBM's Federal System's division (IBM, 1980) suggest that they make successful use of formal verification techniques in the development of large programming systems.

In the author's opinion, formal verification techniques are extremely valuable and have an important role to play in large system development. At present, it is not cost effective to apply these techniques to entire systems but heavily used, critical system components should be proved correct. Other parts of the system might have their correctness demonstrated by non-formal correctness arguments.

3.5.3 Correctness arguments

Correctness can be demonstrated in an informal way by presenting an argument explaining why a program is correct. Although less rigorous, this technique is much easier, quicker and cheaper than more formal correctness verification methods. An example of a non-formal demonstration of correctness is shown below. The algorithm specified takes two strings A and B as input. If B is a substring of A, it returns the index of the first character of B in A otherwise it returns −1.

```
proc match(fix A,B:string; alt offset)
    scalar i:integer
    if |B| > |A| then
        offset := −1
    else
        if |B| = |A| then
            offset := if A = B then 0 else −1 fi
        else
            i := 0;   offset := −1
            do
                if B = A(i,|B|) then
                    offset := i
                else
                    i := i + 1
                fi
            while offset = −1 \/ i <= |A| − |B|
        fi
    fi
corp
```

Termination

The variable i is always increased or offset is assigned a value not equal to −1. Termination is therefore assured.

Correctness argument

(1)   The length of B is greater then the length of A so B cannot be a substring of A. Offset is set to −1.

(2)   If the lengths of A and B are equal, B is contained in A iff A = B, so offset = 0 if equal, otherwise −1

(3)   If $|A| > |B|$ the algorithm moves a pointer i char-
        acter by character along A.   B is compared with
        the selected substring of A each time the pointer
        is moved.   If B is equal to the substring of A,
        offset is set to i, the first character of the
        matching substring.

(4)   The comparison continues until the last substring
        checked is the last $|B|$ characters in A.   The $<=$
        test is OK because the characters in A index from
        0.

Because of the importance of design correctness, the
software engineer should provide some form of
verification - informal or, preferably, formal - with
each program design specification.   The testing of a
design after implementation is so expensive that the
cost of producing this verification is justified.

3.6   DESIGN REVIEWS

Design reviews may be formal or informal.   Informal
reviews(structured walkthroughs) only involve the design
team and are a means of refining and polishing the
design before presenting it for a formal review.   A
formal design review involves members of the design
team, management representatives and, possibly, external
consultants and representatives of the software
contractor.   A formal design review is an important
project checkpoint where major decisions about the
readiness of the project for implementation or even
project viability may be made.
     A formal review ought to be a formality - the design
team should be able to demonstrate that all software
requirements are met and that the software design is
correct.   Formal reviews should not be considered as a
mechanism for detecting design errors. As formal reviews
are not intended as a design validation mechanism, they
will not be discussed here.
     The objective of an informal design review is to
evaluate all aspects of a software design. They should
consider the design in much more detail than formal
reviews. Assuming that some design verification has been
carried out, the principal task of the review is to
check the correspondence between the software
requirements and the software design. Its secondary task
should be to check the correctness of the designer's own
verification of his design.   In practice, however, as

design verification is not yet widely used, the review team may also be required to evaluate the correctness of the software design. The section below describes how an informal design review might be conducted.

3.6.1 Conducting an informal design review

The aim of an informal design review should be to detect design errors. It should not be considered as a mechanism for evaluating either the design team or individuals within that team. Nor should it be concerned with management considerations such as the project cost or schedule – its objective is to validate the design. Ideally, the software will have been verified by the designer so the task of the review team is to check this verification. This checking can normally be carried out by a qualified individual who, given the design and its verification, can check the work of another member of the team. In fact, a verification review can be avoided if the normal working practice in a design group is to exchange designs and conduct this checking procedure as soon as a program unit has been designed and verified.

In situations where formal or informal verification is not used, the software designer should present his design to the review team and should explain and justify that design. The design specifications and software requirements should be distributed before the review for study by the members of the review team. The designer should lead the rest of the team, step by step, through his design explaining the function and need for each statement. The intention is that the review team will detect errors and inconsistencies in the design and point them out to the designer. If errors are detected, they should be noted for subsequent correction by the designer. The review team should not waste time attempting to correct these errors. It must be emphasised, however, that this process is not as effective as verification in detecting design errors.

The checking of the correspondence between software requirements and design is a difficult task. The software requirements should be classified and each member of the design team allocated a number of requirements. It is his responsibility to ensure that these requirements are met. During the design review, each member should present his requirements in turn and describe the design fragments which implement his particular requirements.

   If a requirements specification is ambiguous, the
review team should note the ambiguity and their
interpretation of it. This should then be passed to the
software contractor for clarification and comment.

Implementation 1: The programming language

Programming is a craft, dependent on individual skill, attention to detail, and knowledge of how to use available tools in the best way. Just as a craftsman such as a potter must know his materials, understand the principles of glazing and firing and learn by experience, the programmer must understand the computer system, some theory of programming, and must practise programming. Programming is a practical activity which can only be learned by experience. Nevertheless, the experience of others can be distilled and provide guidelines for the programmer to help him avoid some pitfalls.

This chapter and the following chapter cover aspects of implementation which are of importance to the software engineer – how to choose a programming language, programming language features which affect program reliability, programming style, and programming tools for supporting system implementation.

This chapter concentrates on the programming language used to implement a software system. Although apparently an academic preoccupation, language design is of vital importance to the software engineer. Programming languages are his most basic tools and he must feed back information on the reliability and usability of programming languages to the language designer. The software engineer should have some knowledge of programming languages so that he can make reasoned decisions about which programming language is best suited for particular applications.

In this chapter different classes of programming language are described and this is followed by a discussion of programming language features which affect the readability and reliability of programs. These include declarations, types, modules, control constructs and exception handling. The third major section in the chapter discusses the factors which should be taken into account in choosing a programming language for a major project and the final section discusses the need for

languages to be designed to allow separate compilation
of different parts of a system.

4.1   PROGRAMMING LANGUAGE CLASSIFICATION

Since 1960, literally thousands of different programming
languages have been designed and implemented. The
majority of these languages have been implemented as
part of research projects and only a relatively small
number of them have been widely used. Each of these
languages falls into one of five approximate classes:

(1)   Assembly Languages.
These are machine languages with a one-to-one
correspondence between programming language statements and machine operations. Programming in assembly code involves the programmer mentally
translating his program design into sequences of
machine actions. Because these two notations are
quite dissimilar, assembly code programming tends
to be difficult and error-prone. Each assembly
language is specific to the computer on which it
is implemented.

(2)   Systems Implementation Languages.
This class of programming language evolved from
assembly languages when the difficulty of assembly
code programming was recognised. Systems implementation languages provide some facilities such
as control statements and variable type checking
but they also allow the programmer direct access
to machine operations. In theory therefore, anything which may be programmed in assembly language
may also be programmed in a systems implementation
language. Well known systems implementation
languages which are available on a number of computers are BCPL and C.

(3)   Static High Level Languages.
These are languages which provide the programmer
with some control statements and variable declarations and which have no facilities for the programmer to directly control the machine operations
generated by the compiler. They are characterised
by static storage allocation. The storage space
required for program variables can be computed by
the language compiler and reserved in advance of

program execution. Whilst this has some implementation advantages for the compiler writer, it imposes constraints on the programmer. High level languages in this class were amongst the first high level languages and consequently have become very widely used. The best known examples of this type of language are COBOL and FORTRAN.

(4)   Block Structured High Level Languages.
These languages are developments from static languages, and provide the programmer with a selection of control constructs, and the ability to classify program objects as being of a particular type. They are distinguished by their provision of a limited form of dynamic storage allocation called block structure. The language compiler cannot make all decisions on the amount of store required by program variables and program execution is supported by a store management system which can allocate and deallocate store on entry to and exit from a program block. A program block is a clearly delimited area of a program and execution of the program is interrupted on entry to a block in order to allocate store. The programmer must know on entry to a block exactly how much store is required. Until fairly recently, languages in this class were not widely used commercially but this situation is changing as the advantages of block-structured languages over COBOL and FORTRAN are recognised. Examples of this class of language are ALGOL and Pascal.

(5)   Dynamic High Level Languages.
This class of programming languages is distinguished by a requirement that all storage management is carried out dynamically - that is, the execution of individual language statements can cause store to be allocated and deallocated. In general, the structure of these languages tends to be quite different from the structure of static or block structured high level language - indeed, languages in this class rarely even resemble each other. Dynamic languages tend to be tailored for a particular application and are not general purpose programming languages. They are not widely used commercially but are sometimes useful in research and prototyping applications. Examples of this class of language are APL and LISP.

In general, there is a one-to-many correspondence between high level programming languages and machine code. This means that a number of machine instructions are generated for each high level language instruction. As well as this, high level languages normally allow the user to associate meaningful names to program variables and subroutines where the object name relates to the entity represented by that object. Consequently, high level language programs are easier to read, easier to write, easier to debug, and easier to maintain than assembly code programs.

4.2   PROGRAMMING LANGUAGE CONSTRUCTS

The availability of certain programming language constructs simplifies the construction of reliable and maintainable programs. Some constructs, such as modules, allow a system to be partitioned into independent units and hence enhance program maintainability. Other constructs or the lack of certain features, have inherent disadvantages and cause what are termed, characteristic errors. Examples of characteristic errors are uninitialised variables caused by the lack of an explicit initialisation construct and object mistyping caused by default type allocation based on the initial letter of an identifier.

It is important that the software engineer understands the ramifications of different programming language constructs. Without this understanding, it is not possible to make reasoned technical decisions as to which programming language should be chosen for a project. Therefore, in this section, a number of different constructs are discussed along with their advantages and disadvantages. Where examples are given, the languages Pascal, Ada or FORTRAN are used.

4.2.1 Declarations

The declaration of names for objects used in a program has a dual function; it provides information to the compiler about the storage requirements of that object and it informs the system exactly which names may subsequently be used in the program. A type may be associated with a declaration and this allows the compiler to check that objects of a particular type are only used in operations which are defined for that type. For example, if an object is declared to be type real, the compiler should signal an error if that object is used as an operand in a logical and operation.

Not all programming languages force the user to explicitly declare names for all the objects used in his program. In languages such as FORTRAN or BASIC, the first use of a name is deemed to be its declaration. In FORTRAN, declarations are optional and they may associate one of a limited number of types with a name. If a name is introduced without declaration, the initial letter of that name determines its type - if the name starts with any letter from I-N, it is presumed to represent an integer, otherwise it is taken as a real number.

Optional declarations are dangerous because they leave scope for programmer errors which result in legal but incorrect FORTRAN programs. For example, consider the legal FORTRAN statement:

    IPOINT = IPOINT + 1

The effect of this statement is to set IPOINT to 1. A new integer object called IPOINT is created and initialised to zero and that value plus 1 is assigned to IPOINT. On many printers, the letter O and the character zero (0), are almost indistinguishable and should O be accidentally substituted for zero or vice versa, a new object is created by the use of the misspelt name. This is a characteristic error of FORTRAN.

In programming languages which enforce declarations, the above error is easily detected by the compiler because only IPOINT (say) would have been declared. The use of the name IPOINT would be illegal.

4.2.2 Types

Closely associated with name declarations are type declarations which allow the user to associate a type name with a declared object. This type name serves to classify the object and operations on the object are restricted to operations defined on that class of objects. If the programmer uses an object of a particular type in an invalid manner, this error can be detected and signalled by the compiler.

The notion of type checking was introduced in ALGOL60 and the concept has been considerably refined since then. Programming languages such as Pascal, allow the user to define his own types, relevant to his particular application, and to declare objects of that type. For example, if a traffic light system is being modelled in Pascal, the following declarations might be made:

```
type TrafficLightColour = (red,redamber,amber,green);
var  ColourShowing : TrafficLightColour;
```

The object ColourShowing, which is modelling the colour displayed by the traffic light, may only be assigned the values red, red_amber, amber, and green.

Contrast this with the modelling of such a situation in FORTRAN. Here, integers must be used to represent the entities associated with the traffic light:

```
INTEGER RED,REDAMB,AMBER,GREEN,COLSHW
DATA RED/1/,REDAMB/2/,AMBER/3/,GREEN/4/
```

Integers are associated with each possible colour, and assignments such as

```
COLSHW = RED
```

can be made.

Disciplined programming in FORTRAN, always associating a relevant name with each constant used to represent an entity, improves program readability but there is no mechanism to restrict statements which directly assign integers or real numbers to COLSHW. If names are not associated with constants, assignments such as :

```
COLSHW = 3
```

must be made, forcing the program to consult documentation to find out which colour is actually represented by 3. If a statement such as

```
COLSHW = 13
```

is made, there is no way that the error can be detected either by the compiler or the run time system. Detection of such an error depends on explicit checking code being included by the programmer.

Another important class of Pascal type declarations are subrange type declarations. These allow the programmer to declare a type whose values make up a subset of the values of some other type. For example:

```
type PositiveInteger = 0..maxint;
     LowerCaseLetters = 'a'..'z';
```

These declarations introduce a type called PositiveInteger whose range covers positive integers and the type LowerCaseLetters which encompasses characters between 'a' and 'z'. Objects which are declared as one of these types are restricted to values within the specified range. The Pascal compiler automatically generates code to check, at run time, that assignments to these objects do not cause violation of the range constraint. In languages without the facility of subrange types, the facility can only be modelled by the inclusion of explicit checking code by the programmer.

4.2.3 Structured types

Most programming languages allow the user to declare arrays. Arrays are sequential collections of elements, all of the same type, where each individual element can be identified by its position in the collection. Arrays are an important data type, but they are not particularly suitable for representing objects which model entities made up of a collection of elements of different types. For example, consider a personnel record in an organisation. This might be made up of a number of fields with each field modelling an individual attribute:

    Name : string of letters and blanks
    Address : string of letters, numbers, and blanks
    Age : integer between 16 and 65
    Department : the name of one of a number of known
    departments
    Salary : integer between 3000 and 15000

In Pascal a facility exists for declaring structured types made up of collections of elements, not all of which need be of the same type. A name is associated with each element and reference to the element is made via that name. The fields of the record type have the same names as the entities which they are modelling. If a variable, say employee, is declared to be of type PersonnelRecord, employee.name references the name field, employee.dept references the dept field and so on.

The above personnel record could be represented in Pascal as follows:

    type PersonnelRecord = record
        name : array[1..NAMESIZE] of char;

```
address : array[1..ADDRESSSIZE] of char;
age : 16..65;
dept : (sales,personnel,production,DP,admin);
salary : 3000..15000;
end;
```

In languages which do not provide such structured data types, arrays must be used to represent entities such as the personnel record. Each field of the record is held at a known offset from the start of the array. For example, in a FORTRAN77 character array, the first 20 characters might be the name, the next 30 characters the address, the next 2 characters the age, the next characters a code representing the department and the final 5 characters the salary. This might be declared:

```
CHARACTER PERSRC(40)
```

A disciplined FORTRAN programmer declares names for each field in the record and initialises these names to refer to the appropriate locations in PERSRC. Therefore reference could be made to PERSRC(SALARY), PERSRC(NAME), etc. Because all elements in the array must be of the same type, numbers in the record are represented as character strings and these strings must be converted to numbers before they can be used in arithmetic operations.

Furthermore, it is impossible for the compiler to carry out any checking to ensure that appropriate values are assigned to fields. For example, the following assignment is permitted:

```
PERSRC(SALARY:SALARY+4) = '25500'
```

The FORTRAN77 feature of substring assignment is used to assign the string '25500' to the salary field of PERSRC. As the maximum salary is 15000, this is an invalid value.

Type declarations in a programming language are not just a safety feature. As well as providing information which allows the compiler to carry out some program checking, they are also an important abstraction mechanism. The definition of type names allows reference to be made to entities such as personnel records, traffic light colours, etc, without considering the representation of these entities. The importance of abstraction has already been discussed and the sensible use of typing is a powerful abstraction technique for the system designer.

4.2.4 Pointers

Some programming languages allow objects to be referenced indirectly through pointers. Pointers are objects whose value is a reference to some other object. If a pointer is available, operations on the referenced object may be carried out without its name being explicitly known.

Pointers are particularly useful when used in conjunction with structured types to create linked structures. One or more fields of the structure may be pointers which link that structure to other associated structures. This allows data structures such as linked lists and trees to be implemented.

The unrestricted availability of pointers is, however, a dangerous facility and allows the phenomenon known as aliasing(Hoare 1973, 1975). An aliased object may be referenced in a number of different ways and this can cause problems for program readers, testers, and verifiers. Say an object is named X and pointers Y and Z are created to reference X. Assignment to Y^ (the object referenced by Y) also changes the value of X and Z^.

To avoid such problems, the use of pointers must be limited. In Pascal, pointers may not be assigned a reference to an existing named object but must point to anonymous objects created on the heap. This means that these objects may only be modified via the pointer and not by direct assignment.

Furthermore, Pascal insists that pointers should be constrained in their declaration to refer to a particular type. Pointers declared as references to objects of different types are themselves deemed to be of different types and the usual restrictions on type violations are enforced by the compiler.

4.2.5 Initialisation

One of the most common programming errors is the failure to initialise declared variables before these variables are used. Some languages, such as FORTRAN and ALGOL68, provide facilities for variable initialisation but they do not force the programmer to use them - if a variable is not initialised, it is assigned some standard, system-dependent value.

Other languages, such as Pascal, have no explicit initialisation features and the programmer must use assignment statements to perform initialisations. The separation of variable declarations and program statements in Pascal means that it is impossible to write the initialisation assignment immediately after the variable declaration. This is an aspect of Pascal which is likely to cause programming errors.

Neither the lack of initialisation facilities or purely voluntary initialisation is satisfactory. To reduce the error proneness of a programming language, the programmer should be forced to provide an initial value of the appropriate type for all variables declared in his program. This removes all possibility of a programmer forgetting to initialise some variable and also makes it impossible for a programmer to rely on the system initialising variables to some default value. Relying on system initialisation is particularly dangerous. Should the program be transferred to some other system with different initialisation conventions, an incorrect initialisation will be given to his variables and consequently, the result of executing the program will be unpredictable.

An alternative to enforced programmer initialisation of variables is for the system to assign a special 'not yet initialised' value to a variable when it is declared and to signal an error if an attempt is made to read that variable before an assignment has been made to it. This solves the problem of 'forgotten' initialisation but would have to be enforced on every system if the program were run on different machines. In terms of existing hardware, such a system would be expensive to implement but the design of hardware to support such a system is not difficult and such a design is described by Scowen (1979).

4.2.6 Constants
Many of the entities modelled in a program are not variable but are constant. These may be mathematical entities such as pi, physical constants such as the speed of light or defined constants such as the current standard rate of income tax. During the execution of a program, the values of the objects representing these entities do not change.

There is another class of constant which is commonly used in programming. This is a constant which is a program parameter, used for deriving a particular instance of a program. For example, if a program object represents a name, it may have an associated constant

NAMESIZE, indicating the maximum number of characters in a name. Although constant for any one instance of a program, it may be convenient for NAMESIZE to have different values in different instances of the program.

Of course it is possible to represent constants by using program variables, initialising these variables to the constant value and making no further assignments to that variable. This has the disadvantages that the reader cannot distinguish constants and variables by examining the program and that the compiler cannot enforce constancy – it cannot prevent assignments to a supposedly constant variable.

In FORTRAN77, constants are declared along with other names and a PARAMETER statement is used to associate a value with a constant name. Names used in a PARAMETER statement are declared using the normal FORTRAN mechanism with the result that the constancy or otherwise of a name cannot be ascertained simply by inspecting the declaration. There is no requirement that the PARAMETER statement should immediately follow a declaration so, to determine constancy, PARAMETER statements using the specified name must be searched for in the program listing.

In Pascal, on the other hand, constants are declared explicitly using a const declaration. Constant declarations in Pascal must precede the declaration of types and this imposes the limitation that the type of Pascal constants is restricted to one of the predefined language types – integer, real, char, or boolean. This limitation means that the advantages of Pascal typing only apply to program variables – declarations such as the following are not permitted:

```
type TrafficLightColour = (red,redamber,amber,green);
const GoColour = TrafficLightColour(green);
```

This lack of typed constants is a serious inconsistency in the design of Pascal.

Both Pascal and FORTRAN allow only manifest constants to be declared. That is, constant declarations associate a name with a value which must be known when the program is compiled. Other programming languages such as ALGOL68 and Ada allow the values of constants to be computed and assigned at run time. This latter facility is much less restrictive than the manifest constant facility. Constant values may be determined by reading them in to the program, or they may be calculated from other program variables or constants. This means that the important safety aspects of constants – the ability to guarantee that a name is always associated with the same value, is maintained without forcing the programmer to determine that value at compile time.

4.2.7 The locality and visibility of program names

A general principle of good programming is that the names of objects in a program should be introduced close to where they are used and should only be accessible to those parts of the program where they are required. Almost all programming languages (COBOL is an exception) recognise this and provide some facilities to limit the scope of names used in the program. A name declaration only pertains over part of the program and the declared object may only be accessed from within a clearly delimited area such as a subroutine or a block.

There are 2 common approaches taken in the provision of local variables. FORTRAN and most systems implementation languages offer a single level of locality, whereas block-structured languages such as ALGOL or Pascal offer multiple levels of locality.

Single level locality means that the scope of variables declared in a subroutine or procedure is confined to that subroutine and these variables are not accessible outside that routine. A FORTRAN main program is essentially an unnamed parameterless subroutine and the variables declared in a main program are not accessible to all subroutines – they are not the same as global variables in a block structured language.

Multi level locality is provided by block-structured languages like ALGOL and Pascal. In these languages, declarations are made within a block and the names declared may only be referenced within that block. Storage associated with the name is allocated at run time when the block containing the name declaration is entered and that storage is deallocated when the block is left.

Blocks may be nested so that local variables can be introduced close to where they are required with access to variables in an outer block permitted from an inner block. Consider the example below.

Procedure A has local variables x,y, and z and these may be accessed anywhere within the block defined by procedure A. Because procedure A includes procedure B, these local variables can be accessed from within B.

Procedure B has local variables p,q, and r and these may only be accessed from within B. Procedure A may not access p,q, or r because they are declared as variables in an inner block and hence are inaccessible to outer levels of the program.

```
procedure A;
var x,y,z:integer;
procedure B;
    var p,q,r:integer;
    begin
      ...
    end; {B}
begin
  ...
end; {A}
```

Multi-level locality contributes significantly to program readability as the characteristics of names can be declared close to where these names are used. The reader of the program can easily locate information about these names. The straightforward provision of local names also means that the programmer is not tempted into using the same program variable for different functions in different parts of his program. This is a fairly common practice in some programming languages which is very prone to error.

A consequence of locality provisions in block-structured languages is that variables declared in an inner block may have the same name as variables in an outer block. This does not introduce ambiguity as the declaration of a local variable with the same name as that in an outer block causes the variable in the outer block to 'disappear' whilst the inner block is executing. Therefore, the general rule in block-structured languages is that outer block declarations are accessible to inner blocks except when the inner block contains a declaration of the same name as that used in an outer block.

This inconsistency can be dangerous in situations where blocks are deeply nested. A global variable may be concealed by the declaration of a variable of the same name at block level 1 say. At a much deeper level, the programmer may refer to the global variable, forgetting that it has been concealed by the level 1 declaration. The value he accesses or assigns is therefore that of the level 1 local rather than the

global. This situation is most likely in program
maintenance where a programmer not responsible for the
original code is involved in altering the program.

In spite of this disadvantage, multi level locality
makes for more readable programs than 2 level locality
because declarations clustered around their point of use
rather than at the beginning of a subroutine. However,
languages with only 2 level locality such as FORTRAN are
more amenable to independent compilation of program
units. This will be discussed later in the chapter.

4.2.8 Program modules

Block structured languages provide some control over the
visibility of object names because names that are
declared in an inner block are not accessible from an
outer block. However, the programmer has no control
over the accessibility of outer block objects – they
cannot be protected from access from within an inner
block except by reusing that name. Furthermore, because
of the dynamic storage allocation philosophy of block-
structured languages, it is not possible to preserve the
value of an object from one activation of a block to
another.

Consequently, objects which may only be used by one
or two routines in a program but whose values must be
maintained from one activation of the routine to
another, must be declared globally and must therefore be
potentially accessible by any routine in the program.
Again, this can cause program maintenance problems as
code modifying these objects may be accidentally
introduced into the program. An example where global
objects must be used is shown below in Pascal:

```
    var sp:0..STACKSIZE+1;
        stack:array[0..STACKSIZE] of integer;

    procedure push(v:integer);
    begin
        if sp > STACKSIZE then
            error(stackoverflow)
        else
        begin
            stack[sp] := v;
            sp := sp + 1;
        end
    end; {push}
```

```
function pop:integer;
begin
    sp := sp-1;
    if sp < 0 then
        error(stackunderflow)
    else
        pop := stack[sp];
end; {pop}

function testempty:boolean;
    testempty := sp < 0;
```

Assume that STACKSIZE, stackoverflow, stackunderflow, and STACKSIZE are declared elsewhere.

In this example, the variables sp and stack must be implemented as global program variables because they are shared by the routines push, pop, and testempty. As well as this, they must maintain their values from one access to another and therefore cannot be declared in an inner block.

Block structure on its own is an inadequate mechanism for controlling the visibility of names and there is a need for some additional mechanism which allows the user much closer control over what local names may be accessed from outside the program unit in which these names are declared. It should also be possible to specify that a local variable should maintain its value from one activation of a program unit to another.

A construct providing these facilities has been introduced in several programming languages under a number of different names – a class in SIMULA, a module in MODULA, a segment in ALGOL68, and a package in Ada. In describing this construct, terminology and syntax derived from Ada is used.

An Ada package allows the programmer to declare a named program unit which may contain declarations of local objects. These objects may be strictly local, that is, their names may only be used within the package body or the programmer may choose to 'export' the names of some objects. This means that the names may be used outside that package body and will refer to the objects declared in the package. If those objects are variables, they maintain their value from one activation of the package to another.

The declaration of an Ada package is made up of two parts – a package header which specifies the local package names accessible outside the package and a package body which defines the objects making up the package.

A package is simply a lexical mechanism providing control over the visibility of names. Consequently, a package body consists entirely of declarations – type declarations, variable declarations, and procedure declarations.

The example below is a recoding in Ada of the previous Pascal example of stack implementation:

```
package STACK is
    procedure push(V:in integer);
    procedure pop return integer;
    procedure testempty return boolean;
end STACK;
```

This is the package header which declares the local package names 'exported' from the package. In this case, the user may refer only to the procedure names push, pop, and testempty. A package body declaration specifies the objects associated with these names together with local package objects.

```
package body STACK is

-- declare stack pointer and array to represent the
stack
-- these are local variables but they retain their
value from
-- one activation of STACK to another

sp : integer range 0..STACKSIZE+1 := 0;
stack : array[0..STACKSIZE] of integer;

type errortype = (overflow,underflow);

procedure push(V:in integer);
begin
    if sp > STACKSIZE then
        error(overflow)
    else
        stack[sp] := V;
        sp := sp + 1;
    end if;
end push;
```

```
    procedure pop return integer;
    begin
        sp := sp - 1;
        if sp < 0 then
            error(underflow)
        else
            return stack[sp];
        end if;
    end pop;

    procedure testempty return boolean;
    begin
        return sp = 0;
    end testempty;

    procedure error(T : in errortype);
    begin
        case T of
            when underflow => IO.write('stack underflow');
            when overflow => IO.write('stack overflow');
            when others => IO.write('system error');
        end case;      raise stackerror;
    end error;

end STACK;
```

The package body defines the accessible procedures push, pop, and testempty and local objects stack, sp, STACKSIZE, errortype and error. In order that the package might be self-contained, the error handling procedure is included in the package.

The error procedure illustrates how package names are referenced. This procedure calls the procedure write, declared in a package called IO. A procedure name, exported from a package, is preceded by the package name. Therefore:

```
    IO.write('some message')
```

calls the procedure write in the package IO.

```
    x := STACK.pop
```

calls the procedure pop in the package STACK and

```
    if STACK.testempty then ...
```

calls the procedure testempty declared in STACK.

This mechanism for referencing names exported from a package means that different packages may export the same names and that these names may refer to different objects without ambiguity. For example, a package concerned exclusively with character input/output, say CHARIO, may export a name 'write'. This would be referred to as CHARIO.write. Because the package name precedes the procedure name there is no confusion with the procedure IO.write. The error procedure in this package also illustrates the Ada mechanism for signalling that an exception has occurred. This construct will be covered, along with exception handling in general, later in this chapter.

The provision of modules such as Ada packages offers a number of advantages to the programmer:

(1)   Abstract data types, as proposed by Guttag (1977) may be constructed. These are data types whose representation is concealed from the user. The stack example above, is an instance of an abstract data type. The user may manipulate the stack but its actual representation is concealed. Conceivably, the stack representation might be modified, to a linked list say, without affecting the user's view of the stack and without any changes in the programs which make use of the stack package.

(2)   Related operations may be grouped together and may share variables in a controlled way. An example of this type of module might be the IO package introduced above. Within the package, necessary I/O buffers would be declared and shared by the I/O procedures declared in the package.

(3)   A module is a convenient unit for independent compilation. A module may be constructed as a self-contained unit, making no reference to its outside environment except via other module activations. This means that it can be compiled without the presence of its environment and stored in a library.

Because of these advantages, the availability of modules in a programming language makes that language particularly suitable for major software projects.

4.2.9 Loop control constructs

Loop control constructs are those language control constructs which specify that a statement or a group of statements should be executed a number of times. That number may either be specified explicitly or it may depend on some program variable condition becoming true. The most common loop constructs are for statements, while-do statements and repeat-until statements.

The for statement is used when it is intended to execute a loop a given number of times. It has the general form:

```
for <counter> := <initial value> step <increment> to
<final value>
```

Different languages differ slightly in the exact nature of their for statement.

Normally, the for statement is a very safe construct as, in most languages, loop termination is guaranteed. However, ALGOL60 allows the statement parameters(initial value, step, final value) to be modified by statements within the loop so that it is possible to construct for loops which never terminate.

This problem is circumvented in languages such as Pascal by ignoring any modifications made, within the loop, to the loop parameters. The parameters are evaluated by value rather than by name as in ALGOL60. Pascal does have the disadvantage that the loop counter variable must be declared as any other program variable at the head of a block. However, its value on completion of the loop is, according to the Pascal report, undefined – the user may not assume that it has any particular value on loop termination.

A more satisfactory for statement design causes the loop counter to be implicitly redeclared as a constant after each execution of the loop as implemented by Morrison (1979) in a variant of ALGOL. The value of this constant is one greater than the constant value after the previous loop execution. Not only does this form of implementation ensure that the loop counter cannot possibly be modified within the loop, it also means that the counter name need not be declared in advance by the programmer and that the name disappears on loop termination. There is no possibility of accidental usage. Similarly, the final value and the increment, if any, should also be constant and not subject to modification. This design and its implementation is illustrated below:

```
for i := 1 to N do
    somestatement(i)
```

In low level notation, this is equivalent to:

```
begin
    integer counter := 0;
    constant finalvalue = N;
  1 : begin
        constant i = counter+1;
        if i > finalvalue goto 2
        somestatement(i);
        counter := counter+1
        goto 1
  2 : end
```

Notice that the loop counter value and the value passed as a parameter are distinct so that the constant can be properly redeclared.

Repeat and while statements allow the user to specify that the loop should be executed until some condition is true or while some condition is true.

```
while <condition> do <statement>

repeat <statement> until <condition>
```

These types of loop do not suffer from the same problems as some for statement designs because the loop control variable is under the direct control of the programmer, rather than the language system. The while statement allows the programmer to place the test for loop termination at the beginning of the loop and the repeat statement allows the test to be placed at the end of the loop. Neither construct allows the test for termination to be placed in the middle of the loop.

There are many practical programming situations where it is necessary to place the termination test within the loop. For example, consider the situation where a program reads some input, then processes that input in some way. If the number of input items is unknown but it is known that the last item is -1, an intuitive implementation of this might be:

```
repeat
    read.item
    process.item
until item = -1
```

Unfortunately, this is incorrect because this loop will cause the terminating item -1 to be processed. This can be avoided by the introduction of a boolean variable which is set when the terminator is input:

```
finished := false
repeat
    read.item
    if item = -1 then
        finished := true
    else
        process.item
until finished
```

The implementation of termination from within a loop by the use of if statements and boolean variables is clumsy and normally increases the length of the program. A number of different control constructs have been proposed which provide for the placing of the loop termination test anywhere in the loop. These have been described by Zahn (1974), and Bochmann (1973).

The variety of proposed constructs will not be described here. Rather, the solution adopted in Ada is described. This provides a facility which allows programmer control over the placing of the loop termination test.

In Ada, the loop statement has the form:

```
[<iteration specification>]<basic loop>
```

where the iteration specification is optional. When included, it has the form:

```
for <loop parameter> in [reverse]<discrete range> |
while <condition>
```

The iteration specifier allows the specification of for or while loops. Unlike Pascal, the loop parameter is implicitly declared by its use in the for specifier. The basic loop in Ada has the form:

```
loop <sequence of statements> end loop
```

Examples of Ada loops are:

```
for i in 1..10 loop
    process(i);
end loop;

while i < 10 loop
    process(i);
    i:=i+1;
end loop;
```

It is possible to escape from within a loop by using an exit statement. This has the form:

```
exit[<identifier>][when <condition>]
```

The exit statement causes control to be transferred to the statement following the loop unless it is followed by an identifier, in which case, control is transferred to the statement following the loop labelled with that identifier. The exit-when construct can be used to place the loop terminating condition within the loop. The previous example might be coded:

```
loop
    read_item;
    exit when item = -1;
    process_item;
end loop;
```

4.2.10 Decision constructs
Decision constructs in a high level language are control constructs which allow a statement or group of statements to be selected for execution on the basis of some condition being true. These constructs encompass the one-armed conditional (if-then), the two-armed conditional (if-then-else) and the multi-armed conditional construct (case).

The form of the one-armed and two-armed conditional statements is familiar:

```
if <condition> then <statement>

if <condition> then <statement> else <statement>
```

There are no practical problems in using these statements.

There are a number of different forms of case statement in use but, unlike one- and two-armed conditionals, each form has some disadvantages and may be responsible for certain types of program error.

In ALGOLW and ALGOL68, the case statement takes an integer expression as the case selector and the case statement includes a number of separate executable statements. If the case selector has the value M, the Mth statement is chosen for execution.

```
case <integer expression> of
    <S1>
    <S2>
    <S3>
    ...
    ...
    <Sn>
```

After the selected expression has been executed, execution normally continues with the statement following the case statement.

This form of the case construct suffers from 2 problems:

(1)   The action taken if the value of the case expression is less than zero or greater than N is not specified.

(2)   The correct ordering of the statements to be selected by the case expression is crucial. If an error should be made in this ordering, it is undetectable at compile time or run time and the statement actually executed will not be that statement intended by the programmer. This situation is most likely to arise where the range of the case selector expression is not continuous and dummy statements are inserted into the statement list to ensure that the appropriate statement is selected.

Pascal offers an alternative case statement design which eliminates the dependence on correct programmer ordering of the executable statements. In Pascal, the case selector expression may be any scalar type except real. Each executable statement in the case construct is labelled with one or more special constant labels called case labels. Execution of the case statement involves

evaluating the case selector expression, matching that
value against the case labels and selecting for
execution that statement whose label matches the case
selector value. For example:

```
case inputcharacter of
begin
',' : setcomma;
':' : setcolon;
';' : setsemicolon;
'0','1','2','3','4','5','6','8','9' : setdigit;
'#','.','@' : setotherchar
end;
```

The Pascal case statement makes no attempt to provide a
solution to the first problem identified above - what
action is taken if the case selector fails to match any
of the case labels.

The case statement in Ada has been designed so that
the problem associated with the Pascal case statement
has been eliminated. In Ada, if the case expression is
of type T, cases for all possible values of T must be
included. If explicit mention is not made of all
values, a default statement must be included. For
example, consider a type DAY, defined:

```
type DAY = (mon,tue,wed,thur,fri,sat,sun)
```

and a variable TODAY of this type. An Ada case statement
using TODAY might be:

```
case TODAY of
when mon => first_working_day;
when tue..thur => middle_days;
when fri => last_working_day;
when others => weekend;
end case;
```

The default is stated as 'when others'.

Although the Ada case statement is safe, inasmuch as
user error can always be detected by the compiler and no
undefined situations can arise, it is the author's
opinion that a guarded command mechanism as suggested
by Dijkstra (1975) is superior to the existing form of
case statement. This guarded command construct is a
generalisation of the two-armed conditional so that each
statement is preceded by a boolean expression 'guarding'

that statement. This may be expressed:

```
if
    <condition1> : <statement1>
    <condition2> : <statement2>
    ....
    ....
    <conditionN> : <statementN>
else
    <statement> fi
```

An appropriate shorthand notation might be invented if the left hand side of each condition was identical. Evaluation of the multi armed conditional involves evaluating the conditions until some true condition was found and then executing the statement following that condition.

4.2.11 The goto statement

There has been a good deal of argument over the past few years over the role of conditional and unconditional goto statements in high level programming languages. The controversy was started by Dijkstra (1968), who suggested that the use of goto statements adversely affected the readability and reliability of programs.

It has been demonstrated by Bohm and Jacopini (1966) that any program can be expressed without goto statements as long as language facilities include a while statement, an if-then-else statement and boolean variables. Furthermore, they showed that any program written using goto statements can be transformed into a program without gotos, although this usually involves increasing the program size.

Programs which make extensive use of goto statements to modify the flow of control are more difficult to read and more prone to error than gotoless programs. Undisciplined use of goto statements to share small code sections and to make a program 'more efficient' result in the flow of control in a program being extremely circuitous. In extreme cases, 'spaghetti' programs can result from the uncontrolled use of gotos where the flow of control is as tangled as a bowl of spaghetti.

For these reasons, it has been advocated that the goto statement is so dangerous and powerful that it has no place in high level programming languages. This is true for languages used in specific, very important applications such as the teaching of programming.

Inexperienced programmers cannot be expected to understand the rare circumstances where it may be sensible to use a goto statement and, by removing temptation, the possibility of misusing the goto statement is avoided.

However, experienced programmers who program in a disciplined manner can use the goto statement responsibly and there are certain programming circumstances where it is the most apt construct to apply. Specialised forms of the goto statement such as a statement allowing exit from within a loop or a statement allowing immediate return from a procedure are easier to read and understand than the extensive use of boolean variables and two-armed conditionals which can accomplish the same function. Handling exceptional situations where an error may occur anywhere in a sequence of procedure activations is another circumstance where the goto statement has a role. The situations, where the use of goto statements may be justified, are described in the following chapter.

4.2.12 Exception handling

When an error of some kind or an unexpected event occurs during the execution of a program, this event is termed an exception. Exceptions may be caused by hardware or software errors which may have or have not been anticipated by the programmer. In general, where an exception has not been anticipated explicitly by the programmer, control is transferred to a system exception handling mechanism which handles the exception and, if the exception is serious, terminates the executing program. If an exception has been anticipated by the programmer, he must include code to detect that exception and to take appropriate action when that exception occurs. In general, if a program is running under an operating system, th programmer will not be able to detect or handle hardware exceptions in his program and it is solely the responsibility of the operating system to handle such cases.

Programming languages such as FORTRAN or Pascal offer the programmer little help in detecting and handling exceptions. The programmer must use the normal decision constructs of the language to detect the exception and the control constructs to transfer control to the exception handler.

Whilst this is possible in a monolithic program, in programs where a sequence of procedure calls is nested, there is no convenient and safe mechanism for transmitting the exception from one procedure to another.

Consider the following example:

```
procedure A;
....
B;
....
end {A}

procedure B;
....
C;
....
end {B}

procedure C;
....
....
end {C}
```

Procedure A calls procedure B which calls procedure C. If an exception occurs during the execution of C this may be sufficiently serious to be pointless to continue execution of the statements in B following the procedure call of C. Similarly, it may be necessary to transmit the fact that an exception has occurred from B to A.

The only mechanism which the programmer has for this in Pascal say, is a global boolean variable which is set to indicate that an exception has occurred. This must either be passed as a parameter to every procedure or must be set globally. The programmer must test the value of this variable after each procedure call so that, in a sequence of nested procedure calls, the same test is carried out a number of times. The existing mechanism forces the programmer to test for the exception each and every time that exception might occur. Unanticipated exceptions cause transfer to a system exception handler and normally, program termination.

Whilst such a situation is quite acceptable in some environments such as a student learning environment, it is not acceptable in situations where reliability considerations are paramount. In those situations, usually where the computer is acting as a controller or providing an essential time-critical service, the system must not fail. Furthermore, program size is often critical in such situations and it is unacceptable to include a number of largely redundant statements to test for exceptions which increase program size.

An exception handling facility should be available which does not force the programmer to increase the length of his program inordinately and which makes possible the transmission of exceptions from one program unit to another.

Such exception handling facilities are not easy to design or implement. When designing exception handling constructs, a number of factors must be taken into account:

(1)   How should exceptions be declared?

(2)   Where should exception handlers be placed in a program?

(3)   Should exception handlers be a distinct program structure or should exceptions be handled using existing structures such as procedures?

(4)   How should exceptions be signalled and transmitted from one program unit to another?

(5)   Should exceptions and exception handlers be subject to the normal scope and extent rules of the language? If so, which exception handler should be selected if a number of handlers of the same name are provided at different levels?

(6)   Should exception handlers cause control to be returned to the point where the exception occurred after it has been dealt with?

The majority of widely used programming languages offer no specific exception handling constructs. An exception to this is PL/1 which recognises the importance of exception handling and provides special constructs for this purpose.

In PL/1, the ON statement is used to specify what action should be taken when an exception occurs. As well as built-in exceptions such as end-of-file, integer-overflow, divide-by-zero, etc., the programmer can define his own exception names and can indicate that an exception of that name has occurred. Exception names and actions to be taken are defined using an ON statement:

```
ON end-of-file call closefile
ON condition(HEAPFULL) call garbage_collect
```

The first ON statement above specifies an action to be taken in the event of the standard exception 'end-of-file' occurring. The second example introduces an exception name HEAPFULL and specifies an action associated with that exception.

PL/1 ON statements essentially set up an exception action and this action is triggered either when a built-in system exception occurs or when a SIGNAL statement is used by the programmer to indicate that an exception has occurred. The SIGNAL statement has the form:

```
SIGNAL condition(HEAPFULL)
```

When the SIGNAL statement is executed, this causes control to be transferred to the language statement specified in the ON statement. This action may be a code sequence, a procedure call, or a goto statement. Unless the ON-action branches to a location elsewhere in the program, control returns to the statement following the SIGNAL statement after the ON-action has been executed.

4.2.13 Exception handling in Ada

The programming language Ada is designed for constructing embedded computer systems and a general characteristic of such systems is that they should be highly reliable. Therefore, care has been taken in the design of Ada exception handling facilities and the language provides powerful and adaptable constructs for indicating and handling exceptions.

In Ada, exception names are declared like any other names, that is, as a name associated with some type. Exception names are always declared to be of the special built-in type exception. Drawing attention to an exception is termed raising an exception in Ada and executing a sequence of actions in response to an exception being raised is called handling the exception.

Any program unit in Ada may have an associated exception handler which must appear at the end of the unit. An exception handler is distinguished by the reserved word exception and resembles an Ada case statement inasmuch as it states exception names and appropriate actions for each exception. However, not every exception raised in a program unit need necessarily be handled by that unit — the exception may be propagated to some other unit at a higher level. The example below illustrates the use of exceptions in Ada.

```
-- This program copies characters from an input
-- file to an output file.  Termination occurs
-- either when all characters are copied or -- when a
NULL character is input

nullchar,eof : exception;
    char : character;

loop
    get(input_file,char);
    if end_of_file(input_file) then
        raise(eof);
    elsif         char = ASCII'NULL then
            raise (nullchar);
        else
            put(output_file,char);          end if;
end loop;
exception
    when eof => write(user_console,'no null
characters');
    when nullchar => write(user_console,'null
terminator');
end;
```

In this example, exceptions are handled in the same program unit in which they are declared. To illustrate how exceptions may be propagated to a higher level unit, consider a modification of the above example. Assume that copying of characters ceases whenever any character apart from a letter or a digit is detected:

```
eof,not_letter_or_digit : exception;
function char_is_letter_or_digit(char:in character)
            returns boolean;
begin
    if char in '0'..'9' or char in 'A'..'Z' or
        char in 'a'..'z' then
        return(true)
    else
```

```
            raise not_letter_or_digit;
        end if;
    end;

    loop
        get(input_file,char);
        if char_is_letter_or_digit(char) then
            put(output_file,char);
        end if;      if end_of_file(input_file) then
            raise eof;
        end if; end loop;
    exception
        when eof => write(user_console,'file copied');
        when not_letter_or_digit
    =>write(user_console,'error');
    end;
```

The exception not_letter_or_digit which is raised in the
function char_is_letter_or_digit is propagated to the
calling program because no handler for it exists in the
function.   In   general,   exceptions   are   propagated
outwards until a handler is found or until the Ada
system exception handler is activated.

The exception handling mechanism of Ada, unlike that
of PL/1, does not provide for the exception handler
recovering from the event which caused the exception and
resuming   program   execution   at   the   point   where   the
exception occurred. Instead, an exception occurring
within a program unit always results in the execution of
that unit being terminated.   However, the exception
propagation mechanism can be used to affect recovery if
an exception occurs in a program unit X.   That exception
can be propagated to a higher level unit Y, the
conditions causing the exception corrected or modified
and the program unit X explicitly reactivated.

4.3   CHOOSING A PROGRAMMING LANGUAGE

One of the most important decisions which must be made
when designing and building a large software system is
which programming language is to be used to implement
the system. As most of the costs in a software system
are incurred during the testing and maintenance phases
of the system life cycle, an inappropriate notation
used to represent the system can introduce difficulties
at these later stages of the life cycle.   Choosing an
appropriate   programming   language   minimises   the

difficulties in coding a design, reduces the amount of program testing required, and makes for a more readable and hence more easily maintained program.

There is rarely any justification for choosing assembly code as the programming language for a major project.   Wichmann (1978) has asserted that there appear to be only three application areas where it may be necessary to use assembly code:

(1)   Some aerospace applications where very tight time and space constraints are placed on the program.

(2)   Engineering test programs where arbitrary, perhaps illegal, sequences of instructions must be generated.

(3)   Some microprocessor systems with unusual or special purpose architectures so that it is impossible or uneconomic to construct an efficient high level language compiler for these machines.

As well as these applications, it might be added that the coding of small time critical parts of large systems may be justified.   The identification of which parts are to be coded in a low level language cannot be carried out before the system is implemented.   Only after implementation and evaluation can those parts be discovered and recoded if necessary.

To reduce total life cycle costs, the implementation of the system should be readily maintainable.   This implies that the system should be encoded in a high level language which provides facilities to build the system as a number of autonomous, cooperating modules. The language should have control and data structuring facilities which allow a 'readable' program to be produced.

It should be possible to use meaningful names, structuring facilities such as procedures and functions should be available and the language should have adequate control constructs so that the excessive use of goto statements may be avoided.   As it it obviously desirable that the system should detect as many errors as possible, the language should be typed so that user errors due to object mistyping may be detected by the compiler. These are ideal criteria for selecting a programming language for a major project but pragmatic considerations often mean that the most suitable language, in theory, cannot be used. Some of these important pragmatic criteria are:

(1)   The requirements of the system contractor.
The contractor of a software system may specify that a particular programming language is to be used and, in general, this requirement must be adhered to. Alternatively, the contractor may provide a list of approved languages and one of these must be chosen for the project implementation. It is up to the system designers and implementors to decide which is the most appropriate language for each particular project.

Contractor specification of programming language is the normal practice where the contractor takes over system maintenance from the implementors after an agreed period as is common in systems contracted for defence purposes. As the contractor's staff are involved in program maintenance, the project must be implemented in a language which they can understand.

(2)   The availability of language compilers.
If a project is to be implemented using a particular hardware/operating system configuration, there must be an acceptably efficient translator for the implementation language available.

(3)   The availability of software tools to support program development.
Software tools such as context editors, cross referencers, code control systems and execution flow analysers have an important role to play in supporting the programming process. The availability of such tools for a particular language is likely to make a system easier to implement and validate.

(4)   The size of the project.
If the project is very large, it may be appropriate to design and implement a programming language specifically for that project. This is especially true where no reasonable implementations of existing languages are available. An example of a well known system where this approach was adopted was in the development of the UNIX operating system and its associated programming language C.

(5)   The knowledge of existing programming staff.
        Although it is not particularly difficult for ex-
        perienced programmers to learn a new programming
        language, they require some practice in a language
        before they become fully competent. If other fac-
        tors do not mitigate against it, it is desirable
        to choose a language with which programming staff
        are already familiar.

(6)   The programming language used in previous pro-
        jects.
        This is related to the above consideration
        inasmuch as programmers who have worked on previ-
        ous projects are already familiar with some pro-
        gramming language. Another important considera-
        tion is that program maintenance is made more dif-
        ficult if many languages are in current use. If
        programmers are expected to maintain a number of
        systems, coded in different languages, there will
        inevitably be mistakes made because of confusion
        of language features.

(7)   The need for software portability.
        If the software is intended for only a single
        hardware configuration, and has a limited life-
        time, software portability considerations are not
        important. On the other hand, if the system is
        intended to operate on a number of different
        machines, it is important to select a programming
        language which allows portable programs to be con-
        structed.

(8)   The application being programmed.
        Although so-called general purpose programming
        languages can be used for any application, some
        languages are more suitable than others for par-
        ticular applications. For example, a language
        such as   FORTRAN   is   best   suited   to
        scientific/mathematical applications and is quite
        unsuitable for compiler writing or operating sys-
        tem applications.

    The choice of a programming language is a very
important one and all the above factors should be taken
into consideration when making that choice. At present,
there are no programming languages which are really
suitable for all applications and rigid standardisation
on any one language is not recommended. A better

approach is to have a list of approved programming languages, each tailored towards a particular application. The language on the list which is best suited to an application should be chosen.

4.4   INDEPENDENT COMPILATION

Independent compilation of program units means that units may be compiled separately and subsequently integrated to form a complete program. The integration process is carried out by another program known as a linker or link editor. Without the facility of independent compilation, a language cannot be considered as a viable language for software engineering.

Typically, a large program is made up of a number of distinct program units - procedures, functions or modules. In total, it may consist of several thousand lines of source code and it may take many minutes or even hours to compile the complete program. If every program unit needed to be recompiled each time any one of the units is changed, this imposes significant overhead and increases the costs of program development, debugging and maintenance. If independent compilation is available, compiling the whole system is unnecessary - only the modified unit need be recompiled and the system relinked.

To compile a program unit on its own, that unit must be self-contained. All objects referenced in a unit should either be defined explicitly in that unit or their properties - type, name, parameters of a procedure - should be specified in a special declaration commonly known as an external declaration. As long as the properties of all objects are explicitly specified, compiler checking is not compromised by independent compilation.

An independent compilation facility is vital for the development of large systems and this is one of the principal reasons why FORTRAN, in spite of its shortcomings, has been so widely used in software engineering projects. The design of FORTRAN subroutines is such that independent compilation is straightforward and large libraries of precompiled FORTRAN routines can easily be developed. As well as this, routines specific to some application such as the mathematical routines are available at almost all large FORTRAN installations and this increases the real power of the language enormously.

In FORTRAN, the basic program unit which is independently compiled is the subroutine. Because FORTRAN is not a block-structured language, there is no concept of global names – all names used in a subroutine are either parameters, locally declared or explicitly stated in a COMMON block. A COMMON statement specifies those program variables which are defined outside the subroutine. If reference is made to other subroutines, the FORTRAN compiler assumes them to be externally declared and creates a list of external references to be resolved by the link editor. Because the user need not explicitly specify external references made in a subroutine, the compiler assumes that all external references whether to subroutines or COMMON variables are correct. It cannot check, for example, if a subroutine call has the correct number of parameters and consequently there is no way to detect programmer error.

The design of block-structured languages is such that independent compilation must be implemented as a special feature and restrictions must be imposed on language usage if independent compilation is permitted. The scope rules of block-structured languages are such that all names accessed in a block need not be declared in that block – access to names declared in outer blocks are permitted. Consequently, according to the rules of the language, a procedure may refer to global variables and the compiler must obtain the specifications of these variables by compiling their declarations. Clearly, procedures which refer to global variables cannot be independently compiled and non-standard implementations of block-structured languages like Pascal which offer an independent compilation facility generally forbid the use of global names in independently compiled procedures. In order that independently compiled procedures may make reference to other procedures, the language is usually extended by the provision of an external procedure specification facility.

An external procedure specification allows the programmer to introduce the name of an external procedure and to specify the types of its parameters. There may be a restriction on the parameter types permitted in an external procedure or alternatively, the system may not guarantee compiler checking of external procedure references. Each external procedure which is referenced must be specified and after compilation a special purpose linker is used to create the final program.

Because of the rules governing visibility of names, block-structured languages are not particularly suitable for independent compilation. Procedures which share variables cannot be written and compiler checking is either compromised or the programmer is severely restricted in his use of the language.

The procedure is not a particularly suitable program unit for independent compilation but if a language has module facilities such as Ada packages, independent compilation can be offered at the module level. The fundamental program unit for independent compilation is the module. Because objects declared in a module may retain their value from one activation of a module to another, procedures within a module can share variables. Similarly, because types may also be declared in a module, procedures may use local types and compiler checking is not compromised.

In Ada, the need for separate compilation has been recognised and facilities have been included in the language which allow the user to specify that a program unit has been separately compiled.

Implementation 2: Programming practice

Good programming – the production of reliable and maintainable programs – is a language independent process. Whilst high level languages such as Ada or Pascal simplify the process of converting a design into an implementation, there is no reason why good programs may not be constructed in any language whatsoever. Even assembly code can be written in an understandable way.

The material in this chapter covers some of the language independent aspects of the programming process. These include programming methodology, programming style, the use of software tools to assist programming and how programs may be written so that portability problems are reduced.

The first section in the chapter briefly describes alternative methodologies of programming – top down and bottom up programming. As many of the principles of programming methodology have already been covered in chapter 3, this section simply introduces these different methodologies and discusses which is normally the most appropriate methodology to use.

The second part of the chapter discusses programming style. The style of programming used by an individual programmer is the most important factor affecting the readability and understandability of programs. A well-written program is neatly laid out, makes use of meaningful names, is sensibly commented and makes use of language constructs in such a way that program security and readability is maximised. The creation of such a program requires care, discipline, and pride in workmanship on the part of the programmer.

The third major section describes software tools which can assist the programmer in producing a well-written program. Software tools improve programmer productivity by taking over mundane clerical tasks previously carried out by the programmer himself. The information gathered by software tools about static and dynamic program attributes can be used by the software engineer to refine his work, improving the quality of the developed programs.

This leads on to the following section which covers programming environments. Rather than use a collection of unrelated tools, recent research suggests that an integrated toolkit – a programming environment – could improve programmer productivity. This section describes what this toolkit might contain and introduces the notion of a software engineering environment to support every stage in the software life cycle.

The final part of this chapter addresses program portability. As software costs increase, it is clearly desirable to write programs in such a way that they do not depend on the underlying computer hardware. In practice, complete independence is impossible but the way in which a program is written significantly influences its portability. The material in this section describes how operating system and hardware dependencies can be minimised.

5.1   PROGRAMMING METHODOLOGY

When constructing a program from a design there are two possible methodologies which may be adopted. These are top down program development and bottom up development.

Top down development parallels the top down process which should be used in system design, with the program structure being hierarchical. The programmer implements the higher levels of the design and represents the lower levels by 'stubs' which simulate their function in a simplified way. As the implementation of a level is completed, the programmer moves on to the next lower level and implements that in terms of its sub-levels. Ultimately, the lowest level of the system is implemented using basic programming language facilities.

Bottom up development is the converse of this process. Implementation starts with the lower levels of the system and the system is built up until, finally, the highest design level is implemented. Effectively, the programmer creates basic building blocks and uses these to build more complex blocks which are themselves used as building blocks for higher levels of the system.

Authors such as Wirth (1971), Dijkstra (1968), and Naur (1972) argue that top down development is a superior methodology to bottom up development because it results in the creation of programs which are more readable and more reliable than those implemented using bottom up techniques. Bottom up development, it is argued, tends to result in local optimisations at the expense of system quality because the programmer is never given the opportunity to view the system as an entity rather than as a collection of parts.

Top down development is undoubtedly the best technique to adopt if program design and implementation are considered synonomous. A top down approach to design is essential — the design must progress from the general to the particular. Given a design which has been implemented in a top down manner, it is this author's opinion that strict adherence to top down implementation is not necessary.

In general, top down implementation is the simplest way to implement a design and the practice should be generally adopted. However, the practical limitations of our existing programming languages are such that it may be impossible to implement program stubs in an effective way. It may be necessary to augment the basic programming language constructs with new building blocks created at lower levels of the system. The methodology used is mostly top down but includes some elements of bottom up program development.

As the development process closely parallels top down design in chapter 3, the reader is referred to that chapter for examples of the process.

At this point it is appropriate to introduce the term structured programming. Structured programming is a term which is widely and rather loosely used in discussions of programming. There appears to be no generally accepted definition of the term — in some cases it means programming without the use of gotos, in other cases it means adopting a top down design methodology, and in yet others it means confining programming control constructs to while loops and if statements. It is not the intention here to present an exact definition of the term structured programming. As the term is used, it appears to embrace a philosophy rather than a methodology. The philosophy embraces the design and programming guidelines covered in this book and if these are followed the reader can claim to program in a structured manner.

5.2   PROGRAMMING STYLE

The requirements for the programming language Ada made the cogent observation that a program is read more often than it is written and that it is the responsibility of programming language designers to design languages which allow readable programs to be constructed. However, program readability does not just depend on language facilities. The style in which a program is written determines its readability or otherwise - a well-written program in a language such as FORTRAN might be more readable than a badly written program in Pascal.

The creation of a readable and reliable program is a creative process and it is impossible to lay down rigid rules governing programming style. However, a number of guidelines can be established which, if followed, improve program readability. In addition, recognition and avoidance of error-prone language constructs and the utilisation of language facilities which allow compile-time and run-time checks to be carried out increases the overall reliability of a program. Aspects of programming style relating to the naming of program objects, the use of program comments, the use of control constructs, structuring programs, and paragraphing program listings will be discussed.

5.2.1 The use of names in a program

The objects in a program such as constants, variables, procedures, functions, and types model real-world entities. The function of some entity in the real-world is mirrored by the function of the object representing that entity in a program. Accordingly, the names of objects in a program should be closely related to or, if practical, identical to the names of the real-world entities which are modelled.

For example, if a program is computing satellite orbits, it is concerned with entities such as the mass of the satellite, the mass of the earth, the velocity of the satellite, and the acceleration of the satellite. These should be represented in the program by objects which might be named satellite_mass, earth_mass, satellite_velocity, and satellite_acceleration. It is not enough to use names such as mass, velocity, and acceleration to refer to the satellite mass, velocity and acceleration because it is not immediately obvious to the program reader that these names refer to the satellite rather than some other entity such as the earth.

Even worse, is to choose names which are unrelated to the entities being modelled such as the names of footballers, cryptic abbreviations or single letter identifiers. Poor programmers frequently choose names

which are short and therefore easy to type. This
procedure results in programs which are almost
incomprehensible. Consider the following example,
programmed using short names and compare it with the
next example which is the same program coded using
meaningful names. As well as illustrating the use of
names, the example below also illustrates that the use
of a reasonable programming language such as Pascal does
not guarantee that programs are necessarily readable.

```
program CT(input,output)
    var t,f:real;
    begin
        read(t);          f := t*9/5+32;
        write(f);
    end.
```

```
program ConvertCentigradeToFahrenheit(input,output);
    var FahrenheitTemperature,
    CentigradeTemperature:real;
    begin
        read(CentigradeTemperature);
        FahrenheitTemperature :=
        CentigradeTemperature*9/5+32;
        write(FahrenheitTemperature);
end.
```

In the first instance, if the reader did not know the
formula for converting centigrade temperature to
fahrenheit temperature, it is unlikely that he would
ever deduce what the program was doing. In the second
example, not only does the program name explain the
function of the program, but the conversion formula is
also made explicit. The use of meaningful identifiers
makes it immediately obvious that the program reads in
an input value representing a temperature in degrees
centigrade and outputs a number representing that value
in degrees fahrenheit.

Unfortunately, one of the most commonly used
programming languages, FORTRAN, places an arbitrary
restriction on the length of program names. Early
versions of FORTRAN introduced this restriction to
simplify the task of the compiler writer and revisions
of the language have not removed the restriction. It is
not clear why this is so as our compiler technology is
such that names of any length can easily be handled and
longer names do not invalidate any existing programs.

The FORTRAN programmer has no alternative but to choose abbreviations for program names. There are a number of ways of going about this:

(1)   If the meaningful name is made up of several words such as 'ConvertCentigradeToFahrenheit', the programmer may choose a name made up of the initial letters of each word – CCTF.

(2)   He may choose to abstract important information from the name and abbreviate that. The name 'ConvertCentigradeToFahrenheit' may become CENFAH.

(3)   If a meaningful name consists of a single word such as 'velocity', the best abbreviation convention is to drop vowels from the right in the name so that 'velocity' becomes VELCTY.

Whatever abbreviation technique is chosen, it is important that it is applied consistently. For example, if a program abbreviates 'satellite_velocity' to SATVEL, rocket velocity should be abbreviated to ROCVEL rather than RCTVEL or ROCKV. In addition, the abbreviation convention should be described in a program comment and an index, relating abbreviations to names and their function should be included. For example:

```
C    SATVEL        satellite velocity, real > 0
C    SATMSS        satellite mass, constant = 250kg
C    SATACC        satellite acceleration, real
     ........
```

5.2.2 Information hiding

A security principle which is normally adopted by military organisations is the 'need to know' principle. Only those individuals who need to know a particular piece of information to carry out their duties are given that information and information which is not directly relevant to their work is withheld. When programming, an analagous principle should be adopted to control access to system data by program units.

In principle, each program unit should only be allowed access to program objects which are required to implement that unit's function. Access to other objects, not needed by the unit, should be denied by using the scope rules of the programming language to conceal the existence of these objects.   This is called 'information hiding'.

The advantage of hiding unnecessary information is that there is no way in which the hidden information may be corrupted by a program unit which is not supposed to use that information.   This means that programs are more secure and, in some circumstances, may provide data independence – the data representation may be changed without changing the program units which make use of that data. Furthermore, if objects are declared close to where they are used, this improves the readability of the program.   The reader need not search through pages of listing to find the definition of an object.

Programming languages such as FORTRAN and Pascal do not have constructs which allow access to information on a 'need to know' basis.   FORTRAN's single level locality of declarations in subroutines and Pascal's simple block structure mean that in most programs, unnecessary information is available to some or all program units.

Unfortunately, there is little the user of these languages can do to simulate information hiding constructs and it is left up to the programmer to ensure that system data is not accidentally corrupted.   To avoid such corruption, the programming style adopted should be such that 'tricks' are not used for local optimisations.   These 'tricks' usually depend on altering global information which, strictly, ought to be altered by some other unit in the program.

These practices are sometimes justified by their perpetrators as being necessary for efficiency reasons but they provide immense problems for the program maintainer and can make formal program verification virtually impossible.

In order to implement 'need to know' access, the programming language must have a facility to implement modules.   This is discussed in section 4.2.8 and the reader is referred to that section for examples of how the facility may be used.

5.2.3 Program comments

All programming languages have a facility for including non-executable information in a program as a comment. It is essential that this facility is properly used to create a readable program. Comments in a program should be considered as an integral part of the program – they are as important as any other program statement.   They should never be added to a program as an afterthought, once the programmer considers that his program is finished.

This practice is very common and is frequently justified by the fact that the inclusion of comments when the program is first written means that they must be modified as the program is debugged. If the comments are added later, the amount of work required is reduced. Furthermore, the practicalities of meeting software production deadlines often means that the addition of comments is neglected and program development abandoned with the program in an unfinished state. The nature of the programming task is such that it is not uncommon for a programmer to take over the unfinished work of another programmer who is sick, has been promoted or who has resigned. If the unfinished work is without comments the task of the programmer taking over the work is much more difficult.

It is impossible to present a set of general rules on how to comment a program. The number of comments and the information presented in them should be governed by the program size, the application being programmed and the programming language used. In the previous example, a program to convert from one temperature scale to another, the use of comments is superfluous if meaningful names are chosen whereas if abbreviated names are used, comments would improve program readability.

The function of comments in a well-written program is to relate the program to the real-world entities being modelled by the program. A comment should explain why a section of program has been included or should provide an overall functional description of a program unit. It should not be necessary to include comments explaining how a section of program actually works. If a program is written in a high level language such as Pascal, comments should never be necessary to describe the way in which the program is performing some function. This should always be obvious from the code.

If it is necessary to program in FORTRAN or some low level language, it is virtually impossible to write self-documenting code. As a general rule, every statement in a machine code program should be commented explaining what that statement does in terms of the entities modelled by the program. Similarly, in FORTRAN, as well as comments describing overall functions and why code sections are included, complex code sequences should be commented, explaining the mechanisms used.

5.2.4 Program control constructs

Control constructs in a program should be used so that flow of control is strictly top down. As loops can be considered as single compound statements, execution should commence with the first program statement, each statement should be executed in turn and execution should terminate with the last statement. Program units, loops and decision statements should have a single point of entry and a single exit.

Strictly, this precludes the use of conditional and unconditional goto statements in languages such as Pascal which offer powerful decision and loop constructs. The use of gotos in FORTRAN and machine code should be restricted to simulating the action of higher level constructs such as if statements, case statements and while statements.

However, as long as the rule stating that each compound construct should have a single entry and exit point is observed, goto statements may be used to escape from within a compound construct in the event of some exceptional condition occurring. If a goto is used in this way, the programmer must ensure that it transfers control to the statement immediately after the compound construct and never, under any circumstances, elsewhere. If this discipline is observed, the readability of a program is not compromised and it may even be improved by the use of a goto statement. Knuth (1974) presents a number of examples where the use of a goto is justified.

A circumstance where the use of a goto may be justified is to exit from a procedure in the event of some exception. If the exception is such that it is pointless to continue execution, an immediate return can be made by jumping to the end of the procedure.

Goto statements should only ever be used for the handling of exceptional situations which arise during program execution. They should only be used to skip over code and never to repeat code sections. This means that gotos should only transfer control forward in a program. If higher level constructs are available, there are no circumstances when backward transfers of control using gotos are justified.

Another control construct whose misuse can lead to unreadable programs is the if-then-else two-armed conditional statement. If such statements are deeply nested, it can become very difficult to follow the flow of control and to determine which 'else' is associated with which 'if'. Unfortunately, the nature of the case statement in most languages is such that it cannot be used to code situations where one of a number of conditions may occur, where these conditions involve objects of different types. To encode this situation involves the use of multiple conditional statements:

```
if C1 then
    S1
else
    if C2 then
        S2
    else
        if C3 then
            S3
        else
            if C4 then
                S4
            else
        ........
```

The nesting of conditionals can become so deep that, even with disciplined paragraphing, it is difficult to determine under what circumstances a statement is executed. In a case like this, a more readable program results if multiple single-armed conditionals are used:

```
if C1 then S1
if C2 then S2
if C3 then S3
if C4 then S4
```

Although this introduces inefficiency because conditions are tested even when they must be false, the program is shorter and more readable. A more serious drawback, however, to this form of implementation is that the conditions must be mutually exclusive, otherwise more than one condition might be true. For example, the following conditions could not be directly implemented in this way:

```
if C1 and C2 then
    S1
else
    if C2 or C3 then
        S2
    else
    .......
```

In this example, if both C1 and C2 are true, S1 is executed and the remainder of the statement skipped. However, if this was implemented using single-armed conditionals as shown above, both S1 and S2 would be executed - clearly not what was intended by the programmer.

This situation is one where a goto statement can be used to improve program readability. Using single-armed conditionals and goto statements, a case statement of the form described in the previous chapter can be simulated:

```
if C1 and C2 then { S1;  goto out }
if C2 or C3 then { S2;  goto out }
if C4 then { S3; goto out }
    ....
   out:
```

Any loop construct in a program can be simulated using a while or repeat loop but where a loop is to be executed a known number of times, a for loop should be used. For loops should only be used in situations where no program exceptions should occur - escape should never be made from inside a for loop.

If this convention is observed, the reader of the program can identify the exact circumstances under which a loop will terminate, simply by reading the first statement in that loop. Of course, termination can be compromised in languages such as ALGOL60 or FORTRAN if the user alters the loop parameters. It is very poor programming practice to make assignments to the for loop variable, the increment or the final terminating value within the loop.

If a language without high level constructs is used, the program should be designed as if these constructs were available. It is relatively straightforward to simulate the action of any control constructs using if statements and goto statements. The FORTRAN programmer should translate the higher level control constructs in his design to this form. So called 'facilities' of FORTRAN such as arithmetic IF statements, assigned gotos, alternative subroutine entry and return points are inherently dangerous constructs and should never be used.

5.2.5 Program layout
The majority of programming languages are free format

languages, that is, the meaning of a program is not affected by how it is laid out on a page. Exceptions to this are FORTRAN and some assembly languages where the position of a field in an input record can affect its meaning. This is a hangover from the days when punched cards were used almost universally for preparing programs.

Layout affects the readability of a program. The liberal use of blank lines and consistent paragraphing not only make the program appear more elegant, they also make it easier to read. They act as separators which distinguish one part of the program from another. The example procedure below illustrates how the readability of identical procedures is affected by the way the text is laid out.

```
procedure CountElementOccurrences(var inarray :
intarray; arraysize : integer);
{Given a sorted array of integers, this procedure
prints each
distinct integer and the number of occurrences of
that integer}
var i,count:integer;  begin
count:=1;for i:=1 to arraysize-1 do
begin  if inarray[i] = inarray[i+1] then
count:=count+1 else
begin  write(inarray[i],count); count:=1;
end; write(inarray[arraysize],count);
end;
```

The same procedure laid out using consistent indentation and blank lines is much more readable.

```
procedure CountElementOccurrences(var inarray :
intarray; arraysize : integer);

{ Given a sorted array of integers, this procedure
prints each
   distinct integer and the number of occurrences of
that integer  }

var i,count : integer;

begin
    count := 1;
    for i := 1 to arraysize-1 do
        if inarray[i] = inarray[i+1] then
```

```
            count := count + 1
        else
        begin
           write(inarray[i],count);
           count := 1;
        end;
        write (inarray[arraysize],count);
    end;
```

Distinct parts of the program such as the header comment, variable declarations and the procedure body can be clearly identified by separating them from each other with blank lines. Statements executed in the same loop and in each arm of a conditional statement are picked out by consistent indentation.

It is very difficult to establish hard and fast rules for program layout which cope successfully with each and every program. There are inevitably circumstances such as very long or very short statements where layout rules break down and elegant layout relies on the judgement of the programmer. For this reason, prettyprinters, programs which automatically layout listings are often unsuccessful. However, some general guidelines can be established which are adequate for laying out the majority of Pascal programs. There are a number of possible layout conventions which can be adopted – those used by the author are set out below:

(1)   Label, constant, type, and variable declarations made at the outermost block level (level 0) should start in column 1 of a line. Declarations made at subsequent block levels should start at column T*n, where n is the block level and T is a standard tab indent.

(2)   In procedure declarations, the procedure header should start at column T*n and the procedure body, that is, those statements between 'begin' and 'end' should start at column T*(n+1)

(3)   Local declarations should be separated from the procedure header by at least one blank line.

(4)   If the procedure has a header comment, it should appear before the local declarations and be separated from both the procedure header and the local declarations by at least one blank line.

(5)   The statements within a loop whose initial statement (for,while,repeat) is indented by N blanks should be indented by N+T blanks. If this statement is a compound statement, however, the 'begin' and 'end' brackets of that statement should be on a line by themselves and should be indented by N spaces. Statements within these brackets should be indented by N+T spaces.

(6)   Where a conditional statement is indented by N spaces, the statement in each arm of the conditional should be indented by N+T spaces. If the statement is a compound statement, the rule for compound statements given above should be applied. If the conditional statement is a two-armed conditional, the reserved word 'else' should be indented by N spaces and should be on a line by itself.

(7)   When records are declared, the reserved words 'record' and 'end' should occur on lines by themselves as should the declaration of each field of the record. The indentation of the field name declarations should be consistent and such that the field declaration with the greatest number of characters can fit on a single line.

(8)   Wherever possible, each assignment or input/output statement should appear on a line by itself.

These rules do not describe how each and every Pascal construct is to be laid out. Constructs which are not covered are those for which it is difficult to establish strict rules and the layout of these depends on the actual program text. The important principle which must be adhered to in program layout is consistency - once a set of conventions has been established, the same conventions should be used throughout the same program.

5.3   PROGRAMMING TOOLS

One of the most important developments in the practice of programming has been the realisation that the programming process can be supported by a number of software tools. Before the widespread introduction of timesharing computer systems, the majority of program development was carried out off-line. Programs were prepared and debugged without the aid of the computer

system.   Preparing a program involved punching it onto
cardboard cards, submitting the cards to a batch
processing system and then retrieving the cards along
with a listing of the results of executing or compiling
the program.   Program modifications were made by
repunching those cards in the deck which contained the
program statements to be modified.

Even in this situation, some programming tools were
available.   Apart from compilers, assemblers and other
language processors, most systems provided a link editor
which allowed parts of the program to be independently
compiled then linked together to form an executable
program.   The link editing process also allowed the
creation and maintenance of subroutine libraries.
Subroutine libraries are probably the earliest instance
of organised program sharing.   If a generally useful
subroutine is prepared by one individual, that routine
can be entered in a public library of subroutines and
any other user may refer to that subroutine in his
program.   It is the task of the link editor to search
the appropriate subroutine libraries, abstract the code
of the called routine and link that routine with the
calling program.

As well as these tools, a variety of other software
to assist the process of program development has now
been developed.   The use of timesharing systems allows
interactive editors and debugging tools to be used and
large amounts of backing store means that library
programs to keep track of code and documentation can be
developed.   Some of these software tools are discussed
below and in the following chapter.

5.3.1 Compilers
The most important programming tool available is the
language processing system used by the programmer to
convert his program to machine code.   The provision of a
helpful compilation system can reduce the costs of
program development by making program errors easier to
find and by producing program listings which include
information about program structure as seen by the
compiler. Obviously, the error diagnostic facilities of
a compiler are partially dependent on the language being
compiled.   A Pascal compiler, for example, can detect
many more errors than a FORTRAN compiler. Not only are
the rules which govern the validity of a program more
strict for Pascal than for FORTRAN, the Pascal
programmer should also supply more information to the

compiler about the objects to be manipulated by the
program. This information allows the compiler to detect
forbidden operations on these objects.

As well as providing information to the programmer, a
compilation system must also generate efficient machine
code. This latter task involves a good deal of program
analysis and can be very time consuming with the
consequence that it is uneconomic to carry out this
operation for anything apart from completely developed
programs. A programming environment therefore, should
contain two compatible compilers for each language - a
development compiler and an optimising compiler.

Development compilers should be written to compile
code as quickly as possible and to provide the maximum
amount of diagnostic information to the programmer. An
optimising compiler, on the other hand, should be
tailored to generate efficient machine code without
considering compilation speed and diagnostic facilities.
Programs are developed using the development system and,
when complete, the optimising system is used to produce
the final version of the program for production use.

Within the confines of the language being processed,
development compilers should provide as much information
as possible about the program being compiled e.g:

(1)   The compiler listing of the program should associ-
       ate a line number with each program line.

(2)   When a program syntax or semantic error is
       discovered, the compiler should indicate where it
       found the error and what the error appears to be.
       It may also be appropriate to indicate the possi-
       ble cause of the error.

           The design of meaningful error messages is not
       a simple task as the meaningfullness or otherwise
       of an error message depends on the knowledge and
       experience of the reader of that message. In en-
       vironments where the users of the system are pro-
       fessional programmers, it is acceptable to couch
       error messages in programming language jargon. In
       environments such as engineering laboratories
       where the programmers are those involved in the
       application itself, the compiler should produce
       error messages in plain language which can easily
       be understood. As the users of a system can rare-
       ly be classified exactly, it is a good general
       rule that error messages should be couched in

plain language and should include a reference to a more precise error specification. This is discussed further in chapter 8.

(3)   The compiler should include directives which allow the programmer some control over the program listing generated by the compiler. These directives should allow the suppression of parts of the listing, control over the pagination of the listing and the enhancement of program keywords by bold printing or underlining.

(4)   When a program in a block-structured language is compiled, the compiler should indicate the lexical level at the beginning and the end of each block. This facility allows misplaced 'begin'/'end' brackets to be easily identified.

(5)   The compiler should separate source text provided by the user from information provided by the compiler. This can be accomplished by delimiting the input source using special characters such as '|' and prefacing compiler messages by some string of punctuation characters such as '****'.

(6)   The compiler should identify where each procedure in a program starts and finishes. When a program listing is searched for a particular procedure, the location of that procedure is often not immediately obvious because the name of the procedure is not distinguished from the remainder of the source text. When compiling a procedure heading, the procedure name should be abstracted and, as well as listing the procedure heading normally, the procedure name should be reprinted so that it stands out from the rest of the program text. This can be accomplished in a number of ways but perhaps the most suitable is that used by the XPL compiler (McKeeman et al., 1970). In XPL, the procedure name is abstracted and reprinted on the right hand margin of the listing for each statement in that procedure.

An important tool which may be incorporated with the compiling system is a program cross referencer. Such a system indicates the names used in the program, the types of the named objects, the line in the program where each name is declared and the line numbers where a reference is made to that object. More sophisticated cross referencers can also provide, for each procedure in the program, a list of the procedure parameters and their types, the procedure local variables and the global variables referenced in the procedure.

This latter facility is particularly useful to the programmer who must modify the value of some global variable. By examining the cross reference listing either manually or preferably, automatically, those procedures referencing that variable can be identified and checked to ensure that global variable modification will not affect their actions.

5.3.2 Editors

An important software tool in an on-line programming environment is the editor. The function of the editor is to enable the user to create and modify files kept on-line in the system. A variety of different types of editor have been implemented and these can be broadly classified as follows:

(1)   Line editors. These allow the user to replace one line of his program by some other line. They rely on the user determining the number of the line to be changed. Editors in a BASIC programming environment are inevitably line editors.

(2)   Screen editors. The text to be modified is displayed on the screen of the user's terminal and those parts to be changed are modified by overtyping. Facilities also exist to delete and insert characters.

(3)   Context editors. The editor obeys a sequence of commands which relate to the text to be modified. These commands allow parts of the text to be related by their context and often provide facilities for the repetition of commands.

Many editors include features of all the above types and each type of editor is useful in particular environments. For program development the most generally useful editor is a context editor which also includes line editing facilities.

A context editor should include commands which allow the user to locate text by its position in the file, by its position relative to the text on which the user is currently working and by its context. It should be possible to add, delete and replace complete lines and change text within a line. There should also be a mechanism for the repetitive execution of command sequences so that the same modification may be made at a number of places in the file.

A powerful editing facility, found in the UNIX editor, is the ability to refer to character strings using a pattern definition rather than simply the string itself. For example, the pattern definition:

    proc.*

refers to all strings starting with 'proc', thus allowing all procedure declarations (say), to be found.

5.3.3 Code control systems
A large software project may involve many programmers, hundreds of distinct modules and thousands of lines of code. This code may be distributed over many distinct files and libraries and exist as both source code and object code. A number of distinct versions of a system, tailored to different environments, may be produced at different times. Major problems which exist with any large software system are keeping track of the development and maintenance of program modules, determining the interdependence of modules and ensuring that the common code in different versions of a system is consistent.

If programs are developed under a batch processing system, these problems can be handled by a program librarian. The notion of program librarians was first publicised by IBM in a description of a project management technique known as Chief Programmer Teams (Baker, 1972). The librarian removes much of the administrative burden from programmers, allowing them to get on with constructing the system.

The job of a program librarian is to maintain the information pertaining to a project and all programmers working on a project must funnel their work through the program librarian. The program librarian has no programming responsibilities although he may be involved in file editing. Because all work must be submitted through the librarian, he can ensure that system updates are carried out in such a way that consistency is maintained. Furthermore, the librarian can keep detailed records of which files relate to which system modules and how different system versions can be generated. The program librarian may use specially developed library maintenance programs for this task.

The use of a program librarian is beneficial in a batch environment because it ensures that there is only a single person interface between the programming team and the computer. This is perfectly acceptable when program development is an off-line process but if an interactive system is used, the notion of funnelling work through a single individual is not tenable. In such circumstances, there is a need for an automated system to carry out system housekeeping – maintaining information about files, system modules, updates and different versions of the system.

A number of systems have been developed to automate and extend the task of the program librarian. These include MAKE (Feldman, 1979), SCCS (Rochkind, 1975), and CADES (McGuffin et al., 1979). These systems may be either stand alone systems such as CADES or may operate in conjunction – MAKE and SCCS are both available under the UNIX/PWB operating system.

To illustrate code control systems, MAKE and SCCS will be used as examples of software tools for controlling code modifications and maintenance. These code control systems are complementary – SCCS keeps track of system modifications and different system versions whereas MAKE ensures the consistency of source code and its corresponding object code.

SCCS (Source Code Control System) was originally developed for IBM 370 hardware but now plays a vital role in the UNIX/PWB system. The aim of SCCS is to allow different versions of the system to be maintained without unnecessary code duplication. It controls system updates by ensuring that no part of the system can be updated by more than one programmer at any one time. It also records when updates were made, what source lines were changed and who was responsible for the change.

SCCS is principally a system for storing and recording changes to a system module. Each time a module is changed, that change is recorded and stored in what is termed a delta. Subsequent changes are also recorded as deltas. To produce the latest version of a system, SCCS applies the deltas in turn to the original module until all deltas have been processed. Conceptually, a chain of deltas is involved as shown in Fig 5.1.

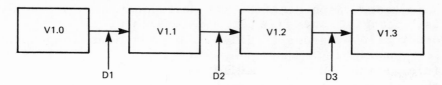

Fig. 5.1   Deltas in SCCS

The user of SCCS can specify that the system should be generated up to any point in this chain, allowing systems at different stages of development to be produced.

An extension of this feature is the ability to freeze a system at any point in the chain. When a module is added to SCCS originally, it is deemed to be release 1.0. Subsequent deltas create 1.1, 1.2, 1.3, etc. At some stage, the programmer may wish to freeze his system, for testing say, although further system development – the addition of more deltas – may be continuing in parallel.

Freezing a system simply involves specifying that new deltas constitute a new release of the system, illustrated in Fig 5.2.

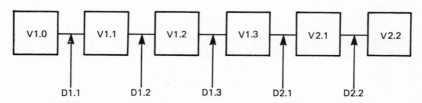

Fig. 5.2   Freezing a system using SCCS

In order to obtain release 1 of the system, the SCCS user requests that release and only those deltas pertaining to release 1 are applied. Furthermore, release 1 can be modified after development of release 2 is in progress by adding new level 1 deltas. In the above example, D1.4 could be inserted between D1.3 and D2.1.

As deltas are date stamped and owner stamped, the user of SCCS can specify that a system version at any particular date should be created and can also generate management reports on system development.

MAKE is a complementary code control system which maintains the correspondence between source code and object code versions of a system. Typically, a system is made up of code abstracted from a number of files. In some cases, dependencies exist between those files, that is, changing one file also necessitates changing some other file or group of files. MAKE provides a mechanism for specifying those dependencies. Using built-in information and user specified commands, MAKE can cause the object code of a system to be recreated when a change is made to part of the system source code.

Using MAKE, the programmer must initially state file dependencies. For example, if the object code file x.o depends on the source code files x.c and d.c, this can be explicitly stated. If d.c is changed, this change can be detected by MAKE and x.o recreated by recompiling x.c and d.c. There is no need for the user to explicitly recompile files after an editing session - MAKE will do this for him and will ensure that only necessary files are recompiled. There is no need for blanket recompilation simply to ensure that nothing has been forgotten.

As an example of how MAKE can be used, consider a situation where a program called comp is created out of object modules scan.o, syn.o, sem.o, and cgen.o. For each object module, there exists a source code module called scan.c, syn.c, sem.c, and cgen.c. A file of declarations called defs.c is shared by scan.c, syn.c, and sem.c. Modifications can be made to any of scan.c, syn.c and sem.c without requiring any other files to be recompiled but a modification to defs.c requires that scan.c, syn.c, and sem.c be recompiled.

A file stating these dependencies which can be processed by MAKE might be created as follows:

```
comp : scan.o syn.o sem.o cgen.o
     cc scan.o syn.o sem.o cgen.o -o comp
scan.o syn.o sem.o : defs
```

This states that comp is dependent (: means dependence) on scan.o syn.o sem.o and cgen.o. The modules scan.o, syn.o, and sem.o are stated to be dependent on defs.

Associated with the dependency of comp is a command sequence stating how comp may be created. Consider a situation where the files defs.c and cgen.c are modified. When MAKE is applied to the dependency information it examines defs.c and notes that its modification time is later than the time scan.o, syn.o, and sem.o were created. It therefore causes the files scan.c, syn.c,and sem.c to be recompiled to create new versions of the object files.

The file comp is now examined and its creation date is seen to precede the creation dates of the object files on which it depends. Therefore, MAKE recreates comp. In this case, there is no need to recompile scan.c, syn.c or sem.c since that compilation step has just been carried out. However, MAKE notes that the file cgen.c has been modified so that it causes that file to be recompiled and the entire system relinked.

Because of its built-in assumptions regarding name conventions such as the assumption that all files ending in .o have .c equivalents, MAKE is strictly UNIX-specific. However, it illustrates a general class of software tool designed for code control.

5.4   PROGRAMMING ENVIRONMENTS

So far, software tools have been discussed in isolation and it has been shown how these tools can aid the practice of programming. An environment designed for program development should provide the tools already discussed and others and should be specifically geared for the production of programs.

Most existing programming environments support the later stages of the software development process and do not provide tools to support requirements specification and software design. However, a number of research projects are underway (Willis, 1981; Standish, 1981; Stucki and Walker, 1981) which aim to develop a software engineering environment. This would provide a consistent environment and a set of tools to support all stages of the software life cycle from requirements definition to maintenance and software management.

Although a programming environment may be provided as a subsystem of some general purpose system, the requirements of a system whose main task is the execution of programs need not coincide with the requirements of a system whose function is to support program development. For example, a mainframe may support a transaction processing system which requires a guaranteed amount of dedicated processor time. Developing programs on such a system can be very frustrating as the programming process must give precedence to the transaction processing system. In some cases, it may even be impossible to develop software for a computer using the facilities of that computer. This is often the case when software is developed for microprocessor systems which have relatively small memories and little support software. For these reasons, it is often better to support a programming environment on a special development machine which is separate from the target machine on which the program will eventually execute.

As well as the software tools to support programming discussed above, a programming environment might provide the following facilities:

(1)   Communications software linking the development computer to the computer on which the software is to execute (the target machine).

(2)   Target machine simulators – these are particularly valuable when microprocessor software is being developed.

(3)   Testing and debugging tools – these might include test drivers, dynamic and static program analysers and test output analysis programs. These tools are discussed in the following chapter.

(4)   Text processing tools – these programs allow documentation to be developed on the same machine as the program. This simplified the task of producing and updating documentation as the program is developed. Documentation tools are discussed in chapter 7.

(5)   Requirements specification and analysis tools as discussed in chapter 2.

(6)   A computer aided design system to support some of the more clerical aspects of software design. Such a tool is included in the AIDES (Willis, 1981) system.

(7)   Project management tools – these software tools allow estimates of the time required for a project and the cost of that project to be made. Furthermore, they may provide facilities for generating management reports on the status of a project at any time. Such tools are at any early stage of development – their current state is discussed in chapter 10.

The best known programming environment is probably the

Unix   Programmers   Workbench (UNIX/PWB)   System (Ivie,
1977; Dolotta et al., 1978).   This system is designed to
support the development of software for IBM, UNIVAC,
XDS, and DIGITAL computers.   The system developers point
out that, as well as providing an environment conducive
to program development, the use of the UNIX/PWB system
means that the same system interface is presented to the
programmer irrespective of which machine is actually
being used for program execution. The programmer need
not learn the details of several different systems.   He
is also preserved from disruptions caused by changes in
the target hardware.

The Stoneman proposals for an Ada programming
environment (APSE) envisage that the APSE should be
portable and available on a variety of different
machines.   To achieve this degree of portability, 3
levels of program support are required - a kernel
environment (KAPSE), a minimal environment (MAPSE) and
the full Ada program support environment (APSE).   The
KAPSE is a minimal system whose purpose is to support a
basic machine independent user interface to an APSE.   It
comprises those facilities required to run Ada programs
and, in general, it must be reimplemented for each
target machine. The MAPSE provides a minimal Ada
programming environment and should support its own
extension. The MAPSE is made up of a number of software
tools, written in Ada, such as an Ada compiler, a link
editor, static and dynamic program analysers as well as
file transfer and manipulation programs.

The highest level environment, APSE, extends this
toolkit providing program editors, documentation tools,
program instrumentation and measurement tools, more
powerful Ada translators such as diagnostic compilers,
code control systems etc.

As well as providing a comprehensive toolkit to
support the development of Ada programs, an APSE must
also provide database facilities for tools to
communicate and to allow relationships between objects
to be recorded and maintained.   The information in the
database may be used to produce management reports
detailing the current state of a project, project
development cost, etc.

Because of the advantages offered by the use of a
comprehensive programming environment, it is inevitable
that more and more software engineering projects will
use such a system. Just as there is no ideal programming
language, there is no ideal programming environment and

different projects will make use of different environments. The identification, development and integration of software tools for use in such environments is still a major research problem.

5.5 PROGRAM PORTABILITY

The rate of change of computer hardware technology is such that computing machinery becomes obsolete long before the programs which execute on that machinery. It is therefore very important that programs should be written in such a manner that they may be implemented under more than one computer/operating system configuration. This is doubly important if a programming system is widely marketed as a product — the more machines on which a system is implemented, the greater the potential market for it.

Techniques for achieving program portability have been widely documented (Brown, 1977; Tanenbaum et al., 1978). They include emulating one machine on another using microcode, compiling a program into some abstract machine language then implementing that abstract machine on a variety of computers, and using preprocessors to translate from one dialect of a programming language to another. A full discussion of program portability requires a book to itself so it is not the intention to cover general techniques of moving programs from one machine to another. Rather, programming practices which reduce and isolate the amount of machine and operating system dependent code in a program are described below.

A characteristic of a portable program is that it is self-contained. The program should not rely on the existence of some external agency to supply required functions. In practice, complete self containment is almost impossible to achieve and the programmer intending to produce a portable program must compromise by isolating necessary references to the external environment. When that external environment is changed, those dependent parts of the program can be easily identified and modified.

Throughout this section, it will be assumed that a high level language is used for programming and that a compiler for that language is available for each machine on which the program is to be implemented. It is also assumed that some standard version of the high level language is used rather than a dialect unique to a particular installation. The work involved in implementing a program on more than a single system is significantly increased if non-standard language 'extensions' are used in the initial coding of the program. Inevitably, compiler writers have different ideas concerning which 'extensions' should be made to a language and different compilers rarely include exactly the same additions.

Even when a standard, widely implemented, high level language is used for programming, it is virtually impossible to construct a program of any size without some machine dependencies. These dependencies arise because features of the machine and its operating system are reflected directly in the language implementation. For example, the precision of numbers is dependent on the machine word size, and the access to backing store files is dependent on the primitives provided by the operating system. Even the character set available on different machines may not be identical, with the result that programs written using one character set must be edited to reflect the alternative character set.

Portability problems which arise when a standard high level language is used can be classified under two distinct headings – those problems caused by language features influenced by the machine architecture and those problems caused by operating system dependencies.

5.5.1 Machine architecture dependencies

The principle machine architecture dependencies which arise in programs are due to the fact that, whatever high level language is used, the language must rely on the conventions of information representation adopted by the host machine. Different machines have different word lengths, different character sets and different techniques for representing both integer and real numbers.

The length of a computer word directly affects the range of integers available on that machine, the precision of real numbers and the number of characters which may be packed into a single word. It is extremely difficult to program in such a way that implicit dependencies on machine word lengths are not introduced.

For example, say a program is intended to count instances of some occurrence where the maximum number of instances which might arise is 500 000. Assume instance counts are to be compared. If this program is implemented on a machine with a 32-bit word size, instance counts can be represented as integers and comparisons made directly. However, if the program is subsequently moved to a 16-bit machine, it will fail because the maximum possible positive integer which can be held in a 16-bit word is 32 767.

Such a situation poses a difficult problem for the programmer. If instance counts are not represented as integers but as real numbers or as character strings this will inevitably introduce unnecessary overhead in counting and comparisons on the 32-bit machine. The cost of this overhead must be traded off against the cost of the inevitable reprogramming which is necessary if the system is subsequently implemented on a 16-bit machine.

If portability considerations are paramount in such a situation and if a programming language which permits the use of user defined types is available, an alternative solution to this problem is possible. The user must define a type, say count_type, whose range encompasses the possible values of the instance counter. In Pascal on a 32-bit machine this might be defined:_

```
type count_type : 0..500000
```

If the system is subsequently ported to a 16-bit machine, then count_type may be redefined:

```
type count_type : array[1..6] of char;
```

Instead of using an integer to hold the counter value, it may be held as an array of digits. Associated with this type must be the operations permitted on instance counters. These can be programmed in Pascal as functions. On 32-bit machines, these functions simply consist of the appropriate integer operations. On 16-bit machines, on the other hand, the functions would be more complex, and must simulate integer operations on digit strings. For example, consider a Pascal function to compare counters for equality. On a 32-bit machine, this might be written:

```
function cequals(c1,c2:count_type) : boolean;
    c_equals := c1=c2
```

On a 16-bit machine, where large integers are represented as strings of digits, the function could be written:

```
function cequals(c1,c2:count_type) : boolean;
var i : integer;
    comp : boolean;
begin
    comp:=true;   i:=1;
    while comp and (i <= 6) do
        comp := c1[i] = c2[i];
    c_equals := comp
end;
```

Irrespective of how the type count_type is represented, the user always has exactly the same operations available and transporting the program simply involves changing the type definition and rewriting the functions which operate on that type.

Ideally, the type definition and its related operations should be grouped together into a self-contained unit like an Ada package. Only the type name and related operations need be visible outside the package with all representation details confined to the package. In languages such as Pascal, where no module facility is available, the operations on each type should be grouped together and clearly delimited by comments.

Different machine word lengths also mean that the precision of real numbers varies from machine to machine. For example, if a real number is represented using 32-bits, 8 digit precision may be possible whereas 64-bit representation allows 17 or 18 digit precision. On a 32-bit machine, no distinction could be made between the numbers 10001.3214 and 10001.3210 whereas they would be considered different numbers on a higher precision machine.

The problem of differing precision has been recognised in Ada and, in defining a numeric type, the user may explicitly state the precision to which values of that type are held. For example, 6 digit precision is specified:

```
type short is digits 6 range 0..SOMEMAX
```

This specifies that numbers of type short lie in the range 0 to SOMEMAX and should be held to 6 digit precision.

This facility eliminates some of the problems involved in porting software which uses real numbers and, theoretically, implementations of Ada should support the specification of any precision whatsoever. In practice, the specification of precisions which cannot be accommodated in one or two machine words is difficult to implement and will probably involve very heavy run-time overhead.

A portability problem related to but distinct from the problems caused by machines having different word lengths is caused by the fact that different machines may represent exactly the same information in different ways. For example, a 16-bit machine which uses two's complement notation to represent negative numbers would represent -1 as 1111111111111111, whereas a machine which uses one's complement notation would represent the same number as 1111111111111110.

In some machines, the most significant bit of a number is the leftmost bit and on others it is the rightmost bit. On 16-bit machines where it is the leftmost bit, the number 2 would be represented as 0000000000000010, whereas if the rightmost bit is significant, 2 is represented 0100000000000000, if two's complement representation is used.

These representation considerations do not normally cause problems for the high level language programmer because the objects which he normally operates on have values which are consistent from one representation to another. If, however, the programmer wishes to generate specific bit patterns and the programming language does not allow the programmer to operate directly on binary objects, the user might simulate these binary objects using integers. The representation of integers on a particular machine must be known if appropriate bit patterns are to be generated. If the program is moved to another machine which uses a different representation for integers, the bitstrings generated from integers will be incorrect. As a general rule, when bitstrings are generated by using integers, absolute integer values should never be used in the program. Rather, the integers representing the bitstrings should be given names appropriate to their function, with these names defined as constants. For example, if it is required to define a mask which will select the rightmost bit of a number, this might be declared:

```
const RIGHTMOST = 1;
```

If the program containing this declaration is subsequently moved to a machine where the most significant bit is the rightmost bit, this constant might be redefined:

```
const RIGHTMOST = -(MAXINT+1);
```

Again, if packages are available, these declarations can be grouped in a package and their representation concealed from the remainder of the program. Otherwise, declarations of such machine dependent constants must be grouped together and clearly identified by comments in the program text.

Unfortunately there is no worldwide standardisation of the character sets used in computers. The majority of systems use a character set named ASCII (American Standard Characters for Information Interchange) but other representations are also used, principally EBCDIC (Extended Binary Coded Decimal) which is used on IBM and IBM compatible systems.

Not only do different character sets use different values to represent each character, they also differ in the punctuation characters provided. As a result, programs written using character set A say, cannot be directly translated to another character set B. The programs in character set A must first be edited to replace characters available in A but not in B by some equivalent. For example, in the original definition of Pascal, it was specified that text enclosed in braces {} is treated as a comment. Many implementations of Pascal execute on machines which do not provide braces so, in these implementations, comments are enclosed within the compound symbols (* and *).

The editing procedure required to resolve character set differences is tedious but does not normally cause serious portability problems. The transformation is clearly defined and easy to implement if a reasonable context editor is available. Portability problems are caused by character representations when the system depends on a character having a particular value. For example, in ASCII, the digits 0-9 have values 60-69 and to obtain the integer value of a digit, 60 is subtracted from the character value. In Pascal:

```
digitvalue := ord(digit) - 60;
```

If this code were transported to machine using the EBCDIC character set, it would be legal but would deliver an incorrect result. In EBCDIC, digits are represented by the values 240-249, so the above statement would consider the character '2' to have an integer value of 182.

Assumptions about the values used to represent characters should never be built-into a program. If the above statement were written:

```
digitvalue := ord(digit) - ord('0');
```

no portability problems arise. Not only is the statement character set independent, it is also a clearer description of the operation being implemented.

A further difficulty which arises because of different character sets results from the fact that different machines use different collating sequences for the letters of the alphabet. In ASCII, the letters 'A' to 'Z' are assigned ascending values in consecutive sequence whereas in EBCDIC, 'A' to 'Z' do not have consecutive values. A program statement may test a value to see if it represents a letter of the alphabet by checking that it lies between the value representing 'A' and the value representing 'Z'. For example:

```
if(someval >= ord('A')) and (someval <= ord('Z'))
then .......
```

On EBCDIC machines, this is not guaranteed to work because the sequence of values between 'A' and 'Z' includes other characters. If the programmer is faced with such a situation and knows that his program may be implemented on machines with differing character sets, the only solution is to isolate such machine dependencies in clearly identified procedures. The above statement might be written:

```
if letter(someval) then......
```

The procedure letter must be rewritten when the program is transferred to a machine with an incompatible character set.

5.5.2 Operating system dependencies

One of the reasons for using high level programming languages is that the languages conceal low level machine details from the programmer. Inevitably, this involves the use of machine operating system facilities. As there is no general consensus on what are operating

facilities are necessary, there is little or no
operating system standardisation. Each implementation of
a particular language reflects the facilities of the
operating system under which that language executes.

In this section, those features of a high level
language program which are dependent on operating system
facilities are discussed. The major problem areas are
libraries, files, input-output and job control.

A well known and widely used operating system
facility is the provision of subroutines which are
available to all users for inclusion in their programs.
Subroutine libraries fall into 2 classes:

(1)   Standardised libraries of routines associated with
        a particular application. An example of such rou-
        tines are the NAG library routines for numerical
        applications. These routines have a standard in-
        terface and exactly the same routines are avail-
        able to all installations which subscribe to the
        library.

(2)   Installation libraries which consist of routines
        submitted by users at a particular installation.
        These routines rarely have a standard interface
        nor are they written in such a way that they may
        easily to ported from one installation to another.

The re-use of existing software should be encouraged
whenever possible as it reduces the amount of code which
must be written, tested, and documented. However, the
use of subroutine libraries reduces the self-
containedness of a program and hence may increase the
difficulty of transferring that program from one
installation to another.

If use is made of standard subroutine libraries such
as the NAG library, this will not cause any portability
problems if the program is moved to another installation
where the library is available. On the other hand, if
the library is not available, transportation of the
program is likely to be almost impossible.

If use is made of local installation libraries,
transporting the program either involves transporting
the library with the program or supplementing the target
system library to make it compatible with the host
library. The user must trade off the productivity
advantages of using libraries against the dependence on
the external environment which this entails.

One of the principle functions of an operating system is to provide a file system – primitive operations which allow the user to name, create, access, delete, protect, and share files. There are no standard governing how these operations should be provided with the consequence that each operating system provides them in completely different ways.

As high level language systems must provide file facilities, they interface with the file system and, normally, the file system operations provided in the high level language are synonomous with the operating system primitives. Therefore, the least portable parts of a program are often those operations which involve access to files.

There are a number of different problems which can arise because of file system incompatibilities:

(1)   The convention for naming files may differ from system to system. Some systems restrict the number of characters in a file name, other systems impose restrictions on exactly which characters can make up a file name and yet others impose no restrictions whatsoever.

(2)   The file system structure may differ from system to system. Some file systems are hierarchically structured where the user may create his own directories and sub-directories. Other systems are restricted to a 2 level structure where all files belonging to a particular user must reside in the same directory.

(3)   Different systems utilise different schemes for protecting files. Some systems involve passwords, other systems use explicit lists of who may access what and yet others grant permissions according to the attributes of the user.

(4)   Some systems attempt to classify files as data files, program files, binary files etc. Other systems consider all files to be files of characters.

(5)   Most systems restrict the user to a maximum number of files which may be in use at any one time. If this number is different on the host machine from that on the target machine, there are problems in

porting programs which have many files open at the same time.

(6)   There are a number of different file structuring mechanisms enforced by different systems. Systems such as UNIX support only character files whereas other systems consider files to be made up of logical records with so many logical records packed into each physical block.

(7)   Related to the structure of the file are the random access primitives supported by the system. Some systems may not support random access, others allow random access to individual characters and yet others only permit random access at the block level.

There is little the programmer can do to make file access over different systems compatible. He is stuck with a set of file system primitives and those parts of the system must be modified if the program is moved to another installation. To reduce the amount of work required, file access primitives should be isolated, whenever possible, in user defined procedures. For example, in UNIX, the mechanism to create a file involves calling a system function called 'create' passing the file name and access permissions as parameters:

    create("myfile",0755)

This creates a file called myfile with universal read and execute access and owner write access. In order to isolate this call, a synonomous user function which calls create can be included:

    create_file("myfile",0755)

In UNIX, create_file would simply consist of a single call to the system routine create. On other systems, create_file could be rewritten to reflect the conventions of the system. The parameters to create_file could be translated into the appropriate form for that system.
    It might be imagined that the input/output facilities in a programming language would conceal the details of the operating system input/output routines.

Input/output should therefore cause few problems when porting a system from one installation to another.

This is true to some extent. In some programming languages, such as FORTRAN, input/output facilities are clearly defined and each implementation of the language provides these facilities. In other languages however, the input/output facilities are poorly defined or inadequate. As a result, the implementors of a compiler 'extend' the I/O facilities to reflect the facilities provided by the operating system. Particular problems arise in many widely used programming languages with interactive terminal input/output. These problems arise because the programming languages were designed before interactive terminals came into widespread use and interactive input/output was not considered by the language designers.

Different systems consider interactive terminals in different ways. In UNIX, a terminal is considered as a special file and file access primitives are used to access it. In other systems, terminals are considered to be devices distinct from files and special terminal access primitives are provided.

There are advantages and disadvantages in considering a terminal as a file. The advantage is that input and output to and from a program can come from either a terminal or a file on backing store. The disadvantage is that the characteristics of a terminal are not exactly those of a file, in fact, a terminal is really like two distinct files, an input file and an output file. If this is not taken into account, portability problems are likely to arise.

Further problems with terminal I/O arise because terminal characteristics differ. Different terminals have different screen sizes, some terminals offer cursor addressability, others do not, some terminals support tab characters and so on. So called 'intelligent' terminals sometimes make use of control characters which differ from terminal to terminal. Again, the only advice which can be given to the programmer wishing to write portable interactive programs is to isolate hardware specific code in clearly defined procedures. These procedures must be rewritten when the system is moved to another installation.

Many systems are made up of a number of separate programs with job control language statements used to coordinate the activities of these programs. There is absolutely no standardisation of job control in different systems with the consequence that all job control must be rewritten when transferring a system from one installation to another. There is nothing the programmer can do to reduce the work involved.

This sad note concludes this section on program portability. Apart from the problems described here which can arise when transferring high level language programs from one installation to another, other portability problems not directly connected with programming also occur. Different installations may have incompatible peripheral devices so that physical media written on the host system cannot be read on the target system. This is a very common and extremely frustrating problem.

An important aspect of portability which is covered in chapter 7 is the portability of documentation. A programming system without documentation is of little use and it is important that documentation is ported along with the program.

Testing and debugging

The validation of a software system is a continuing
process through each stage of the software life cycle.
Program testing is that part of the validation process
which is normally carried out during implementation and
also, in a different form, when implementation is
complete. Testing involves exercising the program using
data which is similar to the real data on which the
program is designed to execute, observing the program
outputs and inferring the existence of program errors or
inadequacies from anomalies in that output.

It is sometimes considered that program testing and
debugging are one and the same thing. Although closely
related, they are, in fact, quite distinct processes.
Testing is the process of establishing the existence of
program errors and debugging is the process of locating
where these errors occurred in the program and
correcting them.

It is very important to realise that testing can
never show that a program is correct. It is always
possible that undetected errors exist even after the
most comprehensive testing. Program testing can only
demonstrate the presence of errors in a program, it
cannot demonstrate their absence. Following Myers (1979)
therefore, a successful test is considered to be one
which establishes the presence of one or more errors in
the software being tested. Notice that this differs
from the normal definition of a successful test which is
a test displaying no output anomalies.

Program testing is a destructive process. It is
intended to deliberately cause a program to behave in a
manner which was not intended by its designer or
implementor. As it is a natural human trait for an
individual to feel some affinity with objects which he
has constructed, the programmer responsible for system
implementation is not the best person to test a
program. Psychologically, the system programmer will not
want to 'destroy' his creation with the result that,
consciously or subconsciously program tests will be

selected which fail - that is they will not be adequate
for demonstrating the presence of system errors.

On the other hand, detailed knowledge of the
structure of a program or programming system can be
extremely useful in identifying appropriate test cases
and the system implementor plays an important part in
this.   The key to successful program testing is to
establish a working environment where system
implementors and outsiders involved in program testing
can play a complementary role.   This must involve the
management premise that program 'errors' are inevitable
because of the complexity of the systems involved and
that errors are not blameworthy.   The testing process
must not be seen as threatening those individuals
involved in implementation otherwise they are liable to
be uncooperative with outsiders responsible for testing.

Although only a part of the overall validation
process program testing is the only technique used to
validate a program in many if not most programming
organisations .   Formal verification and inspection are
not widely used validation techniques. Unfortunately,
testing, on its own, cannot completely validate a
program with the result that unreliable systems are very
common indeed.

As well as covering program testing techniques, this
chapter also briefly discusses the role of verification
and formalised inspections in the software validation
process.   Test case design is illustrated by example and
software tools which may be used in the testing process
described.   The final section in the chapter discusses
debugging.   It describes how a program can be written to
facilitate debugging and discusses a number of automated
debugging aids.

6.1   PROGRAM VERIFICATION

The notion of formal software verification was
introduced in chapter 3. The verification of a software
design was described and, obviously, the same
verification process can be carried out on a completed
program as part of the overall system validation
procedure.

It can be argued that the logical place for formal
verification is after the implementation stage of system
development rather than after the design stage.   If a
design is verified, it is quite possible to introduce
errors during the implementation which would be detected

if the verification process was carried out on the finished program.

However, there are a number of disadvantages in verifying a program rather than a design. These are:

(1)   The program may be written in such a way that verification is very difficult. Implementation dependent constructs whose semantics are not clear may have been used in order to satisfy efficiency requirements.

(2)   The programming language used may be so low level that formal verification is impossible – there is no way a FORTRAN or machine code program can be verified without the use of considerable abstractions.

(3)   If verification follows implementation and design errors are discovered, this may involve considerable work in redesign and reimplementing the program. It is far better to detect these errors at the design stage and accept the possibility of implementation errors which are usually relatively cheap to correct.

(4)   As an implementation is usually larger than a design, program verification is longer, more complex and more expensive than design verification.

Ideally both the design and the implementation should be formally verified but because of the cost of the verification process, this is quite unrealistic. The only exception to this is critical real-time systems whose failure could be disastrous causing an aircraft to crash or an industrial process to go out of control. The reliability required of such systems is so high that it may be cost effective to verify both the program design and the program implementation.

The need for testing is not eliminated if a program is verified. Because program proofs are lengthy, it is quite possible that errors will be made in the course of the verification process. The software will not be 'correct'. Furthermore, verification does not demonstrate that software meets its non-functional requirements so testing is necessary to check that the dynamic attributes of the program are acceptable.

Verification should be carried out at the design

stage in order that the amount of testing required by a program can be minimised. Verification and testing are not mutually exclusive — they are complementary parts of the process of software validation.

6.2 CODE INSPECTIONS

Whether or not a formal verification has been carried out at some stage in the software development process, a useful validation technique is code inspection. Code inspection is a formalisation of egoless programming, described in chapter 9, and involves a programmer conducting an inspection team through his code.

Fagan (1976) suggests that the best size for an inspection team is four members. These are:

(1)   A moderator who is a competent programmer but not personally involved in the project.

(2)   The designer of the program.

(3)   The programmer involved in the implementation.

(4)   The individual responsible for testing the code.

If the same individual is responsible for the design and coding or the coding and testing, another outsider should be brought in to take over one of those roles.

The code inspection process involves distributing the design specifications to the inspection team in advance who study these and attempt to understand the design. This may be supplemented by a preliminary overview presented by the designer. During the inspection itself, the programmer explains how the design is implemented to the rest of the team. They follow his explanation closely and attempt to detect errors in it.

When an error is detected, it is noted by the moderator and the inspection continues. No attempt is made to correct the error even if the correction seems obvious. The task of the inspection team is detection, not correction.

The advantage of code inspections over testing is that the inspection finds many errors in a single session. When errors are discovered by testing, they often require correction before further testing can continue with the result that errors are discovered and corrected one by one. The time required to correct many

errors all at once is much less than that required to
detect and correct them one by one with the result that
the inspection process results in a decrease in the
overall system validation effort.

6.3   STAGES OF TESTING

Except for very small computer programs, it is
unrealistic to attempt to test systems as a single
entity. Large systems are built out of subsystems which
are built out of modules which may themselves be built
out of procedures. If an attempt is made to test the
system as a single entity, it is unlikely that more than
a small percentage of the system 'errors' will be
identified. The testing process, like the programming
process, must proceed in stages with each stage being a
logical continuation of the previous stage. The stages
involved in a system testing are:

(1)   Function Testing
      Function testing is the basic level of testing
      where the functions making up a module are tested
      to ensure that they operate correctly. In a prop-
      erly designed system, each function should have a
      single, clearly defined purpose and it should be
      relatively straightforward to design test cases to
      ensure that the function operates correctly.
      Functions should not depend on other functions at
      the same level so it should be possible to test
      each function as a stand alone entity, without the
      presence of other functions.

(2)   Module Testing
      A module is made up of a number of functions which
      may cooperate with each other. After each indivi-
      dual function has been tested, it is necessary to
      test the cooperation of these functions when they
      are put together as a module. It should be possi-
      ble to test a module as a stand-alone entity,
      without the presence of other system modules.

(3)   Subsystem Testing
      Subsystem testing is the next step up in the test-
      ing process where modules are put together to form
      subsystems. As modules cooperate and communicate,

subsystem testing should concentrate on testing module interfaces.

(4)   System Testing
System testing (sometimes called integration testing) is carried out when the subsystems are integrated under some controller to make up the entire system. At this stage, the testing process is concerned not only with finding errors in design and coding but also with validating that the overall system provides the functions specified in the requirements and that the dynamic characteristics of the system match those required.

(5)   Acceptance Testing
Until this stage, all testing is carried out using data generated by the organisation responsible for constructing the system. Acceptance testing is the process of testing the system with real data – the information which the system is intended to manipulate. The process of acceptance testing often demonstrates errors in the requirements specification for the system. The requirements may not reflect the actual facilities and performance required of the system with the result that acceptance testing demonstrates that the system does not perform as was envisaged.

Normally function testing and module testing are carried out by the implementor of the function without a formal test specification. The programmer makes up his own test data and may incrementally test his code as it is being developed.

The other stages of testing involve integrating work from a number of programmers and must be planned in advance. They are usually undertaken by an independent team of testers. The testing procedure should be formally specified. It is desirable to start test planning at a relatively early stage in the software development process. Module and subsystem testing should be planned as the design of the subsystem is formulated with system test and acceptance test specifications prepared either at the system design stage or while system implementation is in progress.

This description of the stages involved in the testing process is the classical one which, up till now, has been almost universally adopted in the testing of large systems. However, if strict top down testing, as described below, is used, the order of the stages of testing may be changed. Subsystem testing may precede module testing with function testing as the final stage in the testing process.

System testing is not part of this top down testing process but is carried out after subsystems have been completely developed. Rather than simultaneously combining all subsystems into a single unit, they should be incrementally integrated so that errors may be more easily detected and localised.

6.4   TOP DOWN AND BOTTOM UP TESTING

There are two different testing philosophies which have been used in subsystem, module and function testing. These are top down testing and bottom up testing. Each have distinct advantages and disadvantages.

Top-down testing involves starting at the subsystem level with modules represented by stubs - objects which have the same interface as the module but which are very much simpler. After subsystem testing is complete, each module is tested in the same way - the functions are represented by stubs. Finally, the functions are replaced by the actual code and this is tested.

Bottom-up testing reverses the process. Firstly the functions making up a module are tested individually. Then they are integrated to form a module and this is tested. After each module has been tested, the modules are integrated and, finally, the subsystem is tested.

Top down testing is not an activity which should be carried out in isolation. Rather it is used in conjunction with top down program development so that a module is tested as soon as it is coded. In principle, therefore, coding and testing are a single function with no clearly defined program testing phase.

If top down testing is used, it is likely that unnoticed design errors will be detected at any early stage in the testing process. These errors are usually built into the top levels of the system and if they are detected early, a good deal of time can be saved in the testing and possibly the implementation of code which must subsequently be scrapped because of the design error.

As well as this, top down testing has the advantage that a working, albeit limited, system is available at an early stage in the development process. Not only does this provide an important psychological boost to those involved in the system it also demonstrates the feasibility of the system to management.

Unfortunately, strict top down testing can be extremely difficult because of the requirement that program stubs, simulating lower levels of the system must be produced. The mechanism for implementing these program stubs involves either producing a very simplified version of the function required, returning some random value of the correct type or interacting with the tester who inputs an appropriate value, simulating the action of the function.

If the function is a complex one, it may be virtually impossible to produce a program stub which simulates that function accurately. For example, consider a function which converts an array of objects into a linked list. The result of that function involves internal program objects - the pointers linking elements in the list. It is unrealistic simply to generate some random list and return that, nor is it possible for the programmer to input the created list as he has no knowledge of the internal representation of pointers.

A further disadvantage of top down testing is that test output may be difficult to observe. In many systems, the higher levels of that system do not directly generate output but, in order to test these levels, they must be forced to do so. The tester must create an artificial situation, in order to generate test results.

Bottom up testing, on the other hand, involves first testing the modules at the lower levels in the hierarchy, and then working up the hierarchy of modules until the final module is tested. The advantages of top down testing are the disadvantages of bottom up testing and vice versa.

If bottom up testing is used, drivers must be constructed for the lower level modules which present these modules with appropriate inputs. Using a bottom up approach to testing usually means that it is easier to create test cases and observe test input. Bottom up testing has the disadvantage that no demonstrably working program is available until the very last module has been tested. Furthermore, if design errors exist in high level modules these are not detected until a late stage in the system test. Correction of these errors might involve the rewriting and consequent retesting of lower level modules in the system.

In view of the advantages and disadvantages of each

method of testing, there can be no definitive statement made about which is the best method of testing a program. The techniques adopted must depend on the programming organisation, the application being programmed and the individual programmers working on a project.

In practice, some combination of top down and bottom up testing is usually used to test a system. There are obvious advantages in developing a working system even if it has only limited facilities and this requires the top level modules to be tested at an early stage.

If limited facilities are provided it is better that a few facilities are provided completely rather than many facilities in only an extremely primitive state. For example, if an operating system is being developed in language D say, and this operating system is designed to offer language processing, text processing, editing and other facilities to many users a strict top down approach would make limited versions of all these facilities available as early as possible.

However, all facilities are not equally important and, as the system is being programmed in D, it is obviously advantageous to make a full compiler for D available as early as possible. A practical testing strategy therefore involves a controlled top down approach, carried out in conjunction with program development. The system facilities can then be ranked, developing them in order of importance and ignoring any formal top down/bottom up testing techniques.

6.4.1 Incremental testing
One approach to testing is to test each system module individually and, once satisfied that these modules are fully tested, all modules are put together to make up the final system and that system is then tested as an integrated whole. This approach leads almost inevitably to a non-working system with no clear indicators of exactly which aspects of the system are causing the problems. A much better approach which should be adopted irrespective of whether a top down or bottom up strategy is being used, is to introduce modules incrementally, one at a time.

The system should start off as a single module and thus should be tested using appropriate test cases. Once satisfied with the testing of this module a second module can be introduced and further testing carried out. The process continues until all modules have eventually been integrated into a complete system. If a module is introduced at some stage in this process and tests, which previously did not detect system errors, now detect system errors it is certain that these errors are due to the introduction of the new module. The source of the error is localised, simplifying the task of locating and correcting the error.

6.5   THE DESIGN OF TEST CASES

Planning the testing of a programming system involves formulating a set of test cases. Test cases consist of an input specification, a description of the system functions exercised by that input and a statement of the expected output. Thorough testing involves producing cases to ensure that the program responds as expected to both valid and invalid inputs, that the program performs to specification and that it does not corrupt other programs or data in the system.

It is important to distinguish between test cases and test data. Test data is simply the input which has been formulated to test the system whereas test cases are made up of input and output specifications plus a statement of the function under test.

It is impossible to present an example of the test cases for a large system - they would normally occupy a volume much thicker than this book. Rather, a very simple example is presented - the testing of a routine to search a table of integers to determine if some given integer is present in that table.

Assume that this routine is called as follows:

    S:= SEARCH (somearray, somearraySize, RequiredValue)

If somearray has an element equal to RequiredValue, the index of that element is returned by SEARCH, otherwise -1 is returned. The size of somearray is passed to SEARCH as somearraySize. If SEARCH is written in a programming language which permits type checking, such as Pascal, the compiler detects parameters of incorrect type. There is no need to test SEARCH with parameters of the wrong type or with incorrect numbers of parameters.

According to our list above, SEARCH must be tested for its reaction to valid and invalid input, system corruption and performance. As invalid input is trapped by the compiler and performance is not specified there is no need to design specific test cases for them. The requirement that a call of SEARCH should not modify any program variables apart from that assigned the value returned by SEARCH cannot be tested using specific test cases.

To detect if SEARCH actually corrupts global values, a dump of the program global variables is taken. This is taken each time SEARCH is called and repeated immediately after the call of the procedure. These dumps are then compared using a program, to ensure that only the variable assigned a value by search has been changed. It is not realistic to require this process to be explicitly programmed into the system as the extra work involved is considerable. Rather a specialised software tool designed for program testing is used.

Now let us consider the test cases which are required simply to establish a reasonable level of confidence in SEARCH:

Test 1 - Array is a single value equal to required value.
Input - somearray = 17, somearraySize = 1, RequiredValue = 17
Output - function returns 1

Test 2 - Array is a single value not equal to required value.
Input - somearray = 17, somearraySize = 1, RequiredValue = 0
Output - function returns -1

Test 3 - Array is empty
Input - somearray = -, somearraySize = 0, RequiredValue = 1
Output - function returns -1

Test 4 - Array has even number of values, the first of which is the required value.
Input - somearray = 17,23, somearraySize = 2, RequiredValue = 17
Output - function returns 1

Test 5 - Array has even number of values, the second of which is required value.
Input - somearray = 17,23, somearraySize = 2, RequiredValue = 23
Output - function returns 2

Test 6 - Array has an even number of values, none of which is the required value.
Input - somearray = 17,23, somearraySize = 2, RequiredValue = 3
Output - function returns -1

Test 7 - Array has an odd number of values, the first of which is the required value.
Input - somearray = 17,23,29, somearraySize = 3, RequiredValue = 17
Output - function returns 1

Test 8 - Array has odd number of values, the last of which is the required value.
Input - somearray = 17,23,29, somearraySize = 3, RequiredValue = 29
Output - function returns 3

Test 9 - Array has an odd number of values, none of which is the required value.
Input - somearray = 17,23,29, somearraySize = 3, RequiredValue = 4
Output - function returns -1

Test 10 - Array has multiple values one of which is the required value.
Input - somearray = 17,23,29,35,41, somearraySize = 3, RequiredValue = 23
Output - function returns 2

Test 11 - Invalid array size
Input - somearray = 17,23,29, somearraySize = 2, RequiredValue = 1
function indicates error, "Invalid array size"

This set of input values is in no way exhaustive - SEARCH may fail if the input array happens to be 1, 2, 3, 4 but there are no grounds for supposing this. Test cases have been designed to check SEARCH for a number of classes of input and it is reasonable to surmise that if it works successfully for one member of a class, it will do so for all members of that class. For example, a test case has been designed to check that SEARCH does not accept invalid values of the array size - if this test produces an error message for the input above, it should produce the same error message for all other invalid values.

The classes which have been identified for possible input values are:

(1)   Array size of 1, element in array.

(2)   Array size of 1, element not in array.

(3)   Empty array.

(4)   Even array size, element 1st element in array.

(5)   Even array size, element last element in array.

(6)   Even array size, element not in array.

(7)   Odd array size, element 1st element in array.

(8)   Odd array size, element last element in array.

(9)   Odd array size, element not in array.

(10)   Multiple-valued array, element in array.

(11)   Invalid array size.

By identifying these classes and selecting a test case from each class, errors in SEARCH, if they exist should be detected. This form of input classification for determining test inputs is called equivalence partitioning. Equivalence partitioning is a technique for determining which classes of input data have common properties so that, if the program does not display an erroneous output for one member of a class, it should not do so for any member of that class.

The equivalence classes must be identified by using the program specification or user documentation and by the tester using his experience in 'guessing' which classes of input value are likely to detect errors. For example, if an input specification states that the range of some input values must be a 5-digit integer − that is, between 10000 and 99999 − equivalence classes might be those values less than 10000, values between 10000 and 99999 and values greater than 99999. Similarly, if from 4 to 8 values are to be input, equivalence classes are less than 4, between 4 and 8 and more than 8.

In some cases, program specifications may not be precisely detailed so the tester must use his experience to determine equivalence classes. For example, if a program accepts an integer as input, it should be tested using integers less than zero. If a program manipulates tables it should be tested using tables with no entries, a single entry and many entries.

When equivalence classes have been determined, the next step is to choose values from each class which are most likely to lead to a successful test. The values chosen should cause the program to display an erroneous output. Testing experience has shown that the most useful values to select for test input are those at the boundaries of each equivalence class.

Not only input equivalence classes should be considered. Output equivalence classes should also be taken into account and the input values which generate outputs at the boundary of each output class should be chosen as test input. For example, say a program is designed to produce between 3 and 6 outputs, with each output lying in the range 1000-2500. Test input should be selected which produces 3 values at 1000, 3 values at 2500, 6 values at 1000 and 6 values at 2500. Furthermore, input should be selected so that erroneous output values would result if that input was processed as correct input. This input should attempt to force the program to produce less than 3 values, more than 6 values, values less than 1000 and values greater than 2500.

To illustrate this technique of choosing test input, consider how a procedure designed to convert a string of digits to an integer. Assume that the procedure is implemented in Pascal in an environment where 16-bit two's complement notation is used to represent integers.

The conversion procedure is implemented as a function whose declaration is:

```
function StringToInteger (digitstring : shortstring)
: integer;
```

The input parameter is of type shortstring which is an array of 6 characters:

```
type shortstring = array [1..6] of char;
```

The string of digits to be converted to an integer is right justified in digitstring and may be positive or negative. If less than 6 characters long, digitstring is padded with blanks on the left and, if the input is negative, a minus sign occupies the character position immediately to the left of the most significant digit. Because of built-in compiler checking, there is no need to test this function using arrays of more or less than 6 characters or to test it with any other invalid type of parameter.

Inspection of the function specification results in the identification of the following input equivalence classes:

(1)   Inputs with 1 - 6 non-blank characters.

(2)   Inputs with no digits.

(3)   Inputs with a - sign as the most significant character (negative inputs).

(4)   Inputs with a digit as the most significant character (positive inputs).

(5)   Inputs which are left-padded by some character apart from a blank or zero.

(6)   Inputs which are left-padded with zeros.

(7)   Inputs whose most significant character is a digit but which contain non-digits mixed with digits.

(8)   Inputs where the minus sign is not immediately to the left of the most significant digit.

Output equivalence classes can also be identified:

(1)   Negative integers between the minimum integer which it is possible to represent and zero.

(2)   Zero.

(3)   Positive integers between zero and the maximum possible integer which may be represented.

Using 2's complement 16-bit representation for integers means that the minimum integer which may be represented is -32 768 and the maximum positive integer is 32 767.

By selecting test input values at the boundaries of each of these equivalence classes and eliminating possible duplicate values derived from consideration of input and output classes, the following test cases can be constructed .

INPUT	EXPECTED OUTPUT
"-32769"	Error-invalid input
"-32768"	-32768
" 0"	0
" 32767"	32767
"132767"	Error - invalid input
" -1"	-1
" 1"	1
" "	Error - no digits
"xxxxx1"	Error - bad pad
"000001"	1
"-00001"	-1
" 1x2"	Error-invalid digit
" 1 2"	Error-invalid digit
" - 1"	Error-misplaced minus

Twelve input and output equivalence classes can be identified and from these 15 distinct test inputs identified. Notice that tests derived from input and output equivalent classes can overlap - for example, testing the function with the input -32768 tests the function's reaction to an input containing 6 significant characters and also if it converts strings representing negative integers correctly. The technique of equivalence partitioning is a useful one for selecting instances of each possible input for test. However, even when a program operates successfully for individual test inputs, combinations of these inputs may detect program error. Equivalence partitioning provides no help in selecting these combinations.

Generally, the number of possible input combinations for even a relatively small program will be immense. It is quite impossible, usually, to carry out tests of all possible combinations and the experience and intuition of the tester must be used to select combinations likely to cause program failure.

The most productive way of choosing input combinations is to combine the process of testing with code examination. For example, code examination may reveal that 2 separate program routines use and modify shared variables. This is potentially error prone as incorrect or unthinking modification of these variables by one routine could cause the other routine to fail. A useful test case would cause both routines to be exercised during the same program execution.

Code inspection may also reveal the pointlessness of testing other input combinations. If routines are entirely self-contained, it is impossible for the execution of one routine to affect the execution of other routines. Dependencies, also, may be revealed by code inspection. For example, an arithmetic function may accept character strings as input and depend on conversion functions such as the StringToInteger function above to translate its input into numeric quantities. Not only the conversion function must be tested but also routines which call that function for their reaction when the conversion function is presented with invalid input.

6.6   TESTING REAL-TIME PROGRAMS

Real-time systems are those systems which interact with their environment in 'real-time'. That is, the processes in the system must respond to events under time constraints – if the system response is not timely, information may be lost. Examples of real-time systems are operating systems, message switching systems, and process control systems. The effective testing of such systems poses particular problems for the tester.

Real-time systems are usually made up of a number of distinct cooperating processes and, commonly, are interrupt driven. This means that an external event such as the input from a sensor causes control to be transferred from the currently executing process to the process which handles that event.

The peculiar problems of testing real-time systems are caused by the subtle interactions which may arise between the various processes in the system. System errors may be time dependent, only arising when the system processes are in a particular state. The exact state of the system processes when the error occurred may be impossible to reproduce.

The testing of real-time systems is often further complicated because the reliability requirements of these systems are often greater than the requirements for systems which are not time critical. The reason for this lies in the applications for which real-time systems are used - controlling complex machinery, air traffic control, military communications etc. The consequences of system failure are potentially disastrous with the result that system testing must be extremely stringent.

Because real-time systems are composed of a number of processes, the first step in testing such systems is to test each process individually. Following this, it may be appropriate to test threads, that is, test the systems reaction to a single event. This will normally involve control passing from process to process - actions 'thread' their way through the system. After a single thread has been tested, that thread can then be exercised by introducing multiple events of the same class but without introducing events of any other class. For example, a multi-user system might first be tested using a single terminal then multiple terminal testing gradually introduced.

After the system's reaction to each class of event has been tested, it can then be tested for its reactions to more than one class of event occurring simultaneously. At this stage, new event tests should be introduced gradually so that system errors can be localised. Finally, the system must be tested in an operational environment, again gradually increasing the number of operations which the system must perform.

An important software tool which has been developed to assist the construction of real-time programs is the MASCOT system (Jackson, 1977). This system provides a framework for constructing real-time systems and is particularly useful for testing such systems as it allows processes to be introduced and removed without halting other processes in the system. Furthermore, it strictly controls process communications so that the possibility of one process corrupting another is reduced.

6.6.1 The use of simulators

A simulator is a program which imitates the actions of some other program, hardware device, or class of devices. Simulators are often used in testing to replace hardware which is expected but not immediately available. They are particularly important in the testing of real-time programs because they allow a sequence of events to be repeated, thus allowing timing dependent errors to be detected.

In some cases, it may be essential to use simulation to mimic the events which a real-time system must process. For example, if a program is used for controlling a nuclear reactor that program must obviously be able to deal with failure of the reactor cooling system. This failure will normally be signalled by sensor inputs indicating a rise in temperature, drop in temperature, drop in pressure etc. Obviously, this cannot be tested operationally so it is necessary to simulate these sensor inputs using some other program. The reactions of the reactor control program may then be observed.

The ability of simulators to reproduce sequences of events exactly is of vital importance. Consider a situation where a system is accepting input from many user terminals and a system failure occurs.

Each terminal will normally be presenting different commands and the failure may be due to particular terminal commands being processed simultaneously or may be due to some historical event sequence which has caused corruption of information. If the system is tested using real terminals with human operators it is impossible to exactly reproduce the command sequences input at each terminal. However, if a terminal simulator is used, this accepts command sequences from prepared script and the exact sequence and its timing can easily be repeated.

As well as providing repeatable inputs, terminal simulators also allow the system to be tested under load. If a system is required to support n terminals with an average response time of m seconds, a terminal simulator can be set up to imitate n terminals. The simulator can then measure the system response using different combinations of input to ensure that the average response is that required.

The UNIX/PWB system discussed in the previous chapter provides a general purpose terminal simulator called LEAP (Dolotta et al., 1978). This simulator is designed

to run on the UNIX/PWB machine and test programs running
on some other mainframe connected to the PWB machine.
This has the advantage that uncontrolled interactions
between the program under test and the simulator are
eliminated. Furthermore, high level languages have been
developed for use with LEAP which allow the actions of
terminal-operator pairs to be simulated.

6.7   PROGRAM TESTING TOOLS

The program testing process is laborious, complex and
difficult. As a supplement to program development
tools, a number of software tools have been developed to
help the programmer test his program. These include
test data generators, execution flow summarisers, and
file comparators.

6.7.1 Test data generators
Test data generators are programs which automatically
generate a large number of test inputs for some system.
Unfortunately, it is not possible for test data
generators to produce the corresponding outputs –
otherwise they would be equivalent to the program under
test. Their usefulness is therefore limited.

   Test data generators are most useful in situations
where the performance of a system in a practical
environment must be tested. For example, testing of a
database management system may start by using very small
databases and the testing is initially designed to
detect program errors resulting in incorrect output
being produced. This small scale testing does not
actually reflect the actual environment where the
program is to be used – it may be operating using very
large databases. Given the specification of a database,
a test case generator can generate large amounts of data
so that the performance of the system may be tested in a
more realistic environment.

   Another instance where test data generators can be
useful is that situation where the syntax of the output
from a system can be formally specified. A program can
be written which checks that syntax. Given an input
specification, the test data generator can produce a
large volume of input data which is presented to the
system under test. The output is presented to the
syntax checker and if discrepancies are found, this may
be due to errors in the program under test.

   An example of such a situation might be the testing

of the syntax analysis phase of a compiler. The output
from such a phase for a correct program may be simply
whatever program was input whereas, if an incorrect
program is presented the output also includes error
indicators. A test data generator might accept a
specification of the syntax of the language being
compiled and from that generate correct and incorrect
programs. The output from the compiler can be checked
automatically to ensure that error messages are not
generated for correct programs and, conversely, error
messages are generated for incorrect programs.

6.7.2 Execution flow summarisers

Execution flow summarisers , such as that for ALGOLW
described by Satterthwaite (1972), are programs used to
analyse how many times each statement in some other
program has been executed. They are sometimes called
dynamic analysers and have two fundamental parts:

(1)   An instrumentation part which adds instrumentation
       statements to a program either whilst it is being
       compiled or before compilation. When the program
       is executed, these statements gather and collate
       information on how many times each program state-
       ment is executed.

(2)   A display part which collects the information pro-
       vided by the instrumentation statements and prints
       it in a form which can be understood by the
       reader. Typically, this produces a program list-
       ing where each line is annotated with the number
       of times that line has been executed.

In order to instrument a program, all decision
statements and loops must be identified and
instrumentation code placed at the beginning of each
loop and decision. A sequence of statements without
loops or decisions need only have a single
instrumentation section at the beginning of the
sequence. Because the instrumentation phase needs
knowledge of the language syntax, the easiest way to
provide this instrumentation facility is to build it
into the compiler. The user may switch it on with a
compiler directive. Alternatively this phase of the
system may be implemented as a preprocessor which adds
high-level language statements to collect information
about the program execution.

Flow summarisers are useful for program testing as they allow those program statements which have not been executed during a test run to be detected. Subsequent tests can therefore be designed to exercise these statements. They also have an important role as a debugging tool, used in locating program errors and their use in this context is discussed later in this chapter.

6.7.3 File comparators

The process of testing frequently involves the examination of large volumes of test output. This is a tedious process and it is quite possible for the reader to accidentally miss erroneous output. To avoid this, as much of the process as possible should be automated.

Automation involves preparing a file containing the expected output from a program if the tests are unsuccessful - that is, if no errors are detected. The tests are executed and the output directed to some other file. Both files are then compared using a file comparator and differences in the files highlighted. If the expected output and the actual output are the same, the program tests failed to detect any errors.

The use of file comparators is particularly helpful when many tests are submitted to a program at once. Generally, only some of these tests will succeed and a file comparison program can detect these successful tests and bring them the attention of the tester.

File comparators may be completely general purpose, comparing any 2 files character by character for equality. Alternatively, such programs can be constructed for a specific application and information about the structure of the test output built into the program. General purpose comparators are most useful when the expected output from a program is itself generated by a program. For example, when a program is to be extended, a set of tests might be run before the program is altered and the test output saved. After the program enhancement is made, the same tests can be rerun and the output file produced should be the same as that produced before modification.

General purpose comparison programs are less useful when the expected output file is manually input. A trivial input error such as the input of an extra blank will cause a character by character file comparison to fail. However, special purpose programs can be useful in this situation as they can identify and abstract the important items of information from each file and compare these items.

6.8   PROGRAM DEBUGGING

Program debugging is related to program testing in that it relies on test output to signify the presence of errors. Debugging is the process of identifying those areas of the program which are in error and modifying them to correct the error. General principles of debugging are discussed below and the role of software tools in the debugging process described.

The process of debugging involves firstly, locating those parts of the program code which are incorrect or which cause some specification not to be met and secondly, correcting the error or modifying the program so that it meets its requirements. After modification, program testing must be repeated to ensure that the change has been carried out correctly.

The second stage of the process in many instances is straightforward. If the error is a simple coding error it is usually fairly easy to correct that error without affecting other parts of the program. On the other hand, if the error is a design error or involves a misunderstanding of the program requirements correcting this may involve much work.

In such a case, it may be necessary to completely redesign parts of the program and consequently, retest the whole system. It is vitally important, therefore, that such errors be avoided wherever possible by making use of design reviews and validation before coding commences. Apart from avoiding such errors, all the programmer can do to minimise their effect is to program in such a way that the program is made up of independent functional units. If a design error is discovered, the chances are that it will affect a single unit and only that unit need be redesigned and recoded. The remainder of the programming system can remain unchanged.

If, on the other hand, the program units are logically dependent and make use of many shared variables this is a recipe for disaster, should a major redesign be required. In such a program, it is very difficult to determine the effects on the overall system caused by redesigning one module. An apparently straightforward modification can result in errors in functionally unrelated modules and this process may snowball as these errors are corrected causing other errors whose correction then causes more errors and so on.

Probably the most important aid for the debugger is the listing of the test results which display the error to be corrected. If the programmer is familiar with the code, the nature and location of the error can often be determined by examination of these results. Code examination can then determine which statement or statements are incorrect.

Many programmers approach code inspection thinking that they know what the program does and, subconsciously, they read the code as if its operation is what the programmer thinks it is. The most useful debugging aid is the ability to approach code in an open-minded, sceptical manner and to perform a 'thought execution' of that code. This ability, combined with good programming practice, significantly reduces the chore of debugging.

In some circumstances, however, code inspection alone is inadequate. Those circumstances arise where programming errors do not cause immediate failure or obvious corruption to test output. Rather, these errors may cause incorrect although not necessarily invalid output to be generated. In these cases, the execution of the program must be traced to determine where the corruption causing the error is taking place.

The most commonly used technique for this is to include program statements which print important data values at appropriate places in the program. Examination of the output involves comparing subsequent values of the same object and when an anomaly is detected, the coding error must lie between the output statement which printed the correct values and the output statement which printed the incorrect values.

The process of adding output statements can be continued if necessary, until individual statements are bracketed. At this stage, the statement where the error manifests itself can be determined. This need not necessarily mean that an individual statement is incorrect - the error may be a design error or may involve the failure of some program component, previously thought to be correct.

This technique is certain to detect the program statement where the error is manifested, irrespective of how 'correct' the program appears to be. It is, however, a laborious and time consuming process to include output statements and recompile the program after it has been written. It is much better to anticipate that there will be program errors and include some of these output statements when the program is first constructed.

Clearly, when the program is finally delivered, it should not produce debugging output so it is necessary to somehow switch off the statements used to produce diagnostic information. This can be accomplished in 3 ways:

(1)   Each statement can be identified by some string such as ***DEBUG*** and, using this string as an identifier, can be edited out of the final program.

(2)   The output statements can be conditionally compiled into the program. When the program is being tested, a compiler directive can cause the output statements to be included, when the production version of the program is delivered the compiler directive is switched off so that no debugging code is included.

(3)   The output statements can be conditionally executed depending on some global debugging switch which may be set by the program user. The switch is set whilst the program is being debugged and unset in the production version of the program.

Each of these techniques has disadvantages. Editing out diagnostic statements is a final process - it requires time and effort to put them back. Conditional compilation although potentially the best technique is not offered by many existing compilers and the permanent inclusion of diagnostic information increases the size of the program. The user must choose a technique appropriate to his own circumstances.

The inclusion of anticipatory diagnostic statements shares a disadvantage with a number of other error location techniques provided by software tools. Unless carefully controlled, voluminous amounts of information can be generated. Examining all this information is a time consuming process. Excessive output is most easily controlled by controlling diagnostic output via a multi-way, rather than a two-way switch. Levels of output detail can be controlled by switch settings - setting 1 say, may cause global information to be printed only at important checkpoints whereas setting 5 might cause diagnostics to be output more frequently and in greater detail.

6.8.1 Debugging tools

Because of the problems involved in including output statements in programs a number of debugging tools have been developed which perform the same function – they provide information which helps the programmer to locate errors. The debugging tools which have been developed are all concerned with the first stage. They help the user locate the source of the error. At present there is no way to automate the second stage and provide automatic error correction.

The most crude and primitive debugging aid is the core dump. The name is historical as core store is not now widely used, but essentially the core dump is a printout of the machine store content when the program error manifested itself. Manual analysis of core dumps is boring, detailed work and is frequently a waste of time. In order to be useful, debugging tools must present information in terms of the source program being executed. As core dumps present object information rather than information relating to the source program, they are of little use for debugging programs written in a high level language.

6.8.2 Symbolic dump programs

Debugging tools which rely on the user manipulating store addresses are of little use to the high-level language programmer. When using high-level language the programmer needs a debugging tool which relates the names of the objects used in his program to their values. A symbolic dump program is such a tool.

Symbolic dumps can take two forms – an interactive form or a batch form. In the batch form the system lists the names of all program variables along with their values either when the program terminates or at the specific inclusion of a program directive to produce. Such a system saves the programmer including explicit output statements to trace the values of his variables.

A properly designed symbolic dump will not only generate information about global variables but will also present information about local variable values in all activated procedures. It should associate the name of the appropriate procedure with the variable name in order to avoid confusion where variables of the same name are used in different procedures.

Symbolic dumps of this kind are much useful than core dumps but they produce a voluminous amount of information, much of which is irrelevant. A more powerful tool is an interactive program for analysing the symbolic information. This allows the user to request the value of individual variables by name so that only relevant values been be examined. Again, local variables should be accessible by specifying the procedure name followed by the variable name.

An example of an interactive symbolic dump program is the debugging program db, available under UNIX. Using a core dump, db allows the programmer to request the values of variables by name, to examine the content of the machine registers and to display the results in various different formats. Another analysis tool which uses a core dump is an incremental dump program described by Malone and McGregor (1980). This program compares store images before and after program execution and only displays information taken from those parts of the store image which have been changed by the program execution.

Potentially, interactive tools of this kind are extremely useful if they allow the user to scan the dump information in a number of ways. He should be allowed to specify conditions relating to object values and all name/value pairs satisfying these conditions should be printed. It should also be possible to display structures involving pointers in some readable way. Many program errors are the result of misdirected pointers and a facility to detect these is invaluable. The provision of such a facility is extremely difficult and the author is not aware of any debugging system offering this feature.

6.8.3 Program trace packages
Symbolic dump systems allow the user to examine values once the program has terminated but they do not provide information about the dynamic execution of the program. Program trace packages provide such information, printing information about procedure entry and exit, transfers of control, branch selection in if statements etc.

Trace packages involve instrumenting the program automatically so that the relevant information can be collected. This instrumentation obviously involves overhead both in terms of space and speed. Trace packages are even worse than other debugging tools for generating enormous amounts of output and unless they can be switched on and off with extreme precision these packages produce unmanageable quantities of output.

6.8.4 Static program analysers

Static program analysers do not require the program to be executed. Rather, when presented with the text of a program, a static analyser scans that text and searches for anomalies which are likely to result in errors in the program.

Static analysers are perhaps most useful when languages, such as FORTRAN, which do not allow much compile time checking are used for programming. The analyser takes over much of the checking which would be carried out by the compiler in a more strict language such as Pascal. For example, an installation may have a rule that all variable names used in a FORTRAN program must be declared – the default conventions of the language are not to be used. A static analyser can scan a program and mark undeclared variables in the same way as a Pascal compiler can detect undeclared names.

As well as syntax checking, a static analyser can also check that no parts of the program are unreachable because goto statements always branch around the code and it can check variable initialisations by flagging instances where a variable name is used on the left side of an assignment statement before it is used on the right side of an assignment.

A number of static analysers such as DAVE (Osterweil and Fosdick, 1976), AUDIT (Culpepper, 1975) and FACES (Ramoorthy and Ho, 1975) have been developed for use with FORTRAN programs. These analysers all detect anomalies and inconsistencies which normally cause errors. These tools check subroutine interfaces to ensure that the number and types of subroutines parameters are consistent with the routine declaration, they locate COMMON block errors and flag error-prone practices such as branching into a DO-loop.

Static analysers are not just useful with FORTRAN – a program called LINT (Ritchie et al., 1978) has been developed for use with C programs and its authors claim that use of LINT provides static checking equivalent to that provided by the compiler in a language such as ALGOL 68. Thus the reliability advantages of a strictly typed language are combined with the ability to generate

very efficient code using a systems implementation
language.

6.8.5 Dynamic program analysers

As well as being a useful program testing tool, dynamic
program analysers can also be used in debugging a
program. Examination of the output from a flow
summariser can identify loops which do not terminate
properly and allow the user to find sections of code
which are being executed when they ought not to be
executed.

6.8.6 Interactive debugging environments

The most sophisticated debugging tools are systems such
as EXDAMS (Balzer, 1969). These systems give the
programmer the impression that he can interact with his
program while it is executing and can display variable
values, reverse execution sequences and so on.

In fact such systems operate by executing the program
and constructing a 'history' file recording all program
state changes. They then provide facilities for
interrogating this history file in program terms. The
user can watch control flow and/or data flow in his
program as each statement executes and the statement
causing the error can then be detected. Such systems
are potentially very useful but require considerable
resources and are not widely available.

Documentation and maintenance

Program documentation and maintenance are unexciting but essential parts of software production and use. There is little point in producing a software system if it cannot be understood, if it cannot be used except by its implementors, and if modifications to that system are difficult or impossible to make. For organisational reasons, documentation and maintenance are considered separately below. The reader should bear in mind however, that this separation is somewhat artificial – without documentation the maintenance of large systems would be impossible.

This chapter is composed of two parts – the first covers aspects of documentation, the second maintenance considerations. The documentation may describe how to use the program, why it was written, the techniques used in its construction and should clarify any obscurities in the program. As maintenance – the process of making modifications after the program has been delivered – requires an understanding of the program, this is achieved by study of the program code and associated documentation.

Documentation is a topic which is often neglected in programming texts in spite of the fact that, for large projects, the documentation effort may be comparable to the programming effort. In this part of the book, the different types of documentation are described, a style of technical writing is proposed and software tools which aid the production and maintenance of documentation discussed.

This chapter will only cover that documentation which is separate from the program itself. Associated with each program is intra-program documentation – comments. The placing and use of these comments has been covered in chapter 5.

As maintainability is considered to be one of the most important characteristics of a software system and is emphasised throughout the book, the section on program maintenance concentrates on maintenance costs and program understandability rather than how an easily maintained program can be constructed. Understanding a program is the key to effective maintenance and techniques of program reading to achieve this understanding are described. This is followed by a brief summary of research aimed at establishing metrics for gauging the understandability of a program.

7.1   SOFTWARE DOCUMENTATION

The documentation associated with a large software system can be classed as either user documentation or system documentation. User documentation is made up of those documents which relate to the functions of the system, without reference to how these functions are implemented. Systems documentation, on the other hand, describes all aspects of systems design, implementation and testing.

   The documentation provided along with the system must satisfy a number of requirements:

(1)   It must describe how to use the system – without this even the simplest system is useless.

(2)   It must describe how to install and operate the system.

(3)   It must describe the overall system requirements and design.

(4)   It must describe the system implementation and test procedures in order that the system may be maintained.

The documentation provided along with a system can be useful at any stage in the lifetime of the system. It need not necessarily be produced in the same order as the system itself. In fact, it is often useful during system specification to have user documentation available so that the specifier is aware of the constraints within which he must operate.

7.1.1 User documentation
The documentation provided for system users is usually the first contact which they have with the system. It should provide an accurate init al impression of the system. This documentation is not sales literature. It

should not emphasise the glamorous system features nor should it be optimistic about the system's capabilities. It should not be necessary for the user to read virtually all the documentation to find out how to make simple use of the system. The documentation should be structured in such a way that the user may read it to the level of detail appropriate to his needs.

There are at least 5 documents which might be considered under the heading of user documentation. These documents are:

(1)   A functional description, which explains what the system can do.

(2)   An installation document which explains how to install the system and tailor it for particular hardware configurations.

(3)   An introductory manual which explains, in simple terms, how to get started with the system.

(4)   A reference manual which describes in detail the facilities available to the user and how to use these facilities.

(5)   An operators guide (if a system operator is required), explaining how the operator should react to situations which arise whilst the system is in use.

Depending on the size of the system, these may be provided as separate manuals or bound together as one or more volumes. If the latter method of presentation is chosen, each document should be clearly distinguished so that readers may easily find and use the document that they require.

The functional description of the system outlines the system requirements and briefly describes the aims of the system implementors. It should describe what the system can and cannot do, introducing small, self-evident examples wherever possible. For example, the functional description of an operating system which has a hierarchical file system might illustrate the structure of the file system as a tree and instructions on how to move up and down the tree may be shown as examples. The functional description of the system should not attempt to go into detail nor need it cover

every system facility. Rather, it should provide an
overview of the system and, when read in conjunction
with an introductory manual, should enable the user to
decide if the system is appropriate for his needs.

The introductory manual should present an informal
introduction to the system, describing its 'normal'
usage. It should describe how to get started on the
system and how the user might make use of the common
system facilities. It should be liberally illustrated
with examples. The introductory manual should also tell
the system user how to get out of trouble when things go
wrong. Inevitably, beginners, whatever their background
and experience, will make mistakes. It is vital that
easily available information on how to recover from
these mistakes and restart work is provided.

The system reference manual is the definitive
document on system usage. The reference manual may
assume that the reader is familiar with both the system
description and introductory manual. It may also assume
that the reader has made some use of the system and
understands its concepts and terminology. As well as
describing, in detail, the system facilities and their
usage, the system reference manual should also describe
the error reports generated by the system, the
situations where these errors arise and, if appropriate,
refer the user to a description of the facility which
was in error. The most important characteristic of a
reference manual is that it should be complete.
Wherever possible, formal descriptive techniques should
be used to ensure that completeness is achieved.
Although the reference manual should not be deliberately
arcane or turgid, it is acceptable to sacrifice
readability for completeness.

The system installation document should provide full
details of how to install the system in a particular
environment. First and foremost, it must contain a
description of the machine-readable media on which the
system is supplied — its format, the character codes
used, how the information was written and the files
making up the system. It should then go on to describe
the minimal hardware configuration required to run the
system, the permanent files which must be established,
how to start the system and the configuration dependent
files which must be changed in order to tailor the
system to a particular application.

For systems which require an operator, an operators
manual must be provided. This should describe the

messages generated at the operators console and how to react to these messages. If system hardware is involved, it might also explain the operators task in maintaining that hardware - for example - how to change the ribbon on a printer.

Some organisations consider that the production of user documentation should not be the task of the software engineer. Rather, professional technical authors are employed to produce such finished documentation using information provided by the engineers responsible for constructing the system. There is some merit in this approach inasmuch as it frees software staff to do their principal job - construct software. However, it does have the disadvantage that communications between authors and software engineers can be almost as time consuming as writing the documentation so, in practice, the use of technical authors may not be cost effective.

7.1.2 System documentation

In this text, the term 'system documentation' is taken to mean all the documents pertaining to the implementation of the system from the requirements specification to the final acceptance test plan. Documents describing the design, implementation and testing of a system are essential if the program is to be understood and maintained. Like user documentation, it is important that system documentation is structured with overviews leading the reader into more formal and detailed descriptions of each aspect of the system. These documents making up the system documentation should include:

(1)   The requirements specification

(2)   An overall systems specification showing how the requirements are decomposed into a set of interacting programs. This document is not required when the system is implemented using only a single program.

(3)   For each program in the system, a description of how that program is decomposed into units and the functions of each unit.

(4)   For each unit, a description of its operation. This need not extend to describing program actions

as these should be documented using intra-program comments.

(5)   A comprehensive test plan describing how each program unit is tested.

(6)   A test plan showing how integration testing, that is, the testing of all units/programs together is carried out.

(7)   An acceptance test plan, devised in conjunction with the system user. This should describe the tests which must be satisfied before the system is accepted.

7.2   DATA DICTIONARIES

A data dictionary is a document which provides details of each and every entity which is relevant to the system being described. The document is normally referenced using the name of the object of interest - hence the term data dictionary. Data dictionaries are an important part of the documentation in some application areas, particularly those involving data base management systems. However, their use is not restricted to database applications. They are an extremely useful form of documentation which can be used with any kind of computing system.

The entities entered in the dictionary include objects which are named in the system being documented such as procedures, records, files, modules etc and also entities in the real-world system modelled by the program. For example, consider a program which records and processes sales of goods made by some organisation. Each sale might be represented by a record made up of the date of sale, the salesman, the quantity of goods sold, the product reference number and the customer. Under 'sale' in the data dictionary, this information would be recorded along with cross references to other relevant dictionary entries. These cross references would include reference to the program objects used to represent the sale.

Data dictionaries are of value to both system users and to those involved in maintaining the system. Users who intend to use the system to obtain information about some entity can look up the dictionary and, by tracing cross references, work out how to retrieve the required information.

The value of data dictionaries to system maintenance staff is obvious. Much of the information conventionally gathered by cross reference programs can be entered but, more importantly, information about the entity modelled by a program object is also available. When a program object is to be changed, reference to the dictionary can be made to ensure that the change is compatible with the modelled entity and that the change does not affect other system entities.

Because of the need for cross referencing in a data dictionary and also because the dictionary may be subject to change, the data dictionary for a system should always be maintained on-line. Unless in exceptional circumstances, there is little point in providing users with a hard copy of the dictionary which is liable to date rapidly and which is slow to use.

7.3 DOCUMENTATION STANDARDS

A standard procedure for producing, checking and laying out documentation is an important aid to document quality control. The importance of quality control mechanisms in document production cannot be overemphasised. Poor quality documentation is likely to confuse rather than help the reader with the consequence that little use is likely to be made of that documentation.

One mechanism which might be used for checking and improving documents is to establish document inspections. These would be used in the way that code inspections can be used for the detection of program errors. During a document inspection, the text is criticised, omissions pointed out and suggestions made on how to improve the document. In this latter respect it differs from a code inspection which is simply an error finding rather than an error correction mechanism.

Documentation standards should describe exactly what the documentation should include and should describe the notations to be used in the documentation. They should also establish a consistent numbering convention for headings and subheadings.

The numbering of headings and subheadings may appear a trivial point. However, when a large number of separate documents are produced which reference each other a consistent numbering scheme is vital. Documents should be subdivided using exactly the same system so that corresponding sections in each document each refer to the same entity. Explicit cross referencing should be avoided wherever possible and when unavoidable, should reference by section heading and section number.

7.4   DOCUMENTATION TOOLS

This section discusses software tools which can be used to develop and maintain project documentation on a computer system, preferably the same system as is used to develop the project programs. There are a number of advantages which accrue from developing documentation in this way rather than manually. These are:

(1)   The documentation is always on hand. The user need not search for a manual if he has access to the computer.

(2)   The documents stored in the computer system are easy to modify and maintain with the consequence that the project documentation is more likely to be kept up to date.

(3)   The documentation text can be automatically formatted and neatly laid out - in some circumstances, printing costs can be reduced by using a computer driven phototypesetter.

(4)   The documentation text can be automatically analysed in various ways to produce different types of index, and to check for spelling and typing errors.

(5)   Several individuals may work on the production of a document at the same time.

(6)   Documentation management is simplified because all the documents can be gathered together under a common heading and the state of development of these documents ascertained.

Clearly, the most important documentation tool is a powerful editing system which allows documents to be generated and modified. A general purpose program editor as described in chapter 5 may be used for this task or a special document editor specifically designed for producing text may be preferred.   There are advantages and disadvantages to each approach.   A special text editor can be screen based and is perhaps better tailored for secretarial use.   On the other hand, programmers who already use an editor do not normally wish to learn how to use another type of editor and, for them, use of a program editor may be more appropriate.

Using an editor, a computer terminal can simply be treated as a typewriter and the document formatted directly by the typist.   Unfortunately, the screen size of most terminals is such that it does not conform to standard paper sizes.   The typist must adapt to the smaller terminal screen and, when typing, mentally translate screen layout to layout on paper. This problem can be avoided by processing input text using a formatting program.   A text formatter allows the typist to input text in free format and it then automatically rearranges that text and lays it out neatly on standard paper.   The final layout of the document may be specified by the typist.

Text processing systems vary in sophistication. Those systems supplied with commercial word processors are usually fairly simple.   They allow the typist to input the text and modify it using a screen editor.   It can then be printed, justifying the lines of text according to a specification built into the system. Formatting information is not included with the text. More sophisticated systems such as the nroff/troff system available under UNIX (Kernighan et al., 1978) allow the user to intersperse text and formatting commands.   In nroff/troff formatting commands are identified by placing them on a line by themself and preceding them with a special character defined by the user.

When the text is processed, these formatting commands are identified and interpreted.   The text is laid out as specified by these commands.   Such a system is much more powerful and flexible than simpler screen based systems as it allows the user to vary the output format in different parts of the document. The nroff/troff system also allows the user to define his own macros − sequences of formatting commands − and provides elementary text storage and decision making capability. Using these facilities, powerful formatting features can be provided such as automatic subsection numbering, automatic contents creation and footnote placement.

The use of an editor in conjunction with a formatting

system means that changes can be made to a document without the chore of retyping the complete document. Not only does this reduce the cost of producing documentation it also means that higher quality documentation is produced. If documents are produced manually, there is a disinclination to make changes and improve the clarity of an explanation say, because of the retyping effort which is involved. Without this retyping effort, authors can be encouraged to rewrite and reword documents to improve their quality.

This rewriting, however, must be carefully controlled. If computerised document editing facilities are readily available, authors may strive for perfection and expend much effort in relatively minor improvements. It is the responsibility of documentation management to ensure that this does not happen.

Although an editor and a text formatter are the most important documentation tools, there are a number of other programs which are useful in document production. These include programs to assist with proofreading, programs to help lay out complicated tables and mathematical expressions, graphics systems to assist diagram production, pattern matching systems for document retrieval and programs to identify and control changes in documents.

Proofreading is one of the most onerous chores associated with authorship. Although the process cannot be completely automated, some help can be given if a machine-readable copy of the document is available. A spelling checker program splits the document into words then looks up these words in a dictionary. Any words not found in the dictionary are indicated to the user.

A spelling checker should be designed so that the dictionary may be passed as a parameter to the program. This means that after a document has been checked using the standard system dictionary, the spelling checker can be rerun, checking those words not found in the standard dictionary against the user's private dictionary. This dictionary might contain specialised terms or proper names which are particular to a user or an application. Although some spelling checkers also carry out spelling correction, it is the author's opinion that the use of spelling correctors is not justified. Such systems are documented by Peterson (1980) and although they have some advantages they involve an immense amount of additional overhead and can only deal with relatively straightforward spelling errors.

Programs which assist the user with complicated layout problems normally operate in conjunction with a formatting system. Rather than the user being forced to devise a complex set of formatting commands he can provide a table specification say, along with the data to be included in that table. A table formatter will read the specification and the data and generate the appropriate sequence of formatting commands for inclusion in the user's document.

Most document production hardware be it phototypesetter or high quality printer has some graphics capability. This can be utilised to produce diagrams, and software to make use of this graphics capability is of great value. Because the syntax of diagrams is complex, the most useful diagram production systems are those where the user draws or at least outlines his diagram on his terminal. The diagram generator program can then translate this picture into the appropriate formatter commands to generate the diagrams on the printer.

Document retrieval software is, of course, generally useful but it has a specialised application in a document production environment. If the document retrieval system includes a sufficiently powerful pattern matching system, a database of existing documents can be scanned to find any text which is associated with that being produced. This text may then, if appropriate, be reused. As in program production, reuse of existing work can increase productivity and reduce the amount of proofreading (testing) and modification (debugging) required.

Information retrieval systems are also useful in bibliography production. When a document is produced, its bibliography may be added to a bibliography database and this database made publicly accessible. Not only does this help the user find source material, it also ensures that making references to other documents is simplified. The appropriate reference can be copied directly from the bibliography database thus ensuring the correctness of the reference.

As documents are modified and new versions of the document produced, it is important that control is kept over these modifications. Furthermore, important new information should be clearly signalled to readers. Mashey and Smith (1977) report that the code control system SCCS (Rochkind, 1975), available under UNIX, has been used to keep control over the different versions of documents and modifications to these documents.

The use of a file comparison program can identify changes made to documents by pinpointing lines in each copy of the document which differ. By combining the output from such a program with an editor preprocessor, those lines can be edited and marked with revision bars, indicating the changes to the user.

7.5   THE MAINTENANCE OF DOCUMENTATION

As a programming system is modified, the documentation associated with that system must also be modified to reflect the changes in the system. Unfortunately, documentation maintenance is often neglected, with the result that the documentation becomes out of step with the associated software. This introduces problems for both users and maintainers of the system.

It is important that all associated documents are modified when a change is made to a program. Assuming that the change is transparent to the user, only those documents describing the system implementation need be modified. If the system change is more than the correction of a coding error, this will mean revision of design and test documents and, perhaps, the higher level documents describing the system specification and requirements.

If the system modification affects the user interface directly either by adding new facilities or extending existing facilities, this should be intimated to the user immediately. In an on-line system, this might be accomplished by providing a system noticeboard which each user may access. When a new item is added to the noticeboard, users can be informed of this when they log in to the system. System changes can also be indicated on a real noticeboard and in a regular newsletter distributed to all system users.

At periodic intervals, user documentation should be updated by supplying new pages which describe the changes made to the user interface.

The updating process is simplified if manual pages are not consecutively numbered but are numbered according to their chapter or section. For example, pages in chapter 3 would be numbered 3-1, 3-2, 3-3..... If this numbering scheme is adopted, parts of the manual may be replaced without disrupting page numbering in the unchanged parts of the document.

Paragraphs which have been added or changed should be

indicated to the reader. New versions of documents should be immediately identifiable – the fact that a document has been updated should not be concealed on an inner page. Rather, the version number and date should be clearly indicated on the cover of the document and, if possible, different versions of each document should be issued with a different colour of cover.

The updating and maintenance of user and system documentation is considerably simplified if the documentation is available in machine-readable form. Tools for producing documentation have already been described and these tools are equally, if not more, useful for implementing and controlling document modification. In addition, if a document retrieval system is available, the user may immediately obtain copies of modified documents – delays due to distribution are minimised.

7.6   THE PORTABILITY OF DOCUMENTATION

When a computing system is moved from one machine to another, the documentation associated with that system must be modified to reflect the new system. In some circumstances, the work involved in this is comparable to the work involved in moving the programs themselves. If portability is a system design objective, the documentation must also be designed and written with the same aim.

Just as the property of self-containedness is the key to program portability, portable documentation should also be self-contained. This means that the information provided in the documentation should be as complete as possible. Reference should not be made to any other documents, such as an operating system manual, which are not directly associated with the system being documented.

For example, say a programming language allows the user access to mathematical functions such as sin, cos, tan, log, etc. In some installations, these functions may be provided in a library of similar functions shared by all programming languages implemented at that installation. When discussing available functions, the programming language documentation should not simply refer to the documentation describing the mathematical library. Should that language be implemented on another machine without a mathematical library the language documentation would be incomplete. The language manual itself should describe fully the functions available.

Those parts of the system which generally cause portability problems are obviously the sections describing non portable parts of the programming system. These include file organisation, file naming conventions, job control, input-output, and so on. When the system is moved from one computer to another, those parts of the documentation must be rewritten

In order to facilitate this rewriting, descriptions of system dependent functions should be confined to separate sections. These sections should be clearly headed with information about their system dependence and they are replaced when the system is moved to another installation. If possible, other references to system dependent features should be avoided. If this is impossible, an index of such references should be maintained so that they may be located and changed when the program is moved.

As transporting a program and its documentation is really a specialised form of system maintenance, the availability of machine readable documentation and appropriate software tools reduces the work involved in producing documentation for a new system. System dependent parts of the document may be located, rewritten and a new version of the document produced automatically.

7.7   WRITING STYLE

In a book of this nature, devoted to a technical subject, it may appear presumptious to include notes on writing style. Nevertheless, it is unfortunately true that some people involved in software production have great difficulty constructing well-written, clear and concise documentation. The underlying cause appears to be that the teaching of composition in schools is geared towards creative rather than technical writing.

As in many other aspects of software engineering, it is impossible to present a set of rules which govern exactly how to set about a particular task. Technical writing is a craft and, in this section, a set of guidelines is presented which suggest how documents might be written. Writing good documentation is not easy nor is it a single stage process. Documents must be written, read, criticised and then rewritten and this process should continue until a satisfactory document is produced. Some guidelines are:

(1)   Use active rather than passive tenses when writing instruction manuals.

(2)   Do not use long sentences which present a number of different facts. It is much better to use a number of shorter sentences.

(3)   Do not refer to previously presented information by some reference number on its own. Instead, give the reference number and remind the reader what that reference covered.

(4)   Itemise facts wherever possible rather than present them in the form of a sentence.

(5)   If a description is complex, repeat yourself, presenting two or more differently phrased descriptions of the same thing. If the reader fails to completely understand one description, he may benefit from having the same thing said in a different way.

(6)   Don't be verbose. If you can say something in 5 words do so, rather than use ten words so that the description might seem more profound. There is no merit in quantity of documentation - quality is much more important.

(7)   Be precise and, if necessary, define the terms which you use. Computing terminology is very fluid and many terms have more than one meaning. Therefore, if such terms(such as module or process) are used, make sure that your definition is clear.

(8)   Keep paragraphs short. As a general rule, no paragraph should be made up of more than seven sentences. This is because of short term memory limitations. These are discussed in chapter 9.

(9)   Make use of headings and subheadings. Always ensure that a consistent numbering convention is used for these.

(10)   Use grammatically correct constructs and spell words correctly. Avoid constructs such as split infinitives.

An example of badly written technical prose, describing how to log in to a computer system, is:

Once the terminal line speed has been set to 9600 baud, a single line feed (LF) character should be typed. The system should then clear the terminal screen, cause the terminal to beep and type the message 'Login' at the top of the screen. In order to log in, your name should be typed and, when the system responds with the message 'Password', your personal password should then be typed which will not be echoed by the system.

This description can be written in a much more understandable way:

Set the terminal line speed to 9600 baud.
Type a single line feed (LF) character.
The system will then respond as follows:

(1)   The terminal screen will be cleared.

(2)   The terminal will beep.

(3)   The message 'Login' will be displayed at the top of the screen.

You should then type your name.
The system will ask for your personal password.
Type your password. It will not be echoed by the system.

7.8   SOFTWARE MAINTENANCE

Historically, the term 'maintenance' has been applied to the process of modifying a program after it has been delivered and is in use. These modifications may involve simple changes to correct coding errors, more extensive changes to correct design errors or drastic rewrites to correct specification errors or accommodate new requirements.

As Turski (1981) has pointed out, this is a gross abuse of the term 'maintenance'. The addition of a new wing to a building would never be described as maintaining that building, yet adding new facilities to a program is considered as maintenance activity. However, as the term maintenance is widely and generally used, it will be used here to mean changing a program by correcting errors and providing new facilities.

Software maintenance falls into 3 categories. These are perfective maintenance, adaptive maintenance and corrective maintenance. Perfective maintenance encompasses changes demanded by the user or the system programmer, adaptive maintenance is maintenance due to changes in the environment of the program and corrective maintenance is the correction of undiscovered system errors. A survey by Lientz and Swanson (1980) discovered that about 65% of maintenance was perfective, 18% adaptive and 17% corrective.

In general, it is impossible to produce systems of any size which do not need to be maintained. Over the lifetime of a system, its original requirements will be modified to reflect changing needs, the system's environment will change and obscure errors, undiscovered during system validation, will emerge. Because maintenance is unavoidable, systems should be designed and implemented so that maintenance problems are minimised.

The costs of maintenance are extremely difficult to estimate in advance. Evidence from existing systems suggests that maintenance costs are by far the greatest cost incurred in developing and using a system. In general, these costs were dramatically underestimated when the system was designed and implemented. As an illustration of the relative cost of program maintenance, it was estimated that one US Air Force System cost $30 per instruction to develop and $4000 per instruction to maintain over its lifetime (Boehm, 1975).

These figures are perhaps exceptional as the system in question was a highly optimised, tightly coded control system. Almost certainly, performance was its principal requirement and this can sometimes be achieved by sacrificing the understandability and hence the maintainability of a program. Maintenance costs certainly vary widely from application to application but, on average, maintenance costs appear to be about 4 times development costs for large software systems.

Furthermore, Lientz and Swanson found that large organisations devoted about 50% of their total programming effort to maintaining existing systems and, as systems age, relatively more effort must be expended in maintaining those systems.

It is certainly worthwhile to invest time and effort when designing and implementing a system to reduce maintenance and hence overall system costs. The guidelines and techniques discussed in previous chapters recognise this. They have been formulated with the explicit intention of explaining how an understandable and maintainable program can be designed, developed, and tested. As the previous chapters are based on the assumption that the software engineer should produce easily maintained programs as a matter of course, no further discussion on how to construct such systems will be presented here.

7.8.1 Factors affecting maintenance costs

Estimating maintenance costs for any particular program is very difficult. The difficulties arise because these costs are related to a number of relatively unpredictable factors. These include:

(1)   The application being supported.
      If the application of the program is clearly de-
      fined and well understood, the system requirements
      may be definitive and perfective maintenance due
      to changing requirements, minimised. If, on the
      other hand, the application is completely new, it
      is likely that the initial requirements will be
      modified as users gain experience with the system.

(2)   Staff stability.
      It is normally easier for the original writer of a
      program to understand and change a program rather
      than some other individual who must understand the
      program by study of its documentation and code
      listing. Therefore, if the programmer of a system
      also maintains that system, maintenance costs will
      be reduced. In practice, the nature of the pro-
      gramming profession is such that individuals
      change jobs regularly and it is fairly unusual for
      one person to develop and maintain a program
      throughout its useful life.

(3)   The lifetime of the program.
      The useful life of a program obviously depends on
      its application. The program will become obsolete
      if the application becomes obsolete or if its ori-
      ginal hardware is replaced and conversion costs
      exceed rewriting costs. Historical evidence sug-
      gests that program lifetimes are much longer than
      originally anticipated - some systems running to-
      day were coded in the early 1960's.

If a program is continually maintained throughout its life, maintenance costs tend to rise as the program ages. This is a result of the inevitable deterioration of program structure which occurs as multiple modifications are made.

(4)   The dependence of the program on its external environment.

If a program is highly dependent on its external environment it must be modified as that environment changes. For example, changes in a taxation system might require payroll, accounting, and stock control programs to be modified. Taxation changes are relatively common and maintenance costs for these programs will be related to the frequency of these changes.

On the other hand, a program used in a mathematical application does not normally depend on human decisions changing the assumptions on which the program is based. Maintenance costs, therefore, are unaffected by changes in human and political systems.

(5)   Hardware stability.

If a program is designed to operate on a particular hardware configuration and that configuration does not change during the program's lifetime, no maintenance costs due to hardware changes will be incurred. However, hardware developments are so rapid that this situation is relatively rare and computing hardware becomes obsolete very quickly . The program must be modified to use new hardware which replaces obsolete equipment.

This process is distinct from moving the program to another computer system as the required modifications normally involve enhancing the program to make use of improved hardware or modifying assumptions built into the program about the hardware.

Maintenance costs are also governed by less unpredictable, technical factors. The cost of maintenance can be minimised if the requirements of the program maintainer are taken into account when the program is designed and implemented. Technical factors affecting program maintenance are:

(1)   Module Independence. It should be possible to modify one program unit of a system without affecting any other unit.

(2)   Programming Language. Programs written in a high level programming language are usually easier to understand (and hence maintain) than programs written in a low level language.

(3)   Programming style. The way in which a program is written clearly contributes to its understandability and hence the ease with which it can be modified.

(4)   Program Validation and Testing. Generally, the more time and effort spent on design validation and program testing, the fewer errors in the program and consequently decreased maintenance costs resulting from error correction.
        Maintenance costs due to error correction are governed by the type of error to be repaired. Coding errors are usually relatively cheap to correct, whereas design errors are much more expensive as they may involve the rewriting of one or more program units. Errors in the requirements specification are normally the most expensive to correct because of the drastic redesign which may be involved.

(5)   The quality and quantity of program documentation. If a program is supported by clear, complete yet concise documentation, the task of understanding the program can be relatively straightforward. Consequently, program maintenance costs tend to be less for well documented systems than for systems supplied with poor or incomplete documentation.

Because of this multiplicity of factors, it is impossible to present any technique of maintenance cost estimation which has general applicability. Such cost estimates can only be made using cost data from past projects and even then are not likely to be particularly accurate.

7.8.2 Understanding programs
Unless a program is properly understood by the maintenance programmer, changing the program is likely

to result in the introduction of errors. Hence, understanding a program is the key to effective maintenance and the following sections cover program reading techniques and briefly describe experimental techniques for measuring the understandability of a program.

The fundamental assumption which must be made at this stage is that the program reader has a thorough knowledge and understanding of the programming language used. Without this knowledge, it is unlikely that he will ever understand the program in sufficient detail to modify it successfully.

In this section, techniques of program reading are described. However, the usefulness of these techniques to any particular program depends on the application of that program, the style in which it was written and the program reader himself. If the reader has some experience of working with or implementing the type of program he is studying he will almost certainly read that program differently from a reader who has no experience of that application.

For example, a program reader who has experience of compiler writing knows that compilers all have a lexical analysis part, a syntactic and semantic analysis part and a code generation part. These parts normally communicate using a symbol table. When attempting to understand a compiler, that individual will naturally look for those parts as the first stage of the program comprehension process. The reader without experience must start at a different level and by studying program components, determine the functions of different parts of the program. Program documentation presetting a system overview can be exceptionally useful in such cases.

There appear to be no general program reading techniques which ensure that the different units in a program can be identified simply by code examination. The use of meaningful names and descriptive header comments, however, can be enormously helpful and it is essential that their use is adopted in any large system.

Given that program units can be identified, the program reader must then discern how these units are activated and used. There are two ways of tackling this problem. The reader may study the functions of each program unit and, by understanding these functions can work out how the units should be used. Reference to the program code can then confirm this usage.

Alternatively, the reader may choose to examine the program code and trace how and where units in the system are called. By examining various parts of the program, the functions and usage of each of the units can be determined.

The first approach roughly corresponds to a bottom up approach where the overall functions of a system are understood in terms of their subfunctions. The latter approach is a top down approach where details of sub-functions are ignored so that a manageable overall picture may be obtained. There appears to be no evidence to suggest that one technique is superior to the other.

Having identified the program units and how they are used, the program maintainer is generally faced with the problem of understanding one or more units in detail, so that they might be modified.

Given that the programming language is understood, there are various strategies which might be adopted in studying the details of a program unit to determine how that unit operates. For example, the reader might first study the input and output statements to determine the unit's interaction with its environment, then may study the units data declarations, then procedure declarations and finally, with this background, the control statements to understand the units operation. On the other hand, the control statements might be studied first, then procedure declarations, then data definitions and so on. The particular approach adopted is entirely at the discretion of the individual and there is no published evidence to suggest that one technique is better than another.

The approach adopted by the author in studying program units is one possible way of tackling the problem of program understanding. A number of steps are involved:

(1)   The program is scanned to determine if program objects are ascribed meaningful names.

(2)   If not, an attempt is made to determine the function of each object in the program - constants, types, variables, and procedures. A table of names and their functions is constructed.

(3)   Linear code sequences, loops and conditionals are then studied to find out their functions and the

program listing annotated accordingly. This is a process of adding low level comments in a form which is particular to the reader. Existing low level comments in the program are deliberately ignored as experience has shown that they are often misleading.

(4)   The program logic is then traced step by step. Depending on the modifications to be made to the unit, this may mean tracing each statement or may involve only a few statements in one procedure.

Wherever possible, this latter step is best carried out with another person who has also studied the program. Logic tracing is easier if one person explains to the other what the program is supposed to be doing. This verbalisation appears to clarify individual thinking and has the additional advantage that the oversights or misunderstandings by one reader may be detected by the other.

7.8.3 Measuring the maintainability of programs

Attempts have been made to devise techniques which quantify the maintainability of programs and to measure that maintainability automatically. These techniques equate maintainability with complexity - the more complex the program, the more difficult it is to understand and hence maintain.

Halstead (1977) suggests that the complexity of a program can be measured by considering the number of unique operators, the number of unique operands, the total frequency of operators and the total frequency of operands in a program. Using these parameters, Halstead has devised metrics allowing program size, programming effort, and program 'intelligence count' to be computed.

McCabe (1976)has devised a measure of program complexity using graph theoretic techniques. His theory maintains that program complexity is not dependent on size but on the decision structure of the program. Measurement of the complexity of a program depends on transforming the program so that it may be represented as a graph and counting the number of nodes, edges, and connected components in that graph.

Both of these techniques have some applicability but both suffer from the same disadvantage that they do not take into account the data structures used in the program, the program comments or the use of meaningful variable names. Shepherd et al. (1979) have conducted experiments using both techniques. Their results were inconclusive.

Boehm et al. (1978) have devised a number of software metrics including a measure of the maintainability of a program. They consider that program maintainability is dependent on testability, understandability, and modifiability. These factors are themselves dependent on program structuredness, program self-descriptiveness, program conciseness etc. and empirical techniques have been devised to measure these characteristics.

Techniques for measuring program maintainability are rarely used in production programming environments and experimental evidence suggests that existing techniques are still in need of considerable refinement. The refinement of existing techniques and the development of new maintainability metrics is an important research area. With reliable metrics, improved programming techniques which reduce maintenance costs can be identified and adopted.

The user interface

This chapter, deals with a topic which is not normally covered in texts on software engineering – the interface of the user with the software system. It may be thought that the user interface is the responsibility of the systems analyst rather than the software engineer but as was made clear in the chapters covering software requirements specification these roles are not distinct.

The user interface is the yardstick by which the user judges system quality. If a system has a poorly designed interface, it is liable to be rejected, irrespective of the facilities which it offers. A badly designed interface can cause the user to make potentially catastrophic errors. If information is presented in a confusing or misleading way, the user may accidentally misunderstand the meaning of an item of information and on that basis initiate a sequence of potentially dangerous actions.

This situation is most likely to arise when the user is dealing with information not normally presented by the system. Such a situation arises when a system malfunction occurs so the consequences of a user error may be to compound that malfunction. The seriousness of a nuclear accident at a power station in the USA in 1979 may have b en compounded by the complexity of the user interface to the reactor control system.

User interfaces can be classified as on-line interactive interfaces and off-line interfaces. In an on-line interface, the user directly interacts with the computer system through his terminal. An off-line interface on the other hand, relies on the user preparing machine-readable input separately then presenting that to the computer system. The results of processing that input are returned to the user, often on specially designed forms.

Although off-line interfaces are fairly common at the moment, in future the majority of direct user interfaces will be interactive. Indirect interfaces such as that of a consumer to the billing computer of an electricity supply utility will still principally be oriented around a specialised form. This class of interface will not be discussed here.

Interactive user interfaces show a remarkable range of variation - a simple mnemonic interface may simply report system status and accept commands from the user. A business system interface may be the forms input to and generated by the system and an engineering design interface may involve the user manipulating graphic representations of structures. To design an appropriate interface requires knowledge of both user procedures and what is practicable to provide using the computer system.

There are a number of styles of user/computer dialogue which may be implemented - mnemonic based, quasi-natural language, forms driven, menu-type and question-answer dialogue. The first three of these may be classified as user initiated dialogues and the latter two as computer-initiated dialogues. Computer initiated dialogues are most useful for untrained users whereas user initiated dialogues are best where the user is trained and interacts with the computer on a regular basis.

Serious consequences can result if a poorly designed or inappropriate interface is used. At best, an inappropriate interface will result in increased training costs and a higher proportion of user errors, at worst, it will result in the system being completely abandoned. Eason et al. (1975) have identified three characteristic responses which result from poor interface design.

(1)   The user refuses to make use of the computer system. After initial 'testing', he deems it inadequate for his needs.

(2)   The user learns a few commands 'parrot fashion' and restricts his usage of the system to these commands. Because the user has no real understanding of the system, he cannot make use of all the system facilities.

(3)   The user interacts with the computer system by using an intermediary who becomes the local system expert.

An individual's particular reaction to an inappropriate

interface depends on the organisation using the system, the status of the individual and the nature of the system itself. Whereas a manager may decide not to use a management information system or may delegate an intermediary to use the system, a secretary using a word processor system will not, generally, have such options. In this case, minimal system facilities are learned and used and the full capability of the system ignored.

As computer systems become more pervasive because of dramatically reduced hardware costs, more and more individuals will use computers as everyday tools. Interface design should reflect this and should ensure that the computer is seen as a useful and powerful tool. The interface should not have human characteristics otherwise the user may ascribe human abilities to the machine. Human abilities and computer power are complementary and it is the task of the interface designer to ensure that they work well together.

The first section in this chapter briefly discusses psychological issues which should be taken into account in designing a user interface. This is followed by a general discussion of user interface design where a distinction is made between user initiated interfaces and computer initiated interfaces. Natural language interfaces are also discussed.

The final sections of the chapter discuss interfaces which are not based on a standard alphanumeric terminal. The need to use graphics to improve the immediacy and readability of output displays is discussed and the final section in this chapter examines situations where a specially designed terminal might be used.

8.1   USER PSYCHOLOGY

In order to design an acceptable user interface, the psychology of the system user should be carefully considered. There are some interface design issues which are directly related to user psychology and are independent of the background or experience of the individual user. Shneiderman (1980) discusses some of these issues. These include information overloading, task complexity, system response time and the degree of control over the system which the user is allowed.

Information overloading is a situation where the interface presents the user with too many distinct items of information. Miller (1957) suggests that human memory is hierarchical with a short-term memory made up of about seven locations. This is supplemented by other more permanent memory to which information is transferred. If a user interface presents more than seven distinct items of information to the user at the same time, they cannot all be retained in short-term memory and some are likely to be forgotten.

In designing an interface, therefore, information should be presented in units rather than in groups so that the user has time to assimilate that information and, perhaps, transfer it to more permanent memory. This allows short-term memory locations to be kept free for use in problem solving operations.

Because of short-term memory limitations, an individual feels relief when an operation has been completed and the short-term memory may be cleared. As a result, there is an inherent desire for closure - the completion of a task and the subsequent relief. Each time a user types a command or completes a session of editing, closure is achieved and relief gained.

Because of this desire for closure, user interfaces are best organised as a sequence of short operations rather than a single large, complex task. Even although this may involve more typing, informal studies reported by Shneiderman suggest that users prefer short operations in sequence rather than a single, more complicated, operation. This fact may account for some of the success of the UNIX system interface which is based on simple operations but which includes mechanisms (pipes and macros) to combine these simple operations, to create more powerful commands.

The response time of an interactive system is possibly the most important factor influencing the user's opinion of that system. If the user considers the response time to be excessive, he will think that the system is a poor system irrespective of the facilities provided. If the response is prompt, he will be quite prepared to overlook some system inadequacies.

It is not possible to provide a standard acceptable response time because user's expectations vary depending on the complexity of the operation being executed by the system. Users expect instant echoing of characters which they have typed and very fast response to editing or login requests. On the other hand, if a user knows that a task is complex or involves a large amount of information processing, he is prepared to wait much longer. Examples of such operations might be compiling a program or retrieving information from a database.

If it is necessary to include facilities which may involve long response times, the user should be given the option of finding out how his task is progressing. This is particularly important when response times are variable and depend on the loading on the system. Without some indication of how long his task will take, the user cannot readily make use of the time spent waiting for the system to respond.

Strangely, there are situations where too rapid a response can cause the user anxiety. This is particularly likely if the users are inexperienced and a computer-initiated interface (described below) is in use. If the response is fast, the user may be surprised and his thinking disrupted. He may feel that he is being driven by the machine to work at an excessive speed. In such situations, it may be desirable to delay responses and minimise the variance in response time.

As users become more experienced in computer usage, their desire to control the computer increases. They are not content simply to be passive and accept the computer as the dominant partner in their interaction. As a result, they feel resentful if system messages suggest that they are not in charge or if they are forced to follow a prescribed verbose routine with which they are familiar.

Because of this need for control, interactions whose progress is controlled by the machine are only suitable for casual, irregular computer users. Regular system users should be provided with an interface which makes them feel that the computer is a tool which they can control.

8.2 USER INTERFACE DESIGN

The design of a user interface should not be undertaken by the software engineer alone. It is essential to consult with system users and discuss their background and their needs. In some situations, it may be impossible to develop a single interface which is suitable for all system users. In such cases, multiple interfaces should be provided, each tailored for a particular class of user.

User interface systems can be broadly classified as:

(1)   User initiated interfaces.

(2)   Computer initiated interfaces.

In the former case, the user is in charge, controlling the progress of the user/computer dialogue. In the latter case the computer system originates the dialogue, the user replies and, on the basis of that reply, the computer selects the next stage in the conversation. As a general rule, user initiated interfaces are most suitable for experienced or regular computer users whereas computer initiated interfaces are best for inexperienced or casual users. Of course, situations exist where the most appropriate interface is made up of combinations of each interface class.

The most fundamental principle in user interface design is that the interface must be designed to suit the needs and abilities of the individual user. Users should not be forced to adapt to an interface which is convenient to implement or which is suited to the systems designer. Tailoring the interface to the user means that the interface must be couched in terms familiar to the user and that the objects manipulated by the system should have direct analogues in the environment with which the user is familiar.

For example, if a system is designed for use by secretarial staff, the objects manipulated should be letters, documents, diary's, folders, etc., at least as far as the secretary is concerned. In practice, these objects will be implemented using different files but the secretary should not be forced to cope with such computing concepts such as workfiles, directories, file identifiers and so on. The allowed operations might be 'file', 'retrieve', 'index', 'discard', etc. However, if a system interface is designed for program development, the use of computer system terminology is acceptable if not essential. Programmers, familiar with systems concepts, prefer a terse interface and the ability to extend that interface using macros.

The second principle of interface design is that the user interface must be consistent. Consistency should be maintained within a system and across subsystems running on the same machine. Interface consistency means that system commands should have the same format, parameters should be passed to all commands in the same way, and command punctuation should be similar.

A consistent interface means that when a user takes time to learn about one command of the interface his knowledge is applicable to all other commands in the system. For example, say system commands accept parameters which may be filenames or which may be flags controlling command operation. If it is necessary to distinguish flags from filenames by some means - such as preceding flags with a '-' character - this should be the convention for every system command whether or not there is any ambiguity in a particular command between filenames and flags.

If a particular flag name is used to signify a particular operation in one system command, exactly the same name should be used in all compatible commands. For example, if a command to print a file takes a flag '-d' specifying that the file is to be deleted after printing, the same flag name should be used in every other command which can delete a file such as archive commands, copy commands etc.

Interface consistency across subsystems is equally important. Many large systems are made up of subsystems which can be independently activated and these subsystems should be designed so that commands with similar meanings in different subsystems are expressed in the same way. It is very dangerous for a command, say 'k', to mean 'keep this file' in a system editor and the same command 'k' to mean 'kill this transaction' in an information retrieval system. Users of both systems will inevitably confuse the commands.

The third principle of interface design is that the interface should have built-in 'help' facilities. These should be accessible from the user's terminal and should provide different levels of help and advice - from very basic information on how to get started with the system up to a full description of system facilities and how to use them. These help facilities should be supplemented by concise, well written user documentation as described in the previous chapter.

8.2.1 User initiated interfaces

In this section, the design of user initiated interchanges with the computer will be considered. Martin (1973) has identified 9 possible design techniques for this type of interface but only more general design principles will be covered here.

User initiated interfaces fall into two approximate classes:

(1)   Command driven interfaces - the user types commands or queries which are interpreted by the computer.

(2)   Forms oriented interfaces - the user calls up an

image of a form to his screen and fills in that
form by overtyping appropriate parts of the
screen.

Under some circumstances, forms oriented interfaces
might be considered as computer-initiated, particularly
where the user has little or no control over what forms
are actually filled in. In other cases, he has virtually
complete control of everything from form layout to the
contents of the form. This simply illustrates that there
is no clear dividing line between the interface classes.

8.2.2 Command driven interfaces

Command driven interfaces involve the user inputting a
command to the computer system which takes some action
depending on the command. The command may be a query,
the initiation of some subsystem or it may call up a
sequence of other commands.

At the time of writing, this class of user interface
is, by far, the most common. The user interacts with
the system via a terminal made up of a typewriter
keyboard and a display screen which can only display
discrete alphanumeric characters. The size of the
screen is such that normally 24 lines of 80 characters
can be displayed.

This class of interface is a direct derivation from
off-line interfaces where data was punched onto cards
and input to the system. It is a relatively
straightforward task to convert from an off-line
interface to a simple on-line text interface. Because
of this, because terminals to support this class of
interface are cheap, and because the software techniques
of text handling are well understood, the majority of
general purpose computer systems support this class of
interface.

For many applications, this form of user interface is
eminently suitable. Much of the information which is
processed by computer systems is best gathered, input,
and displayed as text and there is no need for
capabilities apart from those required to input and
output text. They are particularly suitable for
environments where the majority of work carried out is
program development, documentation, and maintenance.

Unfortunately, because this type of interface is
derived from punched card systems, many user interfaces
of this type are based entirely on upper case letters.

This is completely artificial as text based information
is normally presented using mostly lower case letters.
Upper case letters are only used in distinguished
positions. Upper case only interfaces are obsolete and
text based user interfaces should always support both
upper and lower case letters.

Command systems may involve the user actually
providing a command such as 'print' or 'edit'.
Alternatively, the command may be implicit with the user
simply providing details of the entity to which his
command relates. An example of this latter type of
command might be an information retrieval system which
does not allow users to modify information in a database
– a library catalogue, for example. The retrieval and
display operation is implicit and the user simply inputs
key details about the information he wishes to retrieve.

The design of such interfaces, where the command is
implicit, is usually straightforward and readily derived
from the application. Situations where the user must
actually input commands tend to be more complex and the
design of those systems depends on the application,
experience, background, and ability of the system users.
When designing such an interface, the software engineer
must decide if the commands input by the user are to be
functional mnemonics (such as ed to initiate the editor)
or if they are to be expressed in full.

If a decision is made to implement a system using
mnemonic commands, the system designer is faced with the
problem of choosing appropriate mnemonics to represent
the possible system operations. Mnemonic choice should
be governed by the following criteria:

(1)   Mnemonics should be easily remembered and semanti-
      cally related to the operation they represent.
      For example, an edit operation might be represent-
      ed as 'ed'.

(2)   Mnemonics should be unambiguous – if there are
      more commands than can be accommodated using ini-
      tial letter mnemonics, two or three letter mnemon-
      ics should be used. Single and multiple letter
      mnemonics should not be used in the same system as
      this may cause confusion. For example, a system
      may have a command to print files and a command to
      purge files. It is poor practice to use a mnemon-
      ic 'pr' for print and 'p' for purge as a mix-up,

with serious consequences, is liable to occur. In such a situation, mnemonics such as ´pr´ for print and ´pu´ for purge would be much better choices.

(3)   If mnemonics are chosen by abbreviating the name of the operation, a consistent abbreviation convention should be adopted. For example, the mnemonic may consist of the first 2 or 3 letters of the operation name. Therefore, users who are not completely familiar with available mnemonics but who know which operation is required can make a reasonable guess at the appropriate mnemonic.

The decision on whether to use mnemonics or full commands must be taken by considering the system users. When users become familiar with a system, it is irritating for them to have to type lengthy system commands or to be presented with wordy, well-known system messages. Such users generally prefer a mnemonic system involving the minimum amount of typing and are content with terse system messages.

On the other hand, inexperienced and casual system users are less likely to be intimidated by an interface if it accepts meaningful commands and generates friendly responses. The inexperienced user is far less likely to make mistakes if commands must be given in full. For example, if the user wishes to compile a Pascal program, the command:

    compile myprogram with Pascal

is more meaningful and potentially less error prone than the terse:

    pcom myprogram

Unless a system is intended for a single class of user such as programming staff (who normally want a concise interface), system commands should be expressible in both a concise and a verbose form. This can easily be accomplished by providing a command translation system which includes a macro processor. The basic command may be the concise version but by defining a full version of the command as a macro, both terse and verbose forms of the command can be made available.

The provision of a macro processor system as part of the interface interpreter allows the user to combine commands into a named sequence which may be initiated simply by typing the macro name. The interface translator expands that name into the command sequence and executes each command in turn. In such systems, it is usually possible to parameterise commands, allowing them to be generalised.

Some interfaces provide constructs which may be used to control which interface commands are executed. The user interface is a special purpose programming language manipulating entities associated with the system application. For example, if the interface is an operating system interface, the objects manipulated may be data and program files. Control constructs such as if-then-else conditionals and while loops allow interface commands to be skipped or to be executed a number of times.

The example below illustrates how commands available under the UNIX operating system interface may be combined to produce more powerful commands. The command 'wp' takes one or more parameters which are the names of files. The effect of wp is to call a word processing subsystem and process each file in turn. The results are displayed on the user's terminal and a hard copy is produced on a high quality printer.

```
wp
: check there is at least one parameter
if $# = 0
then echo 'usage is wp <list of one or more
filenames>'
else
: now call word processor for each parameter
: default iteration list is all parameters
for i do
( nroff $i | hqprinter; echo $i printed) &
nroff $i
done
fi
```

The use of such interfaces is most appropriate when the system users have some programming experience (Mashey and Smith, 1977) although non-programmers may be able to make use of some of their facilities.

The notion of translating one form of a command to an equivalent form has not been extended to system replies, except on an experimental basis (Sommerville, 1981). The advantage of this extension is that system replies can be tailored to user's background - casual users can have full explanatory replies, regular users, concise replies. In the absence of such a mechanism, the best approach is to provide concise system messages expressed in a form suitable for regular users. These should be supplemented by an easy-to-use 'help' facility such as the typing of a single question mark. If the user does not understand a reply, he can ask for help and a fuller, more explanatory version of the reply can be provided by the system.

8.2.3 Natural language interfaces

One class of imperative user interface is those interfaces based on natural language. It is argued that computer systems will not become truly accessible to casual users until natural or quasi-natural language exchanges with the computer system become possible. A number of such interfaces to large data base systems such as LADDER (Hendrix et al., 1978) and PLANES (Waltz, 1978) have been implemented and are reportedly successful. The particular systems are information retrieval systems geared to queries concerning a particular type of subject - ships in the case of LADDER, aircraft in the case of PLANES.

The software problems involved in implementing quasi-natural language interfaces are immense - natural languages are inherently ambiguous and resolving ambiguities is generally difficult and sometimes impossible. Systems such as PLANES and LADDER only operate successfully because knowledge about the entities in the database is built-into the user interface. Using this knowledge, many ambiguities can be resolved. All natural language systems presently implemented confine themselves to very specialised applications and techniques for developing a general purpose natural language understanding system have not been devised.

Even if the implementation of a quasi-natural language system such as PLANES is feasible, it is not necessarily the case that a natural language interface is the most acceptable to users. The fundamental problems with such an interface are:

(1)   It is verbose - users have to type long commands.

(2)   The resolution of ambiguities may involve much time wasting system/user dialogue. Thus even more typing is involved.

Whilst the principle means of communicating with a computer system is via a keyboard, quasi-natural language interfaces are generally inferior to other types of user interface because of the unnecessary typing involved. If general purpose speech recognition and understanding systems can be developed, this situation may change. The verbosity of the language will no longer be a problem as users will be able to talk directly with the computer. However, there is no evidence from current research that speech understanding systems are likely to be available in the near future.

A further problem which may result from the use of a natural language interface is that inexperienced users might overestimate the capabilities of the computer system. If the computer appears to communicate like a human, it is natural for those unfamiliar with computers to ascribe other human abilities to the machine, such as the ability to make deductions on the basis of incomplete information. The consequent disappointment may discourage users from investigating the real potential of the system and may even cause them to abandon usage of the system altogether.

8.2.4 Error message design

The design of error messages is an important part of user interface design. As user errors are inevitable, the system's response should be helpful and should provide information on the nature of the error and, perhaps, its possible cause.

The error messages provided by the system should be polite, concise, consistent and constructive. Under no circumstances should they be abusive and, if the user's terminal might be in a public place, the error handling system should not cause audible tones to be emitted, which might embarrass the user. Error messages should include a reference to the appropriate user manual which describes the error in more detail and which might explain how the error can be corrected.

The background and experience of the user should be anticipated when designing error messages. Lengthy, detailed messages are intolerable if the user is experienced but essential if the user is a novice. Because both types of user may make use of a system, error reports should be structured with the initial report being brief and providing little detail. If the user requires more information, this should be easily obtainable by pressing a single key such as '!'.

8.2.5 Forms-oriented interfaces

User interfaces which are forms oriented involve the user calling up an image of a form to his terminal. He then fills in the form by typing in the appropriate screen locations. Such systems rely on terminals with a cursor which may be moved anywhere on the screen.

Forms oriented interfaces are considered to be user initiated because it is assumed that a library of different forms is available. Exactly which form is filled in is under the control of the user. In general, forms oriented interfaces are more limited in scope than command driven interfaces and are most suitable for use in situations where the users have little experience or understanding of computing.

This type of interface is often the best choice when an existing manual paperwork system, based on standard forms, is to be automated. The interface design may be based on forms already in use. If that automated system resembles the existing manual system, users are unlikely to be intimidated by the system and will accept the new automated system. Furthermore, both manual and automated systems may easily run in parallel without confusion and without the overhead of high user training costs.

One of the most sophisticated forms oriented interfaces is the OfficeTalk (Ellis and Nutt, 1980) system. This is intended to automate the activities in any office and provides powerful facilities for creating and manipulating forms. Individual forms may be examined in more or less detail. The OfficeTalk terminal is designed to mimic a desk, with several forms on it. OfficeTalk avoids one of the limitations of conventional forms oriented systems namely that forms can only be viewed singly. By using a graphics display, several forms may be viewed simultaneously by the user on different parts of his screen.

Forms oriented interfaces must be combined with a simple version of some other interface type which allows forms to be called up, saved, and printed. This may be a command driven interface where the user requests the form by its number or a menu-type interface where the user is presented with a list of possible forms and operations. He selects from this list by indicating the appropriate entry using a device such as a light pen or by positioning the cursor at that entry. Menu type interfaces are covered in the following section.

8.3   COMPUTER-INITIATED INTERFACES

Computer-initiated user interfaces are those user interfaces where the computer system guides the progress of the user/computer dialogue. Information is displayed, the user responds in some simple fashion, and, on the basis of that user response, the computer takes action or displays further information. The computer leads the user through his terminal session by presenting alternatives and acting according to the user's reaction.

Computer-initiated interfaces are most suitable for situations where the users have little or no experience in using computers and who do not make regular use of a computer system. This type of interface has the advantage that the user need remember little or nothing about how to interact with the system – all necessary information is presented to him as his terminal session proceeds.

Computer initiated interfaces fall into two rough classes:

(1)   Menu systems where the user is presented with a list of alternatives and chooses one of these alternatives.

(2)   Question-answer systems where the computer asks the user a question and takes action on the basis of his reply.

The general problem with computer-initiated interfaces is that as they become familiar to the user, he feels frustration over his lack of control over the computer system. He knows the system questions and replies and is angered by unnecessarily verbose communications between him and the machine. It is therefore important that the user should be allowed to abbreviate his replies and shorten system messages once he becomes used to the interface.

8.3.1 Menu systems
In a menu-type interface, the user must select one of a number of possibilities and indicate his choice to the machine. This indication can be made by typing the chosen possibility, by 'touching' the chosen response with a light pen or the terminal cursor or by typing an

identifier associated with the user's choice. An example of a menu system is an information retrieval system where the user is presented with a number of document names and a summary of each. Associated with each document is a number and to display a document, the user simply types that document number.

Menu systems suffer from the restriction that there must be sufficiently few choices so that all possibilities can be displayed on the terminal screen at the same time. In some cases, this is no problem but, in others, there may be tens, hundreds or thousands of possibilities. Techniques must be devised to classify these possibilities and to allow the user to identify his requirements with the minimum number of interactions.

An example of a menu driven system with thousands of possibilities is the UK's Prestel system. This is an on-line information retrieval system containing pages of information. It is publicly accessible via the telephone network and the pages may be displayed on a domestic television set. Prestel offers about 250,000 separate pages and, to allow a menu-type interface to be used, classifies these pages as information pages and index pages. A tree structure of indexes exist and, by starting at the root of this tree, the user works his way through the indexes, keying in an abbreviated version of the page number of the next page required.

All pages in the system have a unique number rather than a number relative to some index so the system does not suffer from the most common drawback of hierarchically indexed systems. On many such systems, the user must progress through every level in the hierarchy from 1 to (n-1), in order to reach level n. This is necessary because items at some level m, are only identified to the higher level (m-1). Using Prestel, the user may access any page by keying in the number of that page.

On the other hand, when there is no such relationship between an index and its entries, it is not normally possible for the user to work his way up the index hierarchy from level n to level 1. There is no physically recorded relationship between an index and its entries. The user must always start at the top and work his way down the indexes.

An alternative to providing an index hierarchy is to present the user with a screenful of information with the added choice of 'go on to next page'. If the user selects this the following page is displayed and the process may continue until the required item is finally displayed. This method is suitable for situations where there are tens rather than hundreds or thousands of possibilities. With such a system, it is important to include a skip forwards and backwards capability so that the user can flip through the pages looking for the one which is required. Otherwise, should the user accidentally miss the required page, he must start all over again at page 1.

8.3.2 Question-answer interfaces

Question-answer interfaces are user interfaces where the progress of the person/computer dialogue is governed by the user's answers to questions posed by the computer. The most widespread use of this type of interface is in computer learning systems but medical interviewing systems using this class of interface have also been developed. This type of interface would be used in preference to a menu-type interface in situations where some overall picture of the user's requirements has to be built up by considering responses to a number of queries.

The design of question-answer interfaces is very dependent on the application being implemented. They appear to be most successful in situations where the number of possible user responses to a question are limited. For example, consider a medical interviewing system intended to find out how many cigarettes a patient smokes in a day. If the system poses the question:

How many cigarettes do you smoke in a day?

There are a variety of possible responses such as:

NONE
0
20
Twenty five
2 packs
about 15

A very sophisticated pattern matching system must be used to recognise the user response as it may be couched in a number of equivalent ways. If the response cannot be recognised, the question must be reformulated and asked again. This may alienate the user particularly as he is liable to have little experience or understanding of computer systems.

In such a dialogue, it is much better to formulate a series of questions which the user can answer simply with 'yes', 'no', or 'don't know'. For example:

Do you smoke cigarettes?

Do you smoke more than 10 cigarettes a day?

more than 20?

more than 30?

....

This particular dialogue terminates when the user answers 'no' to a question.

Question-answer systems of this type have been implemented using a special terminal with only 3 buttons – 'yes', 'no' and 'don't know'. An interesting result that has emerged from the use of the interviewing system is that patients not only enjoy using the system but are actually more honest with it than with medical staff (Lucas, 1977). They appear to feel less inhibited about answering personal questions posed by a machine.

8.4   THE USE OF GRAPHICS

Although interactive computer graphics systems have been available for several years (Newman and Sproull, 1979), their use has been relatively limited. Because of the cost of terminal hardware and the processor power needed to drive the graphics display, user interfaces based on interactive graphics have only been used in systems where there is no possible alternative. Examples of applications which have made use of graphical interfaces include computer-aided design, computer animation and computer aided mapping.

Decreasing processor and memory costs now mean that the cost of graphics display terminals has been significantly reduced. Low cost graphics systems using domestic television technology and based on a microprocessor are now available on almost every personal computer. These systems can act either as stand alone systems or can be used as a graphics terminal connected to some larger system. As a result, it is now realistic to consider using a graphical interface for many types of application system.

Graphical systems have the advantage that the information stored and processed by the computer can be displayed in such a way that the user can gain an overall impression of the entities described by that information. For example, consider a system which records and summarises the sales figures for a company on a monthly basis. These figures may be presented exactly, using alphanumeric text.

Jan	Feb	Mar	April	May	June
2842	2851	3164	2789	1273	2835

By reading those figures, it can be seen that higher sales were recorded in March and much lower sales in May. To abstract this information requires each monthly figure to be studied.

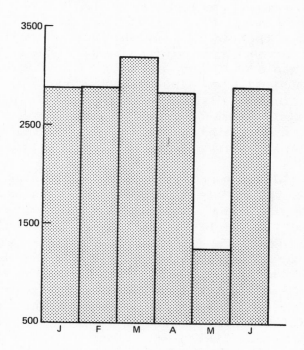

Fig. 8.1   Histogram display

Graphical presentation of this information, as a histogram, makes the anomalous figures in March and May immediately obvious as shown in Fig 8.1. Once an overall impression is gained, further, more precise details can then be obtained about the anomalous figures.

This type of overall impression is what many computer users require. A manager, using an information system, is often more interested in trends and patterns in his data than in exact figures. These trends can be difficult to discern if the data is presented alphanumerically, particularly when correlations are sought. Graphic display of the data, on the other hand, makes trends immediately obvious.

The ability of graphics systems to present approximate information in an easily assimilated way can also be used in designing the user interface to built-in computer control systems. Consider, for example, the sensor information available to the pilot of an aircraft. Traditionally, this information is displayed on electro-mechanical dials. Glancing at a dial provides enough information to tell the pilot whether action is needed or not. He does not necessarily need to see the exact value registered on the dial - the needle position is enough to tell him that all is well or that some corrective action is required.

The introduction of computer controlled sensor and display systems has meant that it is easier, cheaper and more reliable to display information electronically rather than using an electro mechanical dial. The most common electronic display is a digital display based on liquid crystal technology which shows exact values. The operator must examine and mentally check the information rather than acquire this information from a needle position.

Where a large number of sensor displays are provided, digital displays are confusing and time consuming to check. Rather than use digital displays in such situations, it is better to convert the display output to an analogue form and display this graphically. A dial can be simulated on a display screen by blocking in segments of a circle or, alternatively, an expanding/contracting line whose length is proportional to the value displayed may be used. When such at-a-glance displays are provided, they may be supplemented by more exact digital displays activated at the request of the user.

Colour is another parameter which can be used to improve the readability and immediacy of graphic displays. Again, the use of domestic TV technology means that colour graphics systems are relatively cheap and they offer an opportunity to the software engineer to improve the ergonomics of his output displays.

Consider the previous example where sensor data is displayed using a graphical interface. If colour graphics are available, data from a number of sensors can be displayed on the same screen and distinguished by their colour. Displays may be programmed to change colour if the sensor values fall below or rise above the acceptable range, with the usual conventions of red for danger, green for safety adopted.

Another reason for making use of colour graphics displays is the increasing audio visual sophistication of the population in general due to exposure to high quality television technology. If a user interface whose technical quality is less than that normally broadcast is used, some potential users will consider the associated system to be of low quality and decline to make use of it.

As well as presenting information in a form which is more acceptable to many classes of user, graphical interfaces can have associated input devices which are easier and more convenient to use than a conventional keyboard. Because some computer users, such as managerial staff, are unable to type and unwilling to learn this skill, they have an inbuilt resistance to keyboard controlled terminals. If such users can be provided with an alternative, easier to use input device and a user interface built around that device, they are more likely to make personal use of the computer system.

Examples of such input devices include graphics tablets, light pens, and cursor 'mice'. Using a graphics tablet, the user draws on a metal board with a stylus. His movements are sensed and the lines drawn on the tablet are displayed on the screen of his terminal. A light pen is a device used to touch the display screen. Its position can be detected by the graphics system and appropriate action taken. Light pens are fairly low resolution devices so they are not suitable for drawing on the screen. They are best used for marking the position of an object of interest on the screen.

Cursor 'mice' are also devices for screen marking. They consist simply of a ball which can be moved in the x-y directions. As this ball (mouse) is moved, the screen cursor follows its movement. This type of device is cheap and simple and a more convenient way of cursor movement than the usual terminal function keys. Cursor mice have been used in a high resolution graphics system incorporated in the OfficeTalk system discussed above.

8.5   SPECIAL TERMINAL HARDWARE

For some types of application, it is not desirable to base a user interface design on standard alphanumeric or graphics terminals. The needs of some classes of user are such that they are best accommodated by providing a special purpose terminal specifically designed to support the application. General purpose terminals may either be too generalised and difficult to use or may not provide the facilities required by the computer system.

For example, the interface of an air traffic control system with the traffic controller consists of a display screen presenting information derived from radar inputs and the aircraft themselves. The traffic controller has special function keys pertinent to traffic control such as a key which allows him to lock on to a particular aircraft and follow its flight path.

Some banking systems use special terminals which can read information from a special plastic card presented by the customer making the transaction. These terminals perform some of the functions of a bank teller such as cash dispensing. Similarly, retail organisations might use cash register terminals which can read product codes and act as a cash dispenser and collector.

Banking and retail terminal systems present very little information to the user – they are designed for a very particular function and there is no need for any complex interactions. Other special purpose terminals, such as those used in some word processing systems, have more extensive interactive capabilities and are tailored to a specific application by dedicating special functions to certain keys.

As well as a normal qwerty keyboard, a word processing system may also have a set of function keys. These keys might initiate actions such as the loading of a document into the machine, the printing of a document or document editing. Because the operations allowed to the user are restricted, the problem of designing user commands can be avoided if a function key is provided for each command.

There are two sets of circumstances where it may be appropriate to use special purpose terminals:

(1)   When the terminal and computer costs represent a relatively small part of the overall system costs.

(2)   When the system is intended for use by people who
       are not familiar with computing equipment.

When the computer system acts as a controller for some
larger system such as a power station or
telecommunications network, the computer is intended for
use by technicians familiar with the application but
not, necessarily, with the computer system itself. In
this case, the cost of the terminal system is only a
small part of overall system costs. The extra costs
incurred by using a special terminal rather than an
off-the-shelf device are justified by the increased
usability of the system.

     In banking and retail systems, where special purpose
terminals may also be required, the terminal costs make
up the major part of system expenditure. Such systems
where the terminal users are untrained in and
uninterested in the computer system need a specially
designed terminal to facilitate speedy and safe
transactions. The cost of a such a terminal, tailored
towards the specific needs of an organisation is such
that it can only be justified in those cases where very
large numbers of terminals are to be purchased.

     Most requirements for this type of terminal are
satisfied by purchasing off-the-shelf banking or retail
terminal systems and designing the application to use
these terminals. The user interface design is completely
dependent on the hardware characteristics. The market
for such systems is sufficiently large, when all
possible users are taken into account, that economies
of scale allow terminals to be built and sold at a
realistic price.

     It is the responsibility of the system designer and
software engineer to decide when it is cost-effective to
use special purpose terminals. In the situations
described above, the decision is straightforward -
special terminals are essential. In other situations,
the decision is not so clear cut. The advantages
offered by special hardware must be offset against the
increased cost of such hardware. Furthermore, building
the user interface into the hardware is liable to be
expensive in situations where the system requirements
and facilities change with time. As the system evolves,
the interface built-into the terminal may become
inadequate. Updating that interface may require
complete replacement of the terminal.

An alternative to designing a special purpose terminal for some application is to use an off-the-shelf intelligent terminal with an extended keyboard. Special functions can be provided by programming the terminal so that each key represents a particular function - there is no need for the same key to mean the same thing on every terminal. Removable key overlays may be used to label each key with the function which it represents.

Programmable terminals avoid the problems of interface obsolescence described above - as the system requirements evolve, the terminal can be reprogrammed and the keys relabelled. As hardware costs fall, intelligent terminals will become widely used and their potential for individually tailored user interfaces exploited.

Software management 1: Psychology

Effective software management is important if large programming projects are to be completed on time, to specification and within budget. To be effective, the software manager must understand the technical aspects of programming, and must also understand his staff as individuals and how these individuals interact with each other. This chapter and the following chapter are devoted to issues of software management. This chapter concentrates on fundamentals – how programmers behave as individuals and in groups. The following chapter is devoted to more practical aspects of software management – software cost estimation and control, project team organisations and management tools.

Because software engineering is a cognitive activity, psychology – understanding thought processes – is of vital importance. A better understanding of the psychology of programming helps us to understand the human limits involved and to tailor software projects so that programming staff are not set unrealisable objectives. With such an understanding, the software manager is less likely to form project groups whose members' personalities clash and can gain insights into aspects of individual behavior such as the ability of a programmer to learn new programming languages and techniques.

The material covered in this chapter is separated into 3 sections – the programmer as an individual, the programmer as a group member and the effects of the working environment on programmer performance.

The first section considers aspects of individual programming process. It presents a cognitive model of the programming process and describes some implications of that model such as why gotoless programming is better than programming with gotos and how programming ability is language independent. This section also discusses programmer aptitude tests and concludes that they are of no value.

The second section discusses programming group

behaviour. It describes different personality types and
how they interact and discusses some of the problems
managers can have in keeping control of groups. Group
communications, the implications of group loyalty, the
relationship between group structure and system
structure, and the role of the group leader are covered
here.

The final part of the chapter concerns the effect of
the physical work environment on performance. It
concludes that there is a need to design that
environment to facilitate both individual working and
group interactions.

9.1   THE PROGRAMMER AS AN INDIVIDUAL

Programming is an individual, creative task. It is
comparable with composing music, designing buildings and
writing books. Although a programmer may work as part
of a team, the team is only necessary because the
required software system is so large that it cannot be
produced by one person in a reasonable amount of time.
Within the team, the work is partitioned and each
individual programmer works on his own, creating his
part of the project. An understanding of individual
programmer performance is therefore of importance to the
programming manager.

In this section, aspects of the psychology of the
programmer as an individual are described. A model of
the cognitive processes used in problem solving is
presented and the implications of that model discussed.
This is followed by an examination of the influence of
personality on programming performance and the section
concludes with a discussion of the reliability of
programmer selection techniques.

9.1.1 A cognitive model of programmer behaviour
This section describes a model of the human cognitive
process and the implications of that model to programmer
behaviour. The model was suggested by Greeno (1972) and
is described in some detail in Shneiderman (1980).

The model suggests that human memory structure is
hierarchical. Input from the outside world first enters
a relatively small short-term memory and, from there, it
is either transferred to a 'permanent' long-term memory
or it is forgotten. The long-term memory seems to have
an unlimited capacity. There may also exist a 'working'
memory which is more permanent than short-term memory

but considerably less permanent than long-term memory.

When problems are posed, new information from short-term memory is integrated with existing, relevant information from long-term memory in a working memory. The result of this integration forms the basis for the problem solution and may be stored in long-term memory for future use. A diagram of this hierarchy, is shown in Fig 9.1.

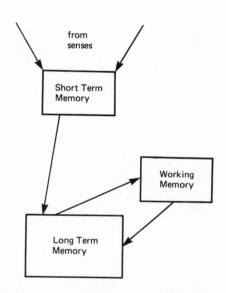

Fig. 9.1   Memory organisation

The knowledge acquired by a programmer and stored in long-term memory can be classified into 2 distinct types:

(1)   Semantic knowledge – the knowledge of concepts such as the operation of an assignment statement, the notion of a linked list and how a hash search technique operates. This knowledge is acquired through experience and learning and is retained in a representation independent fashion. The manner in which the concept was presented to the programmer does not appear to affect the way in which this knowledge is stored.

(2)   Syntactic knowledge – the knowledge of details of a representation such as how to write a procedure declaration in Pascal, what standard functions are available in a programming language, whether an

assignment is written using an '=' or a ':=' sign,
etc. Because this knowledge is detailed and normally arbitrary, it is more likely to be forgotten than semantic knowledge.

Semantic knowledge is acquired by experience and through
active learning where new information is consciously
integrated with existing semantic structures. Syntactic
knowledge, on the other hand, seems to be acquired
mechanically and new syntactic knowledge is not
necessarily integrated with existing knowledge. In
fact, new syntactic knowledge may interfere with
existing knowledge, as it is arbitrarily added to that
knowledge rather than integrated with it.

The different acquisition modes for syntactic and
semantic knowledge explains the typical situation which
arises when an experienced programmer learns a new
programming language. He, normally, has no difficulty
with the language concepts - these are embodied as
semantic knowledge. The language syntax, however, tends
to get mixed-up with the syntax of familiar languages.
For example, the FORTRAN programmer learning Pascal
might write the assignment operator as '=' rather than
':='.

Cognitive processes are constrained by the size of
the short-term memory. In a classic paper, Miller (1957)
found that the short-term memory can store about seven
quanta of information. A quantum of information is not
a fixed number of bits - it may be a telephone number,
the function of a procedure or a street name. Miller
also describes the process of 'chunking' where
information quanta are collected together into chunks.
These chunks can themselves be collected into larger
chunks etc. This chunking process is the basis of our
ability to form abstractions.

Shneiderman conjectures that this chunking process is
used in understanding programs. The program reader
abstracts the information in the program into chunks and
these chunks are built into an internal semantic
structure representing the program. Programs are not
understood on a statement by statement basis. Once the
internal semantic structure representing the program has
been established, this knowledge is not readily
forgotten. Furthermore, the structure can readily be
represented in different notations. Hence, it is
usually straightforward to translate an understood
program from one programming language to another.

9.1.2 Practical implications of the model

This model of how we understand programs may be used to explain a number of aspects of programming practice. For example, it explains why a structured program should be easier to understand; why programmer ability is language independent; and what is the best way to learn a new programming language.

Structured programming should make a program easier to understand because it allows the chunking process to be more effective. If a program can be read top-to-bottom, the abstractions involved in forming chunks can be made sequentially, without reference to other parts of the program. The short-term memory can be devoted to a single section of code rather than having to maintain information about several sections connected by arbitrary goto statements.

For the same reasons, if a programmer actively endeavours to program without the use of goto statements, he is less likely to make programming errors. His short-term memory can be devoted to information relevant to the program section being coded. There is no need to retrieve information from working memory about other parts of the program which interfere with that section.

The process of devising and writing a program is, basically, a problem solving situation. The problem must first be understood, a general solution strategy worked out and, finally, this strategy translated into specific actions. The first stage involves the problem statement entering working memory from short-term memory. It is integrated with existing knowledge from long-term memory and analysed. The second stage uses this analysis to work out an overall solution. A top down development process, as described in chapter 3, is used to develop that solution.

The solution development involves building an internal semantic model of the problem and a corresponding model of the solution. Once this model is built, it may be represented in any appropriate syntactic notation. An experienced programmer who understands a number of programming languages will have approximately the same degree of difficulty in representing that solution, irrespective of which language is actually used. Programming ability is the ability to formulate correct solutions and is language independent.

However, the representation is more likely to be free

of errors if the syntactic facilities of the notation match the lowest level semantic structures which are formulated. Programs written in languages such as Pascal should contain fewer errors than those written in FORTRAN or assembly code. Languages such as Pascal are more expressive than FORTRAN and offer higher level constructs. Consequently, if the final representation is to be in Pascal, the internal semantics need not be developed to such a level of detail as would be required if the program is represented in FORTRAN. Because such a detailed model is not required, more of that model can be retained in short-term memory and programmer errors caused by unexpected interaction of parts of the model are less likely to occur.

Because programming ability is language independent and programming language knowledge is held in a representation independent way, it is relatively easy for programmers who are familiar with one programming language to learn a new language. All that must be learnt is a new syntax — the concepts are already understood.

The managerial implications of this are twofold. Firstly, the common practice of hiring programmers on the basis of programming language knowledge is not justified. Programming ability and programming language knowledge are quite different and knowledge of or even virtuosity with a programming language is no measure of programming ability.

Secondly, when organising programmer education, experienced programmers and inexperienced programmers have quite different requirements. Experienced programmers require to know the syntax of a language whereas inexperienced programmers need to be taught the concepts — how an assignment statement works, the notion of a procedure and so on. It is unlikely that a training course can provide these differing requirements at the same time. Consequently, it is probably cost-effective to provide training courses tailored for inexperienced programmers and to allow experienced programmers to learn a new language using self teaching methods.

9.1.3 Programming and personality

Intuitively, it seems likely that programmer performance is influenced by personality factors. An individual's personality is made up of a number of traits and the presence of one or more particular traits may make that person more or less suited to programming work.

There has been little psychological research carried out to identify those personality traits which might influence programming ability. Using a personality test devised for job aptitude, Perry and Cannon (1966) have produced a programmer profile by testing existing programmers. If new recruits are tested and their profiles matched with this profile, it may be possible to gauge their suitability for programming.

However, as Weinberg (1971) points out, this is not necessarily the case. Different personalities may be suited to different aspects of programming such as systems design, testing etc. Should the tests attempt to identify a 'programming personality' or should they be more precise and identify program design personalities, program testing personalities, and so on?

The ideal personality profile was obtained by testing programmers already in the profession but without reference to their ability. There is no guarantee that the sample of the programming profession chosen is representative of the most competent programmers. Finally, an intelligent programmer filling in personality tests might cheat. Instead of presenting their true personality to the tester, they might present the personality which they think the tester wants. This is a natural human reaction to any kind of assessment and no more culpable than an individual trying to present a favourable picture of himself at a job interview.

Because of the lack of concrete evidence, any attempt to assess the influence of distinct personality traits on programmer performance is conjectural. However, it seems likely that some personality traits play a more important role than others. The ability to withstand stress is one example. The nature of software projects is such that the schedule for the project is imposed on the programmer. Work must be completed by a particular date. As that date approaches, the stress imposed on the programmer becomes greater and his performance may suffer.

Another personality trait which seems likely to be important is adaptive ability. The rate of change of both hardware and software technology is extremely rapid and programmers must be able to adapt to these changes. Without adaptive ability, individuals tend to continue with obsolete techniques to the detriment of overall performance.

Although individual personality traits may be important, there is no evidence to suggest that any one type of personality, as a whole, makes an individual suited or unsuited to programming. Personality factors cannot be ignored however as they are probably most important at the programming team level, when individuals interact. This is discussed later in this chapter.

9.1.4 Programmer selection techniques

Although a personality profile has been devised for programmers it is not widely used to assess the suitability of individuals for programming. Rather, a programming aptitude test is used by many organisations in their selection of programming staff. This section examines aptitude tests and considers their suitability for assessing programming ability.

There have been a variety of different aptitude tests devised. Most of these have derived from a test developed by IBM and made up of a number of components. These include:

(1)   Arithmetic reasoning - the examinee must do sums.

(2)   Geometric relationships - the examinee must choose the next related figure in a series or identify the relationship between figures.

(3)   Number series - the examinee must derive the next number in a series.

(4)   Letter series - the examinee must derive the next letter in a series.

These tests are normally completed in a relatively short time - typically 20 to 30 minutes. Promoters of the tests suggest that high test scores correlate with programming ability.

It has already been suggested that the cognitive process of developing a program involves building an internal semantic model of the problem and its solution. Programming ability is directly related to the ability to construct such a model. Building this model may involve utilising existing knowledge and, except for trivial problems, is an iterative process. A solution if formulated, evaluated and, on the basis of that evaluation, refined so that the final solution is actually approached in a step-wise fashion.

In order to be successful programmer aptitude tests ought to measure the ability of an individual to build internal semantic models. Although definitive evidence does not exist on this point, it is intuitively unlikely that they do so. The reasons for this are:

(1)   The time available for aptitude tests is in no way related to the time available for even the simplest programming task. Aptitude test participants are placed under stress by this time limit and only those able to withstand high levels of stress are likely to succeed in these tests. Although the ability to withstand stress is important for programmers, aptitude tests impose a completely unrealistic stress level.

(2)   The arithmetic reasoning component of aptitude tests simply measures an individual's facility for fast mental arithmetic. Problem solving only occasionally involves arithmetic and then only in a minor role. This part of the aptitude test therefore measures an ability which is quite irrelevant.

(3)   Aptitude tests offer no facilities for refining a solution or presenting reasons explaining how a particular answer was derived. It is often the case that the pattern matching parts of the test are ambiguous with several possible answers to a question. Only one answer is considered 'correct' however, that first thought of by the devisers of the test.

In short, the only aptitude which aptitude tests reliably measure is the aptitude of an individual for aptitude tests. Furthermore, the more often an individual attempts aptitude tests, the better his scores. An individual who is first assessed by aptitude tests as having little programming ability can become an ideal candidate simply by practising aptitude tests!

In view of the model of the programming process described above and our lack of knowledge concerning the personality factors affecting programming ability, it is presently impossible to devise a simple test of programming ability. The psychology of computer programming is not sufficiently understood to allow important factors to be identified and assessed.

9.2   PROGRAMMERS IN GROUPS

The popular image of a programmer is of a lone individual working far into the night, poring over reams of paper covered with arcane symbols. This image of programming as a profession for lone workers is also held by programmers themselves. In a survey by Cougar and Zawacki (1978), it was discovered that data processing professional staff feel that they have a negligible need to work with other individuals.

Whilst there are many programming staff working on their own, the majority of staff working on large projects work in teams which vary in size from 2 to several hundred people. In a study undertaken by IBM (McCabe, 1978), it was discovered that 50% of a typical programmers time is spent interacting with other team members, 30% working alone and 20% of his time was spent non-productively in activities such as travel. Clearly, the interaction between team members plays an important role in overall performance.

The issues covered here are:

(1)   Personality interactions.

(2)   The role of the group leader.

(3)   Egoless programming.

(4)   The influence of group structure on system structure.

Particular programming group organisations such as chief programmer teams are covered in the following chapter.

9.2.1 Personalities in groups
The formation of a software engineering group brings together individuals, each with their own distinct personality. These personalities sometimes work extremely well together and sometimes clash so dramatically that little or no productive work is possible. This section attempts to describe why personality clashes sometimes occur and why some groups work together very successfully.

Very roughly, individuals in a work situation can be classified into 3 types:

(1)   Task-oriented - the individual is motivated by the work itself.

(2)   Interaction-oriented - the individual is motivated by the presence and actions of co-workers.

(3)   Self-oriented - the individual is motivated by a desire for personal success.

Obviously these classes are not rigid and each individual's motivation is made up of elements of each class. Normally, however, one type of motivation is dominant.

In an experiment by Bass and Dunteman (1963), task-oriented persons described themselves as being self sufficient, resourceful, aloof, introverted, aggressive, competitive and independent. Interaction oriented individuals considered themselves to be unaggressive, with low needs for autonomy and achievement, considerate and helpful. They preferred to work in a group rather than alone. Self-oriented individuals described themselves as disagreeable, dogmatic, aggressive, competitive, introvertive and jealous. They preferred to work alone. In the same experiment, it was found that males tended to be task-oriented whereas females were more likely to be interaction-oriented. Whether this is due to natural tendencies or to role stereotyping is not clear.

When individuals worked in groups composed entirely of members belonging to the same personality class, only that group made up of interaction-oriented persons was successful. Task-oriented and self oriented group members felt negatively about their groups - there was, perhaps, an oversupply of leaders. The difficulties encountered when individuals of the same personality class worked together suggest that the most successful groups are made up of individuals from each class with the group leader task-oriented.

With reference to programming groups, Weinberg (1971) suggests that, in practice, two complementary individuals tend to emerge in different roles - a task specialist and an interaction specialist. The task specialist sets, allocates and coordinates the work of the group whereas the interaction specialist sorts out conflicts among group members and between group goals and individual goals.

Observation suggests that the majority of those involved in computer programming work are task-oriented individuals, motivated primarily by their work. This implies that programming groups are likely to be made up of individuals each of whom will have his own idea on how the same project should be undertaken. This is borne out by frequently reported problems of interface standards not being adhered to, systems being redesigned as they are coded, unnecessary system embellishments, etc.

The implication of this for software management is that careful attention must be paid to group composition. Selecting individuals who complement each other in terms of personality may produce a better working group than a group selected on the basis of programming ability. If a selection on the basis of complementary personalities is impossible – a likely situation bearing in mind most programmers are task-oriented – the tendency of each group member to go his own way means that strict managerial control is necessary. Individual goals should not be allowed to transcend group goals.

This managerial control is best accomplished by using formal specifications at all stages of the software production process. Deviation from specification can then be readily detected and corrected. Regular project reviews can ensure that standards are adhered to and that staff conform to the overall objectives of the project.

This conformity is more likely to be achieved if all the members of a project group take an active part in each stage of the project. Individual initiative is most likely when one group member is instructed to carry out a task without being aware of the part that task plays in the project as a whole.

Say a program design is presented to an individual for coding. That individual may see how that design can be improved but, without understanding how that design was arrived at, these improvements could have serious implications. If the programmer is involved in the design right from the start, the individual is more likely to identify with that design and to strive to maintain rather than modify it.

Clearly, the involvement of all group members at each stage of the project is impossible if the group is

large.   This   implies   that,   for   psychological   reasons
alone,   large   groups   are   less   likely   to   be   successful
than   small   groups.   This   is   borne   out   by   a   number   of
experiences   of   project   failure   and   cost   overrun   where
large   programming   groups   were   used.

9.2.2 The role of the group leader

The   group   leader   plays   a   vital   role   in   group   functioning
and   his   performance   frequently   governs   the   success   or
otherwise   of   a   software   project.   While   most   programming
groups   have   a   titular   leader   appointed   by   higher
management,   that   individual   may   not   be   the   real   leader
of   the   group   as   far   as   the   technical   work   of   the   project
is   concerned.   Some   other   more   technically   capable
individual   may   adopt   this   role   with   the   official   leader
being   responsible   for   administrative   tasks.   This   is   not
necessarily   a   bad   organisation   -   technical   competence
and   administrative   competence   and   not   necessarily
synonomous   and   the   roles   of   technical   leader   and
administrative   leader   may   be   complementary.

The   actual   leader   in   a   programming   group   is   that
group   member   who   has   most   influence   on   other   group
members.   The   leadership   may   change   at   different   stages
of   a   project.   Because   of   expertise   or   experience   at   a
particular   stage,   the   best   qualified   group   member   may
command   respect   and   take   over   leadership   for   that   stage.

For   this   reason,   and   because   of   the   similar
motivations   of   each   member   of   the   programming   group,   the
traditional   role   of   a   leader   responsible   for   directing,
disciplining   and   rewarding   in   an   autocratic   fashion   is
not   one   which   is   likely   to   be   successful   with
programming   groups.   In   fact,   a   classic   experiment   by
Lewin   et   al.,   (1939)   suggests   that   the   traditional
leader's   role   as   an   autocrat   is   only   suited   to   a   few
situations,   such   as   military   organisations.

Their   study   showed   that   when   a   democratic   style   of
leadership   is   adopted,   group   productivity   is   higher,
individual   members   work   better   without   supervision   and
are   more   satisfied   with   their   work.   This   confirms   the
intuitive   notion   that   participation   of   group   members   at
all   stages   of   a   project   is   likely   to   result   in   members
adopting   group   goals   and   cooperating   rather   than
competing.

The   leader   of   a   programming   group   will,   in   most
cases,   emerge   as   the   individual   who   is   most   technically
competent   at   each   stage   of   the   project.   If   this   is   not
recognised   by   higher   management   and   an   unwanted   leader

is imposed on the group, this is likely to introduce tensions into the group. The members will certainly not respect the leader and may actively attempt to thwart his leadership.

The implication of this for management is that competent individuals should not be promoted out of programming. It is necessary to provide an alternative career structure for technically able individuals so that they may be properly rewarded yet remain involved in programming. Such a structure has been created by IBM in its use of chief programmer teams, described in the following chapter.

9.2.3 Group loyalties

Being a member of a well led group tends to induce individual loyalty to that group. Each group member identifies with group goals and with other group members. He attempts to protect the group, as an entity, from outside interference. Group loyalty implies that there is a coherence in decision making and universal acceptance of decisions once they have been made.

In general, this is a good thing. Group loyalty means that individuals think of the group as more important than the individual members. If a strong group feeling exists, membership changes can be accommodated. The group can adapt to changed circumstances, such as a drastic change in software requirements, by providing mutual support and help.

There are, nevertheless, two important disadvantages of group loyalty which are particularly obvious when the group is cohesive and tightly knit. The disadvantages are the resistance of group members to a change in leadership if there is a need to introduce a new group leader and a loss of overall critical faculties because group loyalty overrides all other considerations.

If the leader of a tightly knit group has to be replaced and the new leader is not already a group member, the group members tend to band together against the new leader irrespective of whether he is competent or not. The new leader will not have the same feelings of group loyalty as the rest of the group and may attempt to change the overall goals of the group. These changes are likely to be met with resistance from existing group members with a consequent decrease in overall productivity. The only practical way of avoiding this situation is, whenever possible, to appoint a new leader from within the group itself.

Another consequence of group loyalty has been termed 'groupthink' by Janis (1972). Groupthink is the state where the critical faculties of the group members are eroded by group loyalties. Consideration of alternatives is replaced by loyalty to group norms and decisions. The consequence of this is that any proposal favoured by the majority of the group tends to be adopted without proper consideration of alternative proposals. Janis suggests that groupthink is most prevalent under conditions of stress. For a programming group, this may be as deadlines and delivery dates approach when it is particularly important to make reasoned decisions.

Software management should make active efforts to avoid groupthink. This may involve formal sessions where group members are encouraged to criticise decisions and the introduction of outside experts who can offer comments on the group's decisions. Personnel policies can also be used to avoid groupthink. Some individuals are naturally argumentative, questioning, and disrespectful of the status quo. Such people are positive assets as they act as devil's advocate, constantly questioning group decisions.

9.2.4 Group communications
The time which a group member spends on communications is non-productive time. When an individual is communicating, he is not programming. In terms of time alone, therefore, it is desirable to minimise intra group communications.

A further incentive for minimising communications is that the greater the number of separate communications a group member is involved in, the more difficult these communications are to manage. Consequently, when large numbers of interpersonal communications become the norm, errors are more likely to occur.

Effective communication amongst the members of a programming group is essential if that group is to work efficiently. A number of factors affect the effectiveness of intra-group communications:

(1)   The size of the group.

(2)   The structure of the group.

(3)   The status and personalities of group members.

(4)   The physical work environment of the group.

This latter factor will be covered later in this chapter. This section concentrates on the first three factors governing communication effectiveness.

As the size of a programming group increases linearly, the number of potential communication links between individual members increases factorially. For example, if there are 2 members A and B, there are 2 links AB and BA. If there are 3 members A, B, and C, there are 6 links - AB, AC, BA, BC, CA, and CB. Therefore, even in relatively small groups there are a large number of potential communication channels.

There are 2 ways of minimising the number of necessary intra-group communications:

(1)   The group can be structured in such a way that all communications pass through some central coordinator.

(2)   The group size can be kept to a minimum and all communication channels used.

Research by Leavitt (1951) and Shaw (1964, 1971) suggests that the second alternative is the more effective. In their experiments, the group members preferred to work in loosely - rather than rigidly - structured groups and, they also implied, that the problem solving performance of loosely structured groups is superior to that of groups which have a centralised structure. On the other hand, groups where the communication passed through a centralised coordinator seem to be superior for relatively simple tasks such as the collection and dissemination of information.

Further evidence of the superiority of small, loosely structured groups has been provided by Porter and Lawler (1965). They found that the size of an organisation correlates negatively with job satisfaction and productivity. It correlates positively with absenteeism and staff turnover. Although their work related to fairly large organisations, their results probably apply to programming groups.

As well as size and structure, the effectiveness of group communications is also influenced by the status, personalities and sexes of group members. Communications between group members of higher and lower status tend to be dominated by higher to lower communications. The lower status member is inhibited in opening communications because of his status. The effect of status on communications can be minimised by active efforts of the higher status individual to encourage uninhibited communication by lower status members.

The effectiveness of group communication and hence group efficiency can be influenced by personality clashes between group members. These personality clashes may be due to all members being task-oriented (too many leaders) as discussed previously or may be the result of personal likes, dislikes and prejudices. Such clashes are difficult for management to resolve - people cannot be coerced into liking each other. If group effectiveness is hampered by personality clashes, the best solution is to reorganise the programming group, transferring some members elsewhere.

The sexual composition of groups also affects intra-group communication. The importance of interaction-oriented individuals has already been discussed and, as women tend to be more interaction-oriented than men, it seems likely that mixed sex groups will communicate more effectively than single sex groups. Furthermore, a study by Marshall and Heslin (1976) has shown that both men and women prefer to work in mixed sex groups.

9.2.5 Group structure and system structure

It is an observable fact that the structure of a programming system tends to reflect the structure of the group producing that system. For example, if a 3 person group is working on a compiler, the result is likely to be a three pass system, with each pass written by one member of the group. On the other hand, if the group structure is hierarchical, with a dominant leader and subordinates, the resulting system is likely to be hierarchical with the leader coding the 'main program' which calls subroutines coded by his subordinates.

This tendency for systems to reflect the structure of their programming groups, should be recognised by software management and taken into account when the system structure is designed. Ideally, the system is designed using the most appropriate structure and a project group assembled whose structure matches the project structure.

In practice, this is rarely possible. The software manager must use existing staff who are available when the project is to start and only occasionally has the luxury of putting together a new team specifically for each project. Furthermore, the ideal system structure may not be suitable for any type of team structure. If this is the case, the team tends to modify the ideal structure into a suitable form for team implementation, thus negating some of the efforts of the system designer.

This phenomenon appears to be inevitable and attempts to coerce a group into adopting an unnatural working technique are unlikely to succeed. To minimise these clashes between system structure and group structure, the entire programming group should be involved at the system design stage. An appropriate system structure can then be agreed by group members. This structure can take the group structure into account and also the strengths and weaknesses of individual group members. Naturally this is only possible if small programming groups are used.

9.2.6 Egoless programming

The notion of egoless programming was introduced by Weinberg (1971) in his book 'The Psychology of Computer Programming'. Egoless programming is a style of project group working which considers programs to be the common property and responsibility of the entire programming group irrespective of which individual group member was responsible for their production.

If an individual identifies a program as 'his' or 'hers' that individual is loath to accept that the program may contain errors. The validity of this statement is based on the theory of cognitive dissonance, put forward by Festinger (1957).

This theory argues that individuals who hold a set of beliefs or have made a particular decision avoid anything which contradicts those beliefs or that decision. For example, supporters of a political party will normally only attend political speeches made by a member of the same party, in spite of the fact that the material presented in the speech is probably familiar.

On the same basis, the programmer who considers himself personally responsible for a program tends to defend that program against criticism, even if it has obvious shortcomings. The programmer's ego is tied up with the program itself. If, however, the programmer does not consider his work to be a personal possession but instead common group property, he is more likely to offer his program for inspection by other group members and to accept their criticisms of it.

The most important distinguishing feature of egoless programming is that it considers programming errors to be normal and expected and no individual blame is ever associated with these errors. It is not a method of programmer assessment or program quality control. Rather, it is a collective programming effort where the individual who actually coded the program has the same responsibility as all others in the group and is usually undertaken on an informal basis.

The technique of code inspection, described in chapter 6, is a formalisation of egoless programming. However, it differs from egoless programming in that some of the code inspectors are taken from outside the programming group itself.

As well as improving the quality of programs submitted for inspection, the practice of egoless programming also improves intra-group communications. It effectively draws the members of a programming group together and encourages uninhibited communications without regard to status, experience, or sex. Individual members cannot go off and 'do their own thing' but must actively cooperate with other group members throughout the course of the project.

9.3 PROGRAMMER PERFORMANCE AND PHYSICAL ENVIRONMENT

The physical work environment has unquantifiable but extremely important effects on the performance of those working in that environment. Individual behaviour is affected by room size, furniture, temperature, humidity, brightness and quality of light, noise and the degree of privacy available. Group behaviour is affected by factors such as architectural organisation and by available telecommunication facilities.

There has been relatively little attention paid to tailoring the design of buildings specifically for programming. Most programming work takes place in environments designed for other functions, principally business offices. An exception to this is an IBM programming laboratory described by McCue (1978).

The design of this laboratory was carried out in conjunction with the programmers who would use the facilities. The most important environmental factors identified in that design study were:

(1)   Privacy - each programmer requires an area where
       he can concentrate and work without interruption.

(2)   Outside awareness - people prefer to work in na-
       tural light and with a view of the outside en-
       vironment.

(3)   Personalisation - individuals adopt different
       working practices and have different opinions on
       decor. The ability to rearrange the workplace to
       suit working practices and to personalise that en-
       vironment is important.

Obviously, it is not always possible to custom design
buildings specifically for programming. Nevertheless,
software management should recognise the importance of
the working environment to the individual and provide a
pleasant and congenial workplace.

Group effectiveness and communications are also
affected by the physical environment. Programming
groups require areas where all members of the group can
get together and discuss their project, both formally
and informally. Individual privacy requirements and
group communication requirements seem to be exclusive
objectives but the resolution of this problem, described
by McCue, is to group individual offices round larger
central rooms which can be used for group meetings and
discussions.

Intra-group communication is inherently complex and
it is very important that provision for face to face
group meetings be available. These meeting rooms must
be able to accommodate the whole group in privacy - it
is unreasonable to expect group meetings to take place
in the corner of some open plan office.

As well as provision for face to face meetings,
adequate telephone communications are necessary and, if
possible, an electronic mail system should be made
available. Using such a system, users can communicate
via the computer. Indeed, if powerful telecommunication
facilities such as teleconferencing and electronic mail
are available, they may substitute for a good deal of
face to face communication. An example of a successful
project carried out, almost entirely, using
telecommunications was the design of the programming
language Euclid (Lampson et al., 1977).

Effective electronic mail relies on each group member

having ready access to a computer terminal. Decreasing terminal and interactive system costs mean that more and more programmers have their own office terminal and common terminal facilities are no longer required. This has both advantages and disadvantages. The advantages are that a programmer can work at his terminal in conditions of reasonable privacy and that there is no need to devote building space to terminal rooms. However, a disadvantage of eliminating the terminal room is that it reduces the number of informal communication facilities for group members. Weinberg suggests that this informal communication is extremely important and not readily replaceable by formal techniques. Therefore, some common facilities, such as a coffee room, should be provided so that staff may meet for informal discussion and problem solving sessions.

Software management 2: Practice

It is only since the failure of several large projects such as operating system development projects that the peculiar problems involved in software management have come to light. These projects did not fail because the project managers or programmers working on the project were incompetent. Indeed, the nature of these large projects was such that they attracted people of above average ability. The fault lay in the management techniques which were used. As these were the first really large programming projects, management techniques derived from hardware development projects were used and these proved to be inadequate. The delivered software was late, unreliable, cost several times the original estimates and often exhibited poor performance characteristics (Brooks, 1975).

As discussed in the introduction, the experience gained from these project failures was directly responsible for the emergence of software engineering as a discipline. Improved methodologies for specification, design, implementation and validation of software have been developed and some progress has been made in understanding the difficulties in software management. However, much less progress has been made in this than in design and implementation methodologies and it is still not possible to produce a set of general guidelines on how to manage software production.

The software manager is responsible for planning project development and overseeing the work, ensuring that it is carried out to the required standards, on time and within budget. Whilst good management cannot guarantee project success, bad management or inadequate management techniques will almost certainly result in software which is delivered late, exceeds cost estimates and which may be expensive to maintain.

Traditional management structure is hierarchical with individuals at each level in the hierarchy reporting to the level above. Typically, a manager might be responsible for 12-25 subordinates. This hierarchical structure is retained to some extent in software management except that each software manager should only handle about 6 direct subordinates because of the complexity of the software projects under his control.

In a large organisation undertaking a number of simultaneous software development projects, the software management structure might be as shown in Fig 10.1.

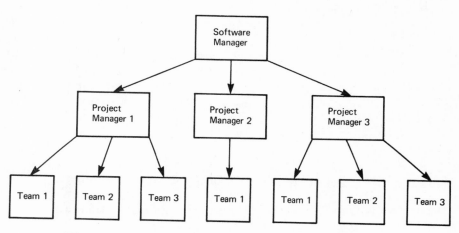

Fig. 10.1   Software management structure

The software department manager is responsible for the running of that part of the organisation devoted to software production. He has little direct contact with the process of software development except, perhaps, when problems arise. The project manager is involved with a particular project and is responsible for 1 to 6 programming teams each working on a particular part of the project. These teams may themselves be organised in the classical hierarchical fashion with a team leader making decisions which are carried out by his subordinates. However, later in this chapter, alternative team organisations will be described which have proved more successful than teams organised in a classical manner.

The material covered in this chapter is relevant to both the project manager and programming team leader who must plan, estimate and control a particular project. The chapter includes sections on project planning, team organisation, programmer productivity and software cost estimation and the final part of the chapter suggests software tools which might be used to aid project management.

10.1   PROGRAMMER PRODUCTIVITY

The productivity of a programmer is a measure of the amount of programming or associated work which can be completed in a given time. In this section, factors which affect programmer productivity are described and the problems of establishing a unit of productivity discussed.

The measurement of programmer productivity is important for two reasons. Firstly, without some estimate of productivity, project scheduling is impossible - productivity measurement provides data which allows estimates to be made. Secondly, some of the advantages accrued from the use of new programming methodologies and management techniques can only be demonstrated by showing that their use results in improved productivity over the whole of the software life cycle.

A number of different units have been devised to measure programmer productivity. These include:

(1)   Lines of code written per programmer month.

(2)   Object instructions produced per programmer month.

(3)   Pages of documentation written per programmer month.

(4)   Test cases written and executed per programmer month.

The most commonly used measure is lines of code per programmer month. This is normally computed by taking the total number of lines of source code which are delivered and dividing that number by the total time in programmer months required to complete the project. This time includes analysis and design time, coding time, testing time and documentation time.

As Jones (1978) points out, this measure of productivity is subject to a number of problems. The most fundamental of these is determining exactly what is meant by a line of code. Programs are made up of declarations, executable statements, and commentary and may also include macro instructions which expand to several lines of code. Different counting techniques adopt different definitions of a line of code. Some consider executable statements only, some executable statements and data declarations, and some each distinct non-blank line in the program irrespective of what is on that line.   Because of these different conventions, published measures of programmer productivity cannot readily be compared.

Another problem which arises when languages such as Pascal are used is how source lines containing more than a single statement should be treated.   If such lines are treated as a single line, this implies that higher productivity can apparently be achieved by the judicious use of newlines!

There is no evidence that any one line counting technique is superior and, as long as the same technique is used consistently, comparisons can be drawn. However, a more serious problem which results from using lines of code/month as a measure of productivity is the apparent productivity advantages which it indicates when assembly code is used.

This paradox results from the fact that all tasks associated with the programming process (design, documentation, testing etc.) are subsumed under the coding task in spite of the fact that the coding time normally represents much less than half the time needed to complete a project. The measure places undue emphasis on coding and considers other stages of the life cycle less important.

For example, consider a system which might be coded in 5000 lines of assembly code or 1500 lines of high level language code. Analysis, design and documentation time are language independent and might take a total of 10 weeks.   Coding time for machine code might be 8 weeks with an associated testing time of 10 weeks.   For the high level language, coding time might be 4 weeks and testing time 6 weeks. In total therefore, 7 months (28 weeks) are required to produce 5000 lines of assembler and 5 months (20 weeks) to complete 1500 lines of high level language code.   The assembler programmer has a productivity of 714 lines/month and the high level language programmer less than half of this – 300 lines/month. Because of this paradox, it is necessary to establish productivity standards for each programming language used and to avoid productivity comparisons between projects coded in different languages.

To avoid some of the problems associated with using lines of code per month as a productivity measure, an alternative is to use the number of object instructions generated per programmer month.   Although this unit is more objective than lines of code - there is no difficulty in defining what is meant by an object instruction - there are also disadvantages in using this measure of productivity. The problem also occurs, to a lesser extent, when programs in different high level languages are compared.

Firstly, it is difficult to estimate the source code/object code expansion ratio with most compilers. This means that object code/month is not useful for productivity estimation before code is actually produced. Secondly, the amount of object code generated by a compiler is very dependent on high level language programming style. A programmer who takes more care over coding and produces tight code is apparently less productive than a programmer who codes in such a way that large object programs are generated.

Other measurements, which have been used, such as pages of documentation/programmer month also suffer from disadvantages. If productivity is measured simply by volume of documentation produced, this mitigates against the documenter who takes time to express himself clearly and concisely.

The problem with all productivity units expressed in volume/time is that they take no account of the quality of the finished system. They imply that more always means better and take no account of the fact that apparently higher raw code productivity may ultimately involve increased system maintenance costs. It is very difficult to measure productivity over the whole of the system life cycle so productivity over the software development stage is measured. If poor quality software is produced quickly, the programmers may appear to be more productive than those programmers who produce reliable and easy to maintain systems. There is a need for a productivity measure which considers software quality as well as the size of the finished system.

10.1.1 Factors affecting programmer productivity

Although the present units for measuring programmer productivity are imperfect, let us assume that productivity can be roughly measured and examine what factors influence productivity.

A study by Sackman et al. (1968) showed that individual productivity differences can be very large - the best programmers may be 10 times more productive than the worst. This aptitude factor is likely to be dominant in individual productivity comparisons.

Accordingly, the factors discussed below are only relevant to programming teams which are made up of programmers who have a range of abilities.

Walston and Felix (1977) carried out a productivity survey to identify productivity improvements which result from using methodologies such as top down development, structured programming, etc. They collected data from over 60 projects ranging from small commercial DP programs to large complex process control systems. They selected 68 variables for analysis and identified 29 of these as correlating significantly with productivity. These variables included characteristics of the system being developed, the experience of the developers, hardware constraints, the use of new system development technology, program design constraints and the quantity of documentation required.

The most important single factor affecting productivity was the complexity of the customer interface. Projects with a low complexity interface showed a productivity of 500 lines/programmer month whereas high complexity interfaces were produced at 124 lines/programmer month.

The other most significant factors were found to be the extent of user participation in requirements definition and the overall experience of the programming team. Where the user did not participate in requirements definition, productivity was measure at 491 lines/programmer month but where there was significant user participation this dropped to 205 lines/month. Teams with a good deal of experience produced at a rate of 410 lines/programmer month whereas inexperienced teams produced at 132 lines/month.

The effects on productivity of customer interface complexity and team experience are what might be intuitively expected although the study by Walston and Felix is useful for quantifying the effects. It might also be expected that if the user had little to do with requirements definition, productivity would be higher although, in such cases, there must be some dubiety that the finished product is exactly what is required by the user.

Design and programming methodologies such as structured programming, design and code reviews and top down development had a positive influence on productivity although this was not as great as the factors previously discussed. However, productivity improvements resulting from the use of these techniques must be seen as a bonus as their principal function is to improve the reliability and maintainability of software.

Another factor which obviously affects productivity is the amount of time that a software engineer actually spends working on software development. Ignoring holidays and leave, each member of a software development team spends time training, attending meetings and dealing with administrative tasks. If a project involves new techniques, training will be required, if the project involves more than one geographical location, travel time between locations is involved and the larger the programming group, the more time must be spent communicating.

Because of the difficulties in establishing a unit of productivity measurement and because of the variety of factors which influence productivity, it is very difficult to give a figure which can be taken as the average productivity of a programmer. For large, complex real-time systems, productivity may be as low as 30 lines/programmer month whereas for straightforward business application systems which are well understood, it may be as high as 600 lines/month. Effective estimation, within an organisation, can only be carried out using historical data derived from previous projects using the same programming language and carried out to the same quality standards. Without such data, productivity estimation is simply guesswork.

10.2 PROGRAMMING TEAM ORGANISATIONS

It is now generally accepted that software projects cannot be tackled successfully by large homogeneous teams of software engineers. Large teams mean that the time spent in communication amongst team members is greater than the time spent programming. Furthermore, it is usually impossible to partition a software system into a large number of independent units with the result that, if a large programming team is used, each member is responsible for a program unit whose interface with the rest of the system is complex. Consequently, the probability of interface error is high and software testing is difficult and time consuming.

Programming team sizes should be relatively small - between 2 and 8 members. When small teams are used, communication problems are minimised - the whole team can get round a table for a meeting. However, if the

magnitude of a project is such that it cannot be tackled
by a single team in the time allowed, multiple teams
must be used. They should work independently with each
team tackling a large part of the project in an
autonomous way. The overall system design should be
such that the interface between the parts of the project
produced by the independent teams is well defined and as
simple as possible.

As well as minimising communication problems, small
programming teams have a number of other benefits.
These include:

(1)   A team quality standard can be developed. Because
      this is arrived at by consensus, it is more likely
      to be observed than arbitrary standards imposed on
      the team.

(2)   Team members work closely together and can learn
      from each other. Inhibitions caused by ignorance
      are minimised as mutual learning is encouraged.

(3)   Egoless programming can be practiced. Programs are
      regarded as team property rather than personal
      property.

(4)   Team members can get to know each other's work so
      that continuity can be maintained should a team
      member leave.

It is usual for small programming teams to be organised
in an informal way. Although a titular team leader
exists, he carries out the same tasks as other team
members. Indeed, as discussed in the previous chapter,
a technical team leader may emerge who effectively
controls software production without having the title of
team leader.

In an informal team, the work to be carried out is
discussed by the team as a whole and the tasks allocated
to each member according to ability and experience.
High level system design is carried out by senior team
members but low level design is the responsibility of
the member allocated a particular task.

Informal teams can be very successful particularly
where the majority of team members are experienced and
competent. The team functions as a democratic team,
making decisions by consensus. Psychologically, this
improves team spirit with a resultant increase in

cohesiveness and performance. On the other hand, if a team is composed mostly of inexperienced or incompetent members, the informality can be a hindrance. No definite authority exists to direct the work causing a lack of coordination between team members and, possibly eventual project failure.

A very serious problem which can arise in some organisation is the lack of experienced team members. Teams tend to be composed of relatively inexperienced members because the career and reward structure of the organisation is such that able and experienced team members are promoted to management positions which do not involve software development. This situation is exacerbated by distinctions made between so-called systems analysts and programmers where design and programming work are separated. Programmers are reduced to simple coders with the result that talented people strive to get out of programming as soon as possible.

In order to utilise the skills of experienced and competent programmers, these individuals should be given responsibility and rewards commensurate with what they would receive in a management position. A parallel technical career path should be established to achieve this without any implication that it is inferior to a management oriented career path. The team organisation discussed below is one way of achieving this.

10.2.1 Chief programmer teams

An alternative programming team organisation to the informal democratic team was suggested by Baker (1972) and also described, in a slightly different form, by Brooks (1975) and Aron (1974). The development of this approach was motivated by a number of considerations:

(1)   Projects tended to be staffed by relatively inex-perienced people as discussed above.

(2)   Much programming work is clerical in nature in-volving the storage and maintenance of a large amount of information.

(3)   Multi way communications are time consuming and hence reduce programmer productivity.

The chief programmer team is based on utilising experienced and talented staff as chief programmers, providing clerical support for these programmers using both human and computer based procedures, and funnelling all communications through one or two individuals.

The chief programmer team has been compared to a surgical team undertaking an operation. The ultimate responsibility in such a team rests with the surgeon but he is helped by skilled, specialised staff members such as an anaesthetist, chief nurse, etc. who carry out particular roles.

The nucleus of a chief programmer team consists of the following members:

(1)   A chief programmer who is experienced and highly qualified. He takes full responsibility for designing, programming, testing and installing the system under development.

(2)   A backup programmer who is also skilled and experienced. He works with the chief programmer and should be able to adopt his role if necessary. His main function is to provide support by developing test cases and analyses to verify the work of the chief programmer.

(3)   A librarian whose role is to assume all the clerical functions associated with a project. The librarian is assisted by an automated library system.

Depending on the size and type of the application, other experts might be added temporarily or permanently to a team. These might include:

(1)   A project administrator who relieves the chief programmer of administrative tasks.

(2)   A toolsmith who is responsible for producing software tools to support the project.

(3)   A documentation editor who takes the project documentation written by the chief programmer and backup programmer and prepares it for publication.

(4)   A language/system expert who is familiar with the idiosyncrasies of the programming language and system which is being used and whose role is to advise the chief programmer on how to make use of these facilities.

(5)   A tester whose task is to develop objective test cases to validate the work of the chief programmer.

(6)   One or more support programmers who undertake coding from a design specified by the chief programmer. These support programmers are necessary when the scale of the project is such that detailed programming work cannot be carried out by the chief programmer and backup programmer alone.

The principal objective of using a chief programmer team is to improve productivity and measurements by Baker (1974) and Walston and Felix (1977) suggest that a chief programmer team is approximately twice as productive as teams which are not organised in this way. However, it is not clear whether this improvement is a result of the team organisation or whether it results simply from using better programmers who would be more productive in any case.

Shneiderman (1980) points out that there may be psychological problems in introducing chief programmer teams. These derive from the position of the chief programmer who is the kingpin of the project and, if the project is successful, takes the credit for this success. Other team members may feel that they have no definite function and be resentful of the status of the chief programmer.

Other political problems in using chief programmer teams are described by Yourdon (1979). In large organisations it may be impossible to fit the chief programmer team into the existing organisational structure and adequately reward the chief programmer. The introduction of chief programmer teams may entail the complete reorganisation of existing staff and this might be resisted. It may be impossible to attract suitably qualified chief programmers to work in certain application areas.

In spite of these disadvantages, the basic premise underlying chief programmer teams - the need to utilise the talent of experienced programmers - is sound. The practice of programming is too difficult and important to be left entirely in the hands of juniors.

10.3   SOFTWARE COST ESTIMATION

The most commonly used technique for estimating software costs is to estimate the size of the programming system to be delivered and hence compute the programmer months required to construct the system using either historic productivity data or by intuition. The overall system cost is based on this figure plus overheads. If the software is being developed for an external agency, a profit figure is added to this cost estimate.

The system size is estimated by carrying out a preliminary design study to establish the units making up the system. An estimate is made of the size of each unit. This estimate is normally based on experience and intuition. These estimates are then summed to give the estimated size of the total system. This method is based on the assumption that programmer productivity for a given part of the system can be predicted in advance. It also assumes that the preliminary design is not over simplified and accurately reflects the system which is to be produced.

We have already seen that programmer productivity is affected by a multiplicity of factors and cannot be accurately estimated by considering the size of each unit to be developed. Other factors such as the programmer's experience, the newness and complexity of the application and the implementation constraints must also be taken into account. Ideally, these factors should be considered for each distinct unit rather than the system as a whole. As a large system may have several hundred units, cost estimation is a time consuming and costly business.

The consideration of productivity factors can be carried out algorithmically and a large number of software costing models have been developed. These are described and compared by Mohanty (1981). The cost models described in his paper have each been developed using different historical data accumulated by the organisations which use the model. It is indicative of the state of the art of software cost estimation that the cost estimates produced by each model for a hypothetical project invented by Mohanty differed greatly. The lowest estimate for a system composed of about 36000 executable machine instructions was $362 000 whereas the highest estimate was $2 766 667.

Rather than estimate costs using historical productivity data expressed in production of code/programmer month, Jones (1977) suggests that cost units based on cost per thousand lines of code are more useful and versatile in cost estimation. Cost units are computed by taking the overall cost of a project and dividing this by the size of the delivered program.

An advantage of using cost units is that all costs associated with a project may be expressed in the same way. This contrasts with estimates based on productivity measures which must compute the production cost as described above then add overheads such as computer costs, support staff costs, documentation costs and travel costs. When cost units are used, all these extra costs can be subsumed under the same heading.

For cost estimation, Jones introduces the notion of a probability rectangle. This technique still relies on an estimate of program size but rather than a specific estimate, best case and worst case estimates are made. Historical data can be used to derive the previous unit costs of programs similar to that being estimated. Typically, these will also lie in a range. To display the minimum and maximum software costs, these can then be plotted as a productivity rectangle as shown below. Assume that the minimum program size estimate is 8 000 lines and the maximum 11 000 lines. If the minimum cost unit is $20 000/thousand lines and the maximum is $26 000 per thousand lines the probability rectangle shown in Fig 10.2 results.

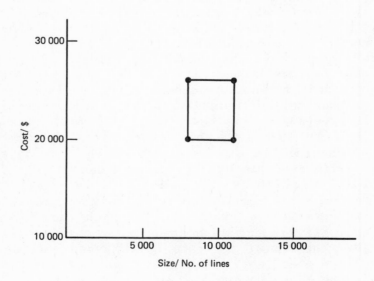

Fig. 10.2   Cost/probability rectangle

The minimum development cost of the program is 8 000 lines at $20 000 per thousand, that is, $160 000 whereas the maximum cost is 11 000 lines at $26 000 per thousand, a total of $286 000. As the project develops and more accurate size estimates are produced, new cost estimates can immediately be produced from the probability rectangle.

So far, cost estimating for complete projects has been discussed but it is also important to estimate costs in more detail and establish estimates for each phase of the project. Figures quoted by Boehm (1975) and Wolverton (1975) suggest that that major costs of software development are incurred in requirements analysis, software design and software testing. The figures vary for the type of system under development. For example, about 50% of the costs were incurred in system testing and 35% in system design in the development of command/control systems whereas for business systems, 44% of the costs were expended in analysis and design whereas only 28% were spent on testing.

In order to estimate the costs of each phase these figures can be used to calculate the proportion of costs incurred at each stage of system development. If costs are monitored as the project progresses, overall estimates can be improved by comparing actual costs and estimated costs of the early stages of the project and updating the overall estimate according to the goodness-of-fit of the estimated and actual costs.

10.4 PROJECT PLANNING

Effective management of a software project depends on thoroughly planning the progress of the project, anticipating problems which might arise and preparing tentative solutions to those problems in advance. It will be assumed that the project manager is responsible for planning from requirements specification to the delivery of the completed system. The planning involved in assessing the need for a software system, the feasibility of producing that system, and the assignment of priority to the system production process will not be discussed. For a discussion of these topics, the reader is referred to Fried (1979).

The planning discussed here is that required for a large programming system which requires multiple teams to tackle the project so that it may be completed in a given time. However, much of the discussion is relevant to the production of smaller systems tackled by a single programming team, although for such systems the

requirement for comprehensive planning can often be met
informally.

Metzger (1973) defines a project plan to be made up
of 11 distinct sections. These are:

(1)   Overview
      This describes the project in general, describes
      the plan organisation and summarises the remainder
      of the document.

(2)   Phase Plan
      This discusses the project development cycle - re-
      quirements analysis, high-level design phase, low
      level design phase etc. Associated with each phase
      should be a date specifying when that phase should
      be complete and an indication of how different
      phases of the project might overlap.

(3)   Organisation Plan
      This defines the specific responsibilities of each
      group involved in the project.

(4)   Test Plan
      This outlines the testing required and the tools,
      procedures and responsibilities for carrying out
      the system test. It does not include specific
      test cases.

(5)   Change Control Plan
      This sets out a mechanism for implementing changes
      which are requested as the system is being
      developed.

(6)   Documentation Plan
      This is intended to define and control the docu-
      mentation associated with a project.

(7)   Training Plan
      This describes training of the programmers in-
      volved in the project and training of the users to
      make use of the delivered system.

(8)   Review and Reporting Plan
      This discusses how the project status is reported.
      The formal reviews associated with the progress of
      the project are defined here.

(9)   Installation and Operation Plan
       This describes the procedure for installing the
       system at the user's site.

(10)   Resources and Deliverables Plan
       This summarises the critical plan details -
       schedules, milestones and all items to be
       delivered under contract.

(11)   Index
       This shows where to find things in the plan.

Some of the sections in this plan have already been
covered in other parts of the book. Here, attention
will be concentrated on project scheduling, reporting
and change control.

10.4.1 Project reporting
It is extremely important that information about the
progress of a project is fed back to management at
regular intervals. Without this information, control of
the project is lost and cost estimates and schedules
cannot be updated.

When planning a project, a series of milestones
should be established. At each milestone, a formal
progress report should be presented to management. As
Metzger points out, it is important that these
milestones each represent the culmination of a distinct
stage in the project . There is little point in planning
indefinite milestones where it is impossible to decide
unequivocally if a milestone has been reached. A good
milestone is characterised by finished documentation,
for example, 'High level design complete' or 'Test plan
formulated'. On the other hand, a poor milestone is
something like 'Coding 80% complete' - what exactly does
this mean and how can it be determined if coding is 80%
complete or not?

Milestones should not necessarily be established for
each and every project activity otherwise the project
team will spend more time on management reporting than
they do on system development. If bar charts are drawn
up for scheduling, these can be annotated with the
project milestones which should occur, roughly, once
every two or three weeks.

10.4.2 Project scheduling
Project scheduling is one of the most difficult tasks of

software management. For many projects, previous experience is of only limited relevance unless the project being scheduled is similar to a previous project. Typically, projects break new ground with the consequence that previous estimates cannot be directly modified. Different projects use different programming languages and methodologies which further complicates the task of estimating the project schedule.

Because of these uncertainties, scheduling is an iterative process. An initial schedule must be estimated but this should not be considered inviolate. As the project progresses, information is fed back to the scheduler and the initial estimate modified.

The preparation of the initial schedule must be based on the experience and intuition of the manager. If the project is technically advanced, the initial estimate will almost certainly be optimistic, in spite of endeavours to consider all eventualities. In this respect, software scheduling is no different from scheduling any other type of large advanced project. New aircraft, bridges and even motor cars are frequently late because of unanticipated problems and it is unrealistic to expect software projects to be different.

Project scheduling involves separating the total work involved in a project into distinct tasks and assessing when these tasks will be completed. When a number of individuals or teams are working on a project, some of these tasks are carried out in parallel. The project scheduler must coordinate these parallel tasks and organise the work so that his workforce is used optimally. The scheduler must strive to avoid a situation arising where the whole project is delayed because a critical task is unfinished.

In estimating schedules, it should not be assumed that every stage of the project will be problem free. Individuals working on a project may fall ill or may leave, hardware may break down and essential support software or hardware may be late in delivery. If the project is new and technically advanced, certain parts of it may turn out to be more difficult and hence take longer than originally anticipated. A rule of thumb in estimating is to estimate as if nothing will go wrong, double that estimate to cover anticipated problems and then add a 'fudge factor' to cover unanticipated problems. This extra factor must be determined by the manager's experience and knowledge of his staff.

As a rough guide for the scheduler, requirements

analysis and design normally take twice as long as coding, as does validation. To estimate the total time required for the project, the system size must be estimated and divided by the expected programmer productivity to give the number of programmer months required to complete the project. The resulting figure is very approximate because of the difficulties involved in estimating system size and the variations in programmer productivity.

Estimating the actual duration of a project cannot simply be carried out by dividing the number of programmer months by the number of available programmers. There are two reasons for this. Firstly, as the number of programmers increases, communication problems arise and productivity falls. Indeed, Fried suggests that once the number of programmers working on a project exceeds a certain maximum, productivity is actually negative. Secondly, some tasks are indivisible and no matter how many programmers work on them, the time required cannot be reduced. Again, experience is required to identify these indivisible tasks and to estimate the duration of a project.

10.4.3 Bar charts and activity networks

Bar charts and activity networks are graphical tools which can be used in project scheduling. Bar charts illustrate who is responsible for each part of the project, when that part is scheduled to start and finish.

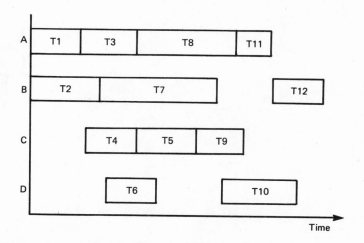

Fig. 10.3   Bar chart for project scheduling

The chart, illustrated in Fig 10.3, shows a project undertaken by four programmers and made up of 11 distinct tasks. Notice that this chart does not show all team members to be occupied all the time - in the slack periods they may be doing other work, have scheduled leave, attend training courses etc.

It is not generally useful to subdivide tasks into units which take less than a week or two to execute. Finer subdivisions means that a disproportionate amount of time must be spent on estimating. It is also useful to set a maximum amount of time for any task on the chart - about 10 to 12 weeks is reasonable.

One of the problems with bar charts is that they do not show task dependencies. In the above chart, T10 might be dependent on T7 and T5 being complete and should T7 be delayed, it may be impossible to start T10. A graphical method which can be used to show these interdependencies is the activity network or PERT chart.

An example of an activity network for showing the interdependencies of the tasks in the above bar chart is shown in Fig 10.4.

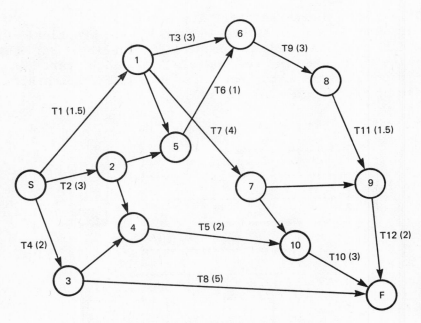

Fig. 10.4   Activity network

Each node on the activity graph is called an event and represents the culmination of one or more

activities.   If an arc is labelled, the label is the
name of the activity followed by the estimated time it
will take to complete that activity.   It is sometimes
necessary to create dummy events to cater for the
situation where mutually independent tasks are each
dependent on the same activity. Arcs from dummy events
are unlabelled and take zero time to execute.

Before progress can be made from one event to
another, all activity paths leading to that event must
be complete. For example, in the above diagram activity
T9 cannot be started until both T3 and T6 are complete.
The diagram shows the interdependence of activities,
illustrating what activities can be carried out in
parallel and what must be done in sequence.

The duration of the project can be estimated by
considering the longest path in the activity graph -
this is called the critical path.   In the above diagram,
the critical path is S-1-6-8-9-F which takes 11 time
units. Delays in any of the activities in the critical
path will necessarily result in delays in the final
project whereas a delay in T8 say, assuming it was not
excessive, would have no effect on the project
completion date.

PERT charts are a more sophisticated form of activity
chart where, instead of making a single estimate for
each task, pessimistic, likely, and optimistic estimates
are made. Considering each of these and combinations of
them makes critical path analysis very complex and is
best carried out automatically.

As well as using activity graphs for estimating, it
is useful for management to construct these charts when
allocating project work. They can provide insights into
the interdependence of tasks which are not intuitively
obvious. In some cases, it may be possible to modify the
system design so that the critical path is shortened.
The duration of the project may be reduced because the
time spent waiting for activities to complete might be
reduced.

Inevitably, initial project schedules will be
incorrect and, as the project develops, it is important
to compare estimates with actual elapsed time.   This
comparison can be used as a basis for revising the
schedule for later parts of the project. When actual
figures are known, it is also important to review the
activity chart and perhaps repartition the later project
tasks in order to reduce the critical path.

10.4.4 Change control

All software development is an iterative process. As software is designed, flaws in the requirements specification are revealed, as it is implemented, flaws in the design are shown up and so on. Changes are both essential and inevitable. However, the changes can easily get out of hand and it is important for management to plan for changes and establish a procedure for documenting and evaluating the effect of these changes.

Changes fall into two categories – those required to correct minor mistakes and those which either add to or remove functions or change the way a function is implemented. The first type of change must be carried out and there is not, generally, any need for managerial approval of the change. However, if a mistake is discovered at a later stage in the project from that in which the mistake was made (say a design error during implementation), it is important that the change be formally documented using a standard change control procedure. If this is carried out, it is possible to check that all documents affected by the change have actually been modified to record the change.

The second type of change should always be subject to managerial approval. Some formal change evaluation procedure should exist and all changes of this type must be subjected to this procedure in order to assess the cost of the change and its ramifications on the rest of the software system. If the cost of the change is relatively low and the change does not affect the rest of the system it should normally be approved.

If, on the other hand, the cost of the change is high or its impact significant, a decision must be made whether to accept the change or not and, if accepted, who is to be responsible for paying for the change. Clearly, if the change is requested by the software customer, they must take the responsibility for paying for that change . Otherwise, some kind of cost benefit analysis must be carried out to determine if the overall benefits resulting from the change are worthwhile. Again, the change should be formally documented and promulgated to all other relevant documents such as the requirements specification, high level design etc.

10.5   SOFTWARE TOOLS FOR MANAGEMENT

Tools for software management fall into two categories – planning tools and reporting tools. Planning tools assist the manager to plan a project by providing information about previous projects and by performing tedious calculations such as cost computations and critical path analysis. Reporting tools analyse machine readable project documentation and generate reports in some standard form.

Unfortunately, little attention has been paid to the development of general purpose software tools for software project management. PERT packages can be used for critical path analyses but this is a tool for project management in general rather than software management in particular. Also, a number of project costing tools have been developed which, given project details, use historic data to compute the probable effort involved and the costs of the different stages of the project. As we have seen, these tools are very organisation specific and give very diverse cost predictions depending on the historic data.

The Stoneman requirements (DoD, 1980) identify two distinct management tools which might form part of an Ada toolkit. A project control system and fault report system. A project control system would keep track of a project against review dates and budgets. Using built-in templates, it might take specifications, designs, and code generated by the programmer and compile them into reports for software management. If documentation was not available in a standard form by a particular date this could be reported to management. A fault report system would be responsible for collecting and collating information about reported errors, managing change control reports and ensuring that the changes are propagated to the relevant documents.

The development of such software tools must be the next major step forward in software management techniques.

References

Alford, M.W. 1977. A Requirements Engineering Methodology for Real Time Processing Requirements. 'IEEE Trans. on Software Engineering', SE-3(1), 60-9

Aron, J.D. 1974. 'The Program Development Process'. Reading, Mass: Addison Wesley

Baker, F.T. 1972. Chief Programmer Team Management of Production Programming. 'IBM Systems J.', 11(1)

Balzer, R.W. 1969. EXDAMS - Extendable Debugging And Monitoring System. 'AFIPS', 34

Bass, B.M. & Dunteman, G. 1963. Behaviour in groups as a function of self, interaction and task orientation. 'J. abnorm. soc. Psychol.', 66, 419-28

Bell, T.E., Bixler, D.C. & Dyer, M.E. 1977. An Extendable Approach to Computer Aided Software Requirements Engineering. 'IEEE Trans. on Software Engineering', SE-3(1), 49-60

Bochmann, G.V. 1973. Multiple Exits from a loop without the Goto. 'Comm. ACM', 16(7), 443-5

Boehm, B.W. 1974. 'Some Steps Towards Formal and Automated Aids to Software Requirements Analysis and Design'. IFIP74, 192-197, Amsterdam: North-Holland

Boehm, B.W. 1975. 'The High Cost of Software'. In 'Practical Strategies for Developing Large Software Systems', Reading, Mass: Addison Wesley

Boehm, B.W., Brown, J.R., Kaspar, H., Lipow, M., Macleod, G. & Merrit, M. 1978. 'Characteristics of Software Quality'. TRW Series of Software Technology, Amsterdam: North-Holland

Bohm, C. & Jacopini, G.   1966. Flow diagrams, Turing machines and languages with only two formation rules. 'Comm. ACM', 9(5),   366-71

Bourne, S.R.   1978. The UNIX Shell.   'Bell Systems Tech.J.', 57(6),   1971-90

Brooks, F.P.   1975. 'The Mythical Man Month'. Reading, Mass: Addison Wesley

Brown, P.J.   ed.   1977.   'Software   Portability'. Cambridge: Cambridge University Press

Chen, P.   1976. 'The entity relationship model - Towards a unifed view of data'. Trans. on Database Systems, 1(1), 9-36

Chu, Y.   1978. 'Introducing a Software Design Language'. In 'Structured Analysis and Design', Infotech State of the Art Report, Maidenhead

Codd, E.F.   1970. A relational model of data for large shared data banks. 'Comm. ACM', 13,   377-87

Constantine, L.L. .& Yourdon, E.   1979. 'Structured Design'. Englewood Cliffs, New Jersey: Prentice-Hall

Cougar, J.D. & Zawacki, R.A.   1978. 'What Motivates DP Professionals'. Datamation, 24(9)

Culpepper, L.M.   1975. A System for Reliable Engineering Software.   'IEEE Trans. on Software Engineering', SE-1(2),   174-178

Dahl, O.J., Dijkstra, E.W. & Hoare, C.A.R.   1972. 'Structured Programming'. New York: Academic Press

Davis, C.G. & Vick, C.R.   1977. The Software Development System.   'IEEE Trans. on Software Engineering', SE-3(1),   69-84

Dijkstra, E.W.   1968. A constructive approach to the problem of program correctness. 'BIT', 8, 174-86

Dijkstra, E.W.   1968. Goto Statement Considered Harmful. 'Comm. ACM', 11(3),   147-8

Dijkstra, E.W.   1975. Guarded Commands, Nondeterminacy, and Formal Derivation of Programs. 'Comm. ACM', 18(8),   453-7

Dijkstra, E.W.   1976. 'A Discipline of Programming'. Englewood Cliffs, New Jersey: Prentice-Hall

DoD 1980. 'Requirements for Ada Programming Support Environments:Stoneman'. US Department of Defense

Dolotta, T.A., Haight, R.C. & Mashey, J.R.   1978. The Programmer's Workbench. 'Bell Systems Tech. J.', 57(6),   2177-200

Eason, K.D., Damodaran, L. & Stewart, T.F.M.   1975. Interface problems in Man-Computer Interaction.   In 'Human Choice and Computers', Amsterdam: North-Holland

Ellis, C.A. & Nutt, G.J.   1980.   Office Information Systems and Computer Science. 'ACM Computing Surveys', 12(1),   27-60

Fagan, M.E.   1976. Design and code inspections to reduce errors in program development. 'IBM Systems J.', 15(3), 182-211

Feldman, S.I.   1979. MAKE - A program for Maintaining Computer Programs. 'Software - Practice and Experience', 9, 255-65

Festinger, L.A.   1957. 'A Theory of Cognitive Dissonance'. Evanston, Illinois: Row Peterson

Floyd, R.W.   1967. Assigning Meanings to Programs. 'Proc. Symposium in Applied Maths.', 19-32

Fried, L.   1979. 'Practical Data Processing Management'. Virginia: Reston

Frost, R.A. 1981. ASDAS - A simple Database Management System, . 'Proc. 6th European ACM Conf. on Systems Architecture', London

Greeno, J.G.   1972. The structure of memory and the process of problem solving. 'Univ. of Michigan : Human Performance Center, Tech. Rep. 37'

Guttag, J. 1977. Abstract Data Types and the Development of Data Structures. Comm. ACM, 20(6), 396-405

Halstead, M.H. 1977. 'Elements of Software Science'. Amsterdam: North-Holland

Hendrix, G.G., Sacerdoti, E.D., Sagalowicz, D. & Slocum, J. 1978. Developing a Natural Language Interface to Complex Data. 'ACM Trans. on Database Systems', 3(2), 105-47

Heninger, K.L. 1980. Specifying Software Requirements for Complex Systems. New Techniques and their Applications. 'IEEE Trans. Software Engineering', SE-6(1), 2-13

Hoare, C.A.R. 1969. An axiomatic basis for computer programming. 'Comm. ACM', 12(10), 576-83

Hoare, C.A.R. 1973. Hints on Programming Language Design. 'ACM Symp. on Principles of Programming Languages', Boston, Mass., 1-30

Hoare, C.A.R. 1975. Data Reliability. 'Proc. Int. Conf. on Reliable Software', Los Angeles, 528-33

IBM 1980. Software Development. 'IBM Systems J.', 19(4)

Iverson, K.E. 1962. 'A Programming Language'. New York: Wiley

Ivie, E.L. 1977. The Programmers Workbench - A Machine for Software Development. 'Comm. ACM', 20(10), October 746-53

Jackson, K. 1977. Language Design for Modular Software Construction. 'Information Processing 77', 577-82, Amsterdam: North-Holland

Janis, I.L. 1972. 'Victims of groupthink. A psychological study of foreign policy decisions and fiascos'. Boston: Houghton Mifflin

Jensen, R.W. & Tonies, C.C. 1979. 'Software Engineering'. Englewood Cliffs, New Jersey: Prentice-Hall

Jones, T.C.   1978. Measuring Programming Quality and Productivity.   'IBM Systems J.', 17(1), 39-63

Kernighan, B.W., Lesk, M.E. & Ossanna Jr, J.F.   1978. Document Preparation.   'Bell Systems Tech. J.', 57(6), 2115-35

Knuth, D.E.   1974. Structured Programming with go to Statements.   'ACM Computing Surveys', 6(4), 261-301

Lampson, B.W., Horning, J.J., London, R.L., Mitchell, J.G. & Popek, G.L.   1977. Report on the programming language Euclid.   'Sigplan Notices', 12(2), 1-79

Leavitt, H.J.   1951.   Some effects of certain communication patterns on group performance.   'J. Abnorm. Soc. Psychol.', 38-50

Lehman, M.M & Belady, L.A.   1976. A model of large program development.   'IBM Systems J.', 15(3), 225-52

Lehman, M.M.   1980. Programs, Life Cycles and the Laws of Software Evolution.   'Proc. IEEE', 68(9), 1060-76

Lewin, K., Lippit, R. & White, R.K.   1939. Patterns of aggressive behaviour in experimentally created "social climates".   'J. Social Psychology', 10, 271-99

Lientz, B.P. & Swanson, E.B.   1980.   'Software Maintenance Management'.   Reading, Mass: Addison Wesley

Linger, R.C., Mills, H.D. & Witt, B.I.   1979. 'Structured Programming - Theory and Practice'. Reading, Mass: Addison Wesley

Lucas, R.W.   1977. A study of patient's attitudes to computer interrogation.   'Int. J of Man-Machine Studies', 9, 69-86

Malone, J.R. & McGregor, D.R.   1980. STABDUMP - A dump interpreter program to assist debugging.   'Software - Practice and Experience', 10, 329-32

Manna, Z.   1969. The Correctness of Programs.   'J. of Computer and System Sciences', 3, 119-27

Marshall, J.E. & Heslin, R.   1976. Boys and Girls Together. Sexual composition and the effect of density on group size and cohesiveness.   'J. of personality and Social Psychology'

Martin, J.   1973. 'Design of Man-Computer Dialogues'. Englewood Cliffs, New Jersey: Prentice-Hall

Mashey, J.R. & Smith, D.W.   1977. Documentation Tools and Techniques.   'Proc. 2nd Int. Conf. on Software Engineering', San Francisco, 177-81

McCabe, T.J.   1976. A complexity measure.   'IEEE Trans. on Software Engineering', SE-2, 308-20

McCarthy, J.   1962. Towards a mathematical science of computation.   'Proc. IFIP Congress', 21-8, Amsterdam: North-Holland

McCue, G.M.   1978. IBMs Santa Teresa Laboratory – Architectural Design for program developement'.   'IBM Systems J.', 17(1), 4-25

Mcgregor, D.R. & Malone, J.R., 1980. The FACT database: A system based on inferential methods . 'Proc. Cambridge Symposium on Research and Development in Information Retrieval', Butterworth.

McGuffin, R.W., Elliston, A.E., Tranter, B.R. & Westmacott, P.N.   1979. CADES – Software Engineering in Practice.   'Proc. 4th Int. Conf. on Software Engineering', Munich

McKeeman, W.M., Horning, J.J. & Wortman, D.   1970. 'A Compiler Generator'.   Englewood Cliffs, New Jersey: Prentice-Hall

Metzger, P.W.   1973. 'Managing a Programming Project'. Englewood Cliffs, New Jersey: Prentice-Hall

Miller, G.A.   1957. The Magical Number 7 plus or minus two: Some limits on our capacity for processing information.   'Psychological Review', 63, 81-97

Mills, H.D.   1981. Principles of Software Engineering. 'IBM Systems J.', 19(4), , 415-20

Mohanty, S.N.   1981. Software Cost Estimation: Present and Future. 'Software - Practice and Experience', 11(2),   103-21

Morrison, R.   1979.   'S-Algol Reference Manual'. CS/79/1, Dept of Computational Science, University of St Andrews, Scotland

Myers, G.J.   1975. 'Reliable Software through Composite Design'. New York: Van Nostrand

Myers, G.J.   1979. 'The Art of Software Testing'. New York: Wiley

Naur, P.   1972. An experiment on program development. 'BIT', 12, 347-65

Newman, W.M. & Sproull, R.F.   1979. 'Principles of Interactive Computer Graphics'. New York: Mcgraw-Hill

Osterweil, L.J. & Fosdick, L.D.   1976. DAVE - A validation, error detection and documentation system for FORTRAN programs.. 'Software - Practice and Experience', 6, 473-86

Perry, D.K. & Cannon, W.M.   1966. A Vocational Interest Scale for Programmers. 'Proc. 4th Annual Computer Personnel Conf.', ACM, New York

Peters, L.J.   1980. Software Representation and Composition Techniques. 'Proc. IEEE', 68(9), 1085-93

Peterson, J.L.   1980. 'Computer Programs for Spelling Correction'. New York: Springer-Verlag

Porter, L.W. & Lawler, E.E.   1965. Properties of organisation structure in relation to job attitudes and job behaviour. 'Psychol. Bull.', 64, 23-51

Ramoorthy, C.V. & Ho, S.F.   1975. Testing large Software with Automated Software Evaluation Systems. 'IEEE Trans. on Software Engineering', SE-1(1),   46-58

Ritchie, D.M., Johnson, S.C., Lesk, M.E. & Kernighan, B.W.   1978. The C Programming Language. 'Bell Systems Tech. J.', 57(6),   1991-2020

Ritchie, D.M. & Thompson, K. 1978. The UNIX Time Sharing System. 'Bell Systems Tech.J.', 57(6), 1905-29

Rochkind, M.J. 1975. The Source Code Control System. 'IEEE Trans. on Software Engineering', SE-1(4), 255-65

Ross, D.T. 1977. Structured Analysis(SA). A Language for Communicating Ideas. 'IEEE Trans. on Software Engineering', SE-3(1), 16-34

Sackman, H., Erikson, W.J. & Grant, E.E. 1968. Exploratory experimentation studies comparing on-line and off-line programming performance. 'Comm. ACM', 11(1), 3-11

Salter, K.G. 1976. A Methodology for Decomposing System Requirements into Data into Data Processing Requirements. 'Proc. 2nd Int. Conf. on Software Engineering', San Francisco

Satterthwaite, E. 1972. Debugging Tools for High Level Languages. 'Software - Practice and Experience', 2, 197-217

Schoman, K. & Ross, D.T. 1977. Structured Analysis for Requirements Definition. 'IEEE Trans. on Software Engineering', SE-3(1), 6-15

Scowen, R.S. 1979. A new technique for improving the quality of computer programs. 'Proc. 4th Int. Conf. on Software Engineering', Munich, 73-8

Sharman, G.O.H. & Winterbottom, N., 1979. NDB:Non programmer Database Facility. 'IBM Technical Report TR 12.179', Hursley, UK

Shaw, M.E. 1964. 'Communication Networks'. In 'Advances in Experimental Social Psychology', New York: Academic Press

Shaw, M.E. 1971. 'Group Dynamics. 'The Psychology of Small Group Behaviour'. McGraw-Hill: New York

Shepherd, S.B., Curtis, B., Milliman, P., Borst, M. & Love, T. 1979. First year results from a research program in human factors in software engineering. 'AFIPS', 44, 1021-7

Shneiderman, B. 1980. 'Software Psychology'. Cambridge, Mass: Winthrop Publishers Inc.

Sommerville, I. 1981. Providing the user with a Tailor Made Interface. 'Proc. 6th European ACM Conf. on Systems Architecture', London

Standish, T.A. 1981. ARCTURUS - An Advanced Highly Integrated Programming Environment. In 'Software Engineering Environments', Amsterdam: North-Holland

Strachey, C. & Milne, R. 1976. 'A theory of programming language semantics'. London: Chapman and Hall

Stucki, L.G. & Walker, H.D. 1981. Concepts and Prototypes of ARGUS. In 'Software Engineering Environments', Amsterdam: North-Holland

Tanenbaum, A.S., Klint, P. & Bohm, W. 1978. Guidelines for Software Portability. 'Software - Practice and Experience', 8, 681-98

Teichrow, D. & Hershey, E.A. 1977. PSL/PSA: A Computer Aided Technique for Structured Documentation and Analysis of Information Processing Systems'. 'IEEE Trans. on Software Engineering', SE-3(1), 41-8

Turski, W. 1981. Software Stability. 'Proc. 6th European ACM Conf. on Systems Architecture', London

Van Leer, P. 1976. Top down development using a program design language. 'IBM Systems J.', 15(2), 155-70

Walston, C.E. & Felix, C.P. 1977. A method of programming measurement and estimation. 'IBM Systems J.', 16(1), 54-73

Waltz, D. 1978. An English Language Question Answering System for a Large Relational Database. 'Comm. ACM', 21(7), 526-39

Weinberg, G.M. 1971. 'The Psychology of Computer Programming'. New York: Van Nostrand

Wichmann, B.A. 1978. Performance of System Implementation Languages. In 'Constructing Quality Software', Amsterdam: North-Holland

Willis, R.R. 1981. AIDES: Computer Aided Design of Software Systems. In 'Software Engineering Environments', Amsterdam: North-Holland

Wirth, N. 1971. Program Development by Stepwise Refinement. 'Comm. ACM', 14(4), 221-7

Wirth, N. 1976. 'Systematic Programming, An Introduction'. Englewood Cliffs, New Jersey: Prentice-Hall

Wolverton, R.W. 1975. The Cost of Developing Large Scale Software. In 'Practical Strategies for Developing Large Software Systems', Reading, Mass: Addison Wesley

Yeh, R.T. & Zave, P. 1980. Specifying Software Requirements. 'Proc. IEEE', 68(9), 1077-85

Yourdon, E. 1975. 'Techniques of Program Structure and Design'. Englewood Cliffs, New Jersey: Prentice-Hall

Yourdon, E. 1979. 'Managing the Structured Techniques'. Englewood Cliffs, New Jersey: Prentice-Hall

Zahn, C.T. 1974. A Control Statement for Natural Top Down Structured programming. 'Symposium on Programming Languages', Paris

Index